HIDING FROM MYSELF: A MEMOIR

BRYAN CHRISTOPHER

TABLE OF CONTENTS

PART III

*A*s *I peer into the cavernous depths, I realize that in this cold, cruel world, Hugh Hefner's closet has become my safe place. It's larger than the bedroom of my apartment and unlike any closet I've experienced. It's not like I've gone around the world and conducted an independent study of people's closets, I just know there are few like this one.*

I could live full time in this closet.

The walls aren't plaster with layers of old peeling paint like mine. These are lined majestically with antique wood intricately carved with details that hark back to the 1920s when the Mansion was originally built. The current resident seemingly has a silk fetish—hundreds of silk pajamas, in a diversity of colors, hang on a rod that extends for eternity, creating a sweeping silk pajama rainbow. As my fingers flirt with the silk, I marvel that I'm holding in my hand the potent signature of the Playboy lifestyle. Pajamas. And they do look comfortable... For a moment, I'm tempted to try a pair on, just to test the magic, but quickly abort the notion because it's...creepy. If there exists a heterosexual vortex in the universe, my theory has been I'd find it here. But after months of using Hugh Hefner's closet as base camp for my hetero expedition, I'm beginning to doubt the pajamas have actual powers as I'd hoped.

I just know I can't keep doing this—this hiding out in Hef's closet. Sooner or later, someone is going to find me.

—Chapter 2: Hugh Hefner's Closet

God grant me the serenity
To accept the things I cannot change,
The courage to change the things I can,
And the wisdom to know the difference.

— The Serenity Prayer

I discovered the hidden stash of *Playboys* in my dad's sock drawer in 3rd grade. By the summer before 7th grade, I was feverishly scoping the bunny herd for the one he might not miss, finally settling on the August 1980 issue featuring a close up of Bo Derek's face: big blue eyes, tousled hair, and a bead of moisture wetting her lips. It read, *"BO ENCORE! A second visit with Hollywood's hottest number,"* and the caption above Bo's left eye: *"Ronald Reagan: Who is this guy anyway?"* When the movie *10* came out, I was nine, but the power the bodacious blonde with beaded cornrows had over all the dads on the block was palpable.

She was "perfect" in ways we boys were "too young to understand."

But at twelve and "old enough," I opened to Bo's encore, hoping to get hardcore, but she was looking at me with those saucer blue eyes—not with lusty desire, but pity. She knew I was in trouble; puberty striking like a tsunami that summer, the first wave changing the landscape of my life irrevocably the moment I spied Brooke Shields and Christopher Atkins swimming naked over coral reefs in the *Blue Lagoon*. I was staked out in the hallway past my bedtime when I made the shameful discovery that my eyes—*against direct orders from my brain*—were spending a worrisome amount of time *not* looking at Brooke.

The second wave slammed later that seismic summer of '82 when I, along with my rat pack of hormone-ravaged homies, slipped out of the heart-warming *E.T.* and into the raunchy sex-comedy *Porky's*. We'd seen E.T. go home twice before, but had yet to witness the infamous "Peeping Tom" *shower scene* that had all the junior high boys buzzing with its full-frontal bounty of sorority girls showering. As the naked coeds soaped onscreen, my friends had a primal response, a *physiological* reaction. A switch had been turned on in each of them as they ogled and drooled. While they were inflamed with lust, I was burning with shame, humiliated that my body *wasn't* reacting as theirs. I was watching the same soapy scene, but while they were getting off, I was getting panicky.

When I got home, I began praying, then pleading: "Please, God, don't let me be..."

I couldn't even say the word.

In the Lone Star buckle of the Bible Belt, I'd never heard the word "gay" used as a compliment. "Faggots" were bullied and "queers" smeared—that message was personally reinforced later that same scratchy summer when Brad Jones, the infamous school bully of Shady Oaks elementary, pedaled past my house. And stopped. The older kids on the block had given fair warning: *All* 7ᵗʰ graders get hazed, and if they make it to 8ᵗʰ grade in one piece, they're *expected* to carry on this time-honored tradition of terror. Since Brad was a year older, we'd been free of his mullet and his malice at the elementary school for an entire year. Seeing him leaning menacingly over the handlebars of his BMX dirt bike and staring at me with the intensity of a pissed-off pit bull was a brutal reminder that he was an 8ᵗʰ grader—and *back in business.*

"Hey, *faggot!* You gonna be a seventh grader, huh?" he snarled from the street.

I was with Helen, my neighbor, and Stacy, my girlfriend (the heart-shaped *Bryan+Stacy* necklace from the school carnival hanging around her neck). I froze. *Is he talking to me? Did he call me a...?*

I'd never had a confrontation with him, but few would forget the day in 5ᵗʰ grade when he smeared Randy Miller during recess. The 6ᵗʰ graders had been playing "Smear the Queer," a variation of dodge ball where the "queers" are hand-plucked from the playground, thrown against a wall, and fired upon by a battalion of ball-throwing classmates chanting, "Smear the queer!" It was my least favorite game, striking an even more sinister tone the day bully Brad singled out Randy "the dandy," hurling him against the wall of the school with such force, Randy's head hit the brick with a grisly thud, silencing his tearful pleas for mercy and sending an eerie chill over the gathering crowd. Randy whimpered quietly, slumping over in a disoriented stupor. Until he saw the blood, the subsequent wailing only fueled Brad's delirious laughter. I knew with Randy, it wasn't anything he'd done. It was what they all thought he was: a "faggot."

Of all the things a boy could be in Texas, that was unquestionably the worst.

As Randy cowered in the tornado-drill position, his skinny arms not armor enough to protect the bloody goose egg oozing above his temple, several of Brad's henchmen were holding volleyballs, aimed-and-ready, waiting for Brad's cue, much like a pack of rabid coyotes circling a toy poodle. It was understood that Brad always got the first throw. "Randy *the dandy!*" Brad taunted. "Only *sissies* play with the girls!"

Randy moaned helplessly as students watched on in stunned silence, no one saying a word.

"If it walks like a queer, talks like a queer, and acts like a queer, it must be a queer! And *we all know* queers *deserve* to be smeared!" Brad said, hurling the volleyball and striking the bloody knot on Randy's noggin. The squeal was bone chilling, the high-pitch inciting the pack to join in on the pelting, all the while howling with laughter and gleefully singing, "*Smear the queer!*"

That was what happened to queers.

"Yeah, I'm talking *to you*, queer!" Brad the bully growled *at me* from the curb.

It was fight-or-flight, and I definitely wanted to flee.

"Leave him alone, moron!" Stacy defended me, unafraid of him or anyone. Her high kicks on the playground, even in skintight Gloria Vanderbilt jeans, kept all the boys running for cover.

"I ain't talking to you, Blondie. I'm talking to the little sissy fag!"

"Like, oh my gawd, he's totally not a fag!" Helen said, a budding "Valley Girl" in Texas.

"Look at him! *Total fag!*" he spat, hurling words like stones aimed at the newly exposed chinks in my armor. "Better watch yourself gay-wad. When I see you in the hallways, I'm gonna kick your faggoty-ass! Ah, hell, what're we waitin' for?" he said, dropping the bike and storming the yard. He made it halfway up the drive before my mom appeared on the porch in a black smock, her hair in the middle of being frosted, resembling an aluminum artichoke. I had the mom on the block all the other kids called "Mom," but at that moment, she looked like the big bad witch—and *mean*, like a mad momma bear about to maul a threat to one of her cubs.

"What's all this yelling?" she shouted, her presence causing Brad to swiftly retreat.

He mounted his Mongoose and pedaled off, but not before threatening one last time. "I'll be looking for you, faggot! Gonna kick your limp-wristed fairy-ass all the way to *San Francisco!*"

As he rode away, his acidic words burned into my twelve-year-old psyche, disfiguring me instantly—and in grotesque ways I knew I'd always see.

"Don't listen to him," Stacy consoled me sweetly. "He totally barfs me out."

But I did listen to him, his voice forever echoing in the hallways of my mind.

That night I was still shaking, as though bully Brad had taken a razor blade to my premature mind and sliced the word "Faggot!". Suddenly the idea of being trapped eight hours a day, five days a week inside a school where a rabid 8th grader was on the loose and hunting the hallways for me with the intent to *smear*, made junior high (and life) not so exciting anymore.

Staring limply at the pages of *Playboy*, I considered the consequences.

I had great parents, but when they brought me into the world in 1970, they were students at Baylor (the world's largest Baptist university) in Waco, Texas—the magical place of my birth, and where hell, fire, and damnation awaited those who drank and danced. Despite their "higher learning" at a Southern Baptist institution (where my dad drank and my mom danced), we didn't pray before meals, spend Friday nights at youth rallies, or pass time on rainy afternoons playing Bible Trivial Pursuit. For our religious inoculation they sent us to Vacation Bible School every summer at the Baptist church where "Smear the Queer" was not only played outside during breaks from learning about Adam and Eve, Moses, and Jesus, but it was also played inside by the pastors, confirming that the schoolyard bully had it right all along. I hadn't heard it from my parents, but the message was clear: there was something wrong, perverted, and downright sinful about my impotent response to Bo running slo-mo on the beach in her cornrows. If I couldn't get the "10" to register on my pubescent radar, it meant one thing: there's a special place in Hell for me.

"God smeared a bunch of 'em in Sodom and Gomorrah," a youth pastor told us, bristling at the thought. "They're *sick* and *sinful*, and now they want equal rights? Not in my country!"

The concept of openly gay people and their civil rights wasn't on my Lone Star radar until that moment. I was in my mother's womb in Waco during the 1969 Stonewall Riots in New York City. I heard the rumor that Rod Stewart had a gallon of suspicious fluid pumped out of his stomach, but I had never heard that gay patrons of a bar in New York, sick of being smeared by the police, fought back, sparking the genesis of a gay civil rights movement.

"You should see 'em at them 'gay pride' parades up there in New York City! Disgustin'! Actually *proud* of their *sin!*" the pastor sneered. "Won't be long before they want to marry!"

From the playground to the pulpit, it was clear: I had a flaw—a fatal flaw—one that could *never, ever* be exposed. And must be fixed.

If God created me, surely He can fix me—at least this broken part of me.

God created male and female; Adam and Eve and all that.

It's all so basic and makes perfect sense.

Unless you're the limp twelve-year-old boy holding the *Playboy* mag, then it becomes a crisis.

PART I

CHAPTER 1:

RINGING DOORBELLS FOR JESUS

It's New Year's Eve, 1992, and I'm on a foggy street corner in San Francisco flanked by two hot sorority girls and we're going door-to-door, Bibles tucked under our arms and pockets stuffed with evangelical tracts. We're in the city for the annual Campus Crusade for Christ Christmas conference. Ringing doorbells for Jesus in the Castro is simply our evangelical outing for the day. Tomorrow we'll be fishing for souls at the Fisherman's Wharf.

Huddling tight on the sidewalk in a cozy neighborhood, I grasp hands with each of the girls, bow my head, and lead the prayer much like a quarterback prepping for the next play.

"Thank you for loving us and sending your Son to save us," I pray, my palms clammy in the hands of two righteous babes. "Be with us today as we seek to spread *your* love and *your* truth."

"Lead us to souls ripe for the harvest, Lord," Monica chimes in.

"Praise you, God. We love you, Jesus! Amen," Heather signs off.

We are all three in our junior year at UCLA.

"Oh my god, I am so excited!" Heather cheers, choking her frizzy blonde hair into a bushy ponytail. If you were to judge a book by its cover, you might peg her for a Hooters waitress, her snug wool sweater unable to restrain her blessed and bouncy bosom. "I'm so ready to win this city for the Lord!" Heather hoots, adjusting her backpack stuffed with Bibles. I've offered to carry it for her but she insists: "Jesus carried a cross *like the size of a telephone pole* on his bloody back for like miles while being ridiculed and spat on—*and did he complain?* Plus, I climbed Mount Whitney last month so forty pounds of God's Word on my back is nothing!"

Monica is the yin to Heather's yang. If you were to line up all the sorority girls at UCLA, she would stand out. The only girl that comes close to her righteous fox-for-Jesus looks is Lisa, one of her identical triplet sisters currently trolling Twin Peaks with her God Squad.

Campus Crusaders have blanketed the City.

If the world is coming to an End—*and we're not saying it is*—but if you know a thief will one day be coming in the night, don't you want to be prepared? This morning our

17

Crusade leaders rallied us to hit the streets with the Word by saying things such as: *"If you had the cure for cancer, would you keep it to yourself?"* Of course not! You'd tell *everyone.* Similarly, Jesus is the cure for our sin-tainted humanity, and the soul-saving Vaccine is just a prayer away. *And with our Campus Crusade-endorsed, Holy Spirit-certified Rapture Insurance, you won't be around (and neither will we) when the locusts start swarming and the moon turns to blood.*

Earlier, our army of Crusaders invaded the food court at an outlet mall, sweeping through the fast-food troughs armed with Bibles and tracts—no one was safe, each table a sinful shopper soul in need of saving. *"Sorry to interrupt your lunch, but we're doing spiritual surveys..."* The "survey" was a slippery ploy to make our pitch: eternal salvation in four easy steps, cartoon-illustrated in the pocket-sized proselytizing tool inside every Crusader's bag of tricks, *The Four Spiritual Laws*, forged by Bill Bright, founder of Campus Crusade for Christ. *Don't have time? We have information that might just change your afterlife.* If we got a nibble, we started reeling: *In planning our eternal retirement, why settle for the crowded beaches of Hades when you can secure your slice of Paradise behind the Pearly Gates?*

While secular society south of the Golden Gate hustles in another year with fireworks and immoralities, we Crusaders are focused on more eternal things, like how many souls we can save before midnight. At this rate, I don't think we'll make our quota. While our mission north of Mission Street is to evangelize, it's also training, an opportunity for us veterans to pass along our sacred skills to the new babes in Christ. Monica is a Jesus Christ superstar, long using her exposure as a Walt Disney-packaged triplet actress in Hollywood to further the Kingdom. The same camera-ready charm that lands her in television commercials also makes her highly effective at selling real estate in the Promised Land. A seasoned fisher of souls, she's able to turn a table of ungodly teenage boys at a Chick-fil-A into believers without cracking a Bible.

But Heather, Monica's little sis' at the Kappa house, is a reformed sorority slut who "totally fell for Jesus" last summer—and in evangelical terms, she's *on fire!*

"Can you imagine the impact we could have, like, *on the world*, if Jesus was Lord of the Kappa house?" Heather muses.

Monica looks at me, gushing at Heather's zeal. But I don't see Heather's budding naiveté as sweet, just naïve. I also happen to know that half my fraternity has slept with her. Thank God I never did while sowing my wild oats on Greek Row. The fraternity was a detour from the straight-and-narrow, but now I'm back on track and living for the Lord.

"Is the Lord leading you in a certain direction?" Monica asks, looking up at me doe-eyed.

It's a loaded question.

The truth is I've become a slightly jaded Jesus freak. Spreading the Good News since my freshman year, I'm now three years into my campus crusade and the fundamentals are choking my faith. It's the ringing doorbells part. I'd even planned on sitting this day out, but since I'm trying to impress Monica so she'll fall in love and marry me, here I am, ding-dong indoctrinating.

I march to the door of one of the historic Victorian homes that line the street and knock. I'm not wearing a tie, so we don't look Mormon. We look like college kids, maybe knocking to ask directions or to solicit support for a local charity.

We definitely don't have that *"Have you signed up for Heaven?"* look.

An elderly woman opens the door, graying, hunched over and at least a hundred years old. She keeps the screen door closed. I look to Monica, who nods to Heather, granting her permission to take off the training wheels—a decision that has Monica and me already bracing for impact.

"Hi ma'am," Heather says. "Do you know where you'll be spending eternity?"

The woman cocks her head, shifting her weight precariously on her cane.

Heather continues, but louder. "If you want to go to Heaven, I have great news!" she pitches, as if selling miracle hand cream on an infomercial.

The wobbly old woman slams the door in our face.

"Did I say something wrong?" Heather asks, crestfallen. "Was it *me*?"

"No, Heather," Monica consoles her. "Some people just aren't ready to hear the truth."

"I'm just saying," Heather scowls. "If she goes to Hell, it's not my fault!"

Gathering on the next porch, Heather prayerfully pouting, Monica looks at me and our eyes agree that she just isn't ready. With Heather on the bench and so many souls to go, as I reach to knock, Monica whispers, "Why don't you take this one?"

I'm not bragging, but when it comes to winning souls for the Kingdom, the leaders of Campus Crusade for Christ all believe I'm gifted. I think most people can learn to be a good salesman for Jesus, but the best and brightest evangelicals are simply born with it. I'm able to effortlessly turn a conversation with a stranger about the weather into a discussion about eternity in less than two minutes. It just comes naturally. My evangelical skills might give one the impression that I can walk on water, or that my mom was a virgin, but it's not me. *It's the Lord.*

At the very least, most heathens figure I've been saving souls all my life, but really I was just like them until my senior year in high school and I was "born again"—the ecclesiastical turning point I talk about when I go around to churches and give my testimony: "New Year's Eve, 1988, I was in Lake Tahoe with my mom and her side of the family. It was a cold, wintry night..." I testify, trying to create drama and suspense. "While most were counting down to a new year, I was staring out of the 13th floor window of a Harrah's casino hotel room, wrestling with the tough questions: *What's the meaning of life? Why are my parents divorcing? Where am I going to college?* Those were some of the questions that led me to Him, and I know most of you have your own questions, but I'm here to tell y'all today, whatever your question, *Jesus Christ is the answer!*" I preach, usually triggering a few Amens from the pews.

That's the version I tell the church folk. Full stop.

The part I leave out, the part I don't dare talk about: the reason I was a tormented Texas 12th grader in Tahoe, the *real* reason I was mulling the merits of jumping from the 13th floor balcony was that I had a girlfriend, Julie, and a best friend, Luke, and I was in love with one of them.

And it wasn't Julie.

As much as a seventeen-year-old high school kid could know about love, Luke was the one that stirred my soul, and that mortified me. Julie had no idea, and neither did he.

The queer affliction that reared its ugly head at the dawn

of puberty had spread from my libido to my heart. I was a high school senior, secretly harboring romantic feelings for my best friend and not my girlfriend—an excruciating detail to keep from the two people who knew me best, but didn't know me at all. *What was I expecting to happen? Luke and I go to prom together? Hold hands in the hallway?* It was all so disturbingly incompatible with the world around me, as I gazed down at Lake Tahoe Boulevard—party horns blaring, fireworks lighting up the sky, my soul suffocating with fear—I was thinking the unthinkable: the only way to spare my parents the shame and stigma of having a gay son, the only way to escape an existence stricken with AIDS (widely believed in 1987 to be God's judgment), the only way to put an end to the amorous sentiments festering inside for Luke was to take just one small step off the 13th floor balcony.

I didn't jump, of course. Instead—and this is where I pick back up on the church-appropriate version of my testimony: "I grabbed a book I'd picked up in the DFW airport entitled *God's way to the Good Life* by Robert Schuller, and as the rest of Tahoe was bringing in the new year, I was on my knees praying that God would give me the good life. And He did. And He'll give it to you as well. All you have to do is ask!"

That was *the* defining moment, New Year's Eve marking the rebirth of my spirit and the genesis of a new identity—one I hoped would be straight.

With a renewed sense of hope, purpose, and direction, I entered Penn State the next autumn as a freshman on a gymnastics scholarship, fired up to learn more about the Bible. When a charismatic sophomore named Brett approached me in front of the dorms the first week and invited me to a Bible study he was leading out of his dorm room, it seemed divine.

He was involved with Campus Crusade for Christ, a campus ministry with the primary goal, *"to help reach the sixty million college students of the world with the message of the Gospel."*

My mind was fertile ground, and the seed of fundamentalism was sown. The first non-negotiable fundamental quickly took root: the Bible was the *literal* and *inerrant* word of God. You didn't question *God's Word*. You just believed it. *"Hey bro, you spend time in the Word?"* was a common question from my fellow Crusaders. As was, *"How's your walk with God?"* God was the Creator of the Universe, but also your best friend, a genie in a bottle, there whenever you called on Him. Since the salvation of others was paramount, if you were up late witnessing and didn't have time to study for your chemistry exam, if you had faith and prayed, God would help you pass. After all, you were doing His work. There was *power* in prayer, and it worked a lot like magic. While most college kids took naps, Crusaders had "Quiet Time"—time scheduled daily for Bible study, reflection, and prayer. To know God, we were taught you must spend time with Him, so I rescheduled my classes to have the hour before gymnastics practice every day free to commune with the Creator in the Penn State campus chapel.

My blind faith and tenacious grip to an inerrant and holy Bible drew ire and skepticism from my teammates who saw my budding fundamentalist Christian worldview as simply ignorant.

"Dude, how can it be the 'Word of God' when it was written by men?" they challenged.

"It's *inspired* by God. He used human hands to write his message," I countered.

"I bet you also believe the world is only six thousand years old and created in six literal days?"

"Yeah, like God made fossils," they joked, mocking my apparent naïveté.

"Uh . . . well," I stumbled, not yet able to explain my blind faith, inspiring me to immerse in serious scholarship of the Bible. I began attending Bible studies, leading Bible studies, and taking my well-worn Bible with me everywhere. If someone had a question, I'd flip through the Bible for the answer. The Apostle Paul wrote in his letter to the Galatians: *"Do not gratify the desires of the flesh, for the desires of the flesh are against the Spirit, and the desires of the Spirit are against the flesh"* (Gal. 5:19). *"But the fruit of the Spirit was 'self-control'"* (Gal. 5:23).

I practiced self-control as if God was handing out gold stars, "denying my flesh" in an attempt to starve the demon of homosexuality. In the men's Bible study I led out of my dorm room my sophomore year, we took vows of celibacy in preparation for our future wives. I'd been taught *if we do our best, God will do the rest*, but when it came to my desire for Eve, God wasn't meeting me halfway! Despite a two-year commitment to celibacy, complete immersion in the Word, and an unwavering faith, I was *still* staring limply at the pages of *Playboy*.

It was like dieting and exercising obsessively for two years and actually gaining weight.

My spirit broke.

After two years (and two ankle surgeries) at Penn State, I traded my scholarship for my freedom, transferring to UCLA in the fall of 1990 and slowly shedding the chains of Christian fundamentalism. It wasn't until the end of my first semester that I'd thawed enough to drink a beer without feeling like I was sinning against the Lord. I'd hoped that by walking the straight and narrow God would reward my celibacy with straightness, but those efforts proved futile.

It was time to change tactics.

I'd been treating my problem as a *spiritual* issue—a gay demon that needed to be exorcised—but what if my problem was *psychological?* Since I was a student at UCLA, home to one of the top Psychology departments in the country, my academic path was sealed. I'd taken classes in statistics, chemistry and computer science, but none ignited my passion like Abnormal Psychology 101. I liked the idea of making a living by helping others. But really I wasn't thinking about future employment when I chose to major in psychology. I was thinking about a *cure,* the *possibility* of a future free of the *abnormal* desire to connect with dudes. If my same-sex affliction had psychological roots, then a degree in psychology would provide scientific insight into the human psyche and the psychological tools to fix what's broken inside.

I hadn't given up on God, but in an effort to provide optimal conditions for the successful cultivation of hetero-desire, I thought it fitting to augment my studies of psychology with intimate exposure to females—the kind found *outside* of church, Bible studies, and prayer meetings. So I joined a fraternity, and by spring I was sitting in the middle of the trophy room at the Lambda Chi frat house surrounded by a brood of bros as a blonde and buxom stripper named "Marilyn" circled me, provocatively shaking a can of Reddi-wip whipped cream.

She'd been hired as a tasty treat for all us new pledges.

"You're a handsome one," she said in a squeaky voice more Minnie Mouse than Marilyn Monroe. A blonde wig was all she was wearing. She leaned in, jiggling her breast implants that hung like overripe melons in an earthquake, as my fraternity brothers whooped and hollered.

"Do you like whipped cream?" she asked, seductively.

On the Reddi-wip can there was a picture of a stack of pancakes with a large dollop of whipped cream on top, and I just didn't have the heart to tell her I preferred my whipped cream on pancakes or sundaes and not on her silver dollar-sized areolas.

"I love whipped cream," I said, acting as hormonally ravaged as I could.

With her creamy nips heading for my face, I closed my eyes and commanded my tongue to start licking, all the while struck by how shocking it was to go from sharing Jesus Christ with the pagans at Penn State to licking Reddi-wip off the breasts of a stripper at a UCLA frat house. When I came up for air, my heart sank when I realized she wasn't finished with me yet. Grabbing the back of my head, she slammed my face into her bouncy bosom and started jiggling. I knew I was supposed to enjoy this, and did my best to seem genuinely thrilled, but her charade was lost on me.

And then my "big brother" did something cruel. He slipped a larger bill to the shady conman husband/manager, granting me access to the mother lode: her shaved pubis. While Marilyn decorated *down there*, I acted like I'd just found the golden ticket. And as I submerged into her whipped abyss, waves of nausea threatening my charade, the husband reminded me of the "no touching" rule. Before I could reply I was more than okay with that, Marilyn pulled my face into her frothy legs, inciting my brothers to go bonkers. There was a powerful testosterone-marinated mob mentality going on, an everybody-else-was-doing-it sort of thing.

But I *still* wasn't like everybody else. Not by a long shot.

At the end of my first year at UCLA, I moved out of the dorms and into the frat house for the summer. No one forced me. I went willingly. My hobbit-sized single room in the basement was private and away from the others, but after a few weeks of fraternal living, reality bit. While it was nice to think I joined a fraternity to canoodle with college sorority co-eds, the truth was I'd followed Eliot onto Greek Row and the bromantic feelings I'd bottled were starting to leak.

I met Eliot my first semester at UCLA. I was a transfer student shaking off the chill of two years in Pennsylvania, and he was a cocky freshman from Newport Beach who sat in the front row in board shorts and sandals asking questions that stumped our professors. I'd met a lot of people at UCLA, but Eliot was my first friend. We studied together, worked out at the campus gym, and even had our own midnight radio show at the campus radio station. I had no plans of joining a fraternity. I just tagged along with

Eliot to a few Rush events for the free food and beer, but when six guys from Sigma Chi took me into a dark room, shined a spotlight on me, and offered me their first "bid," I unwittingly accepted on the spot. Eliot accepted a bid also, but was having second thoughts about Sigma Chi and the next night sneaked off to Lambda Chi without me just to make sure. I panicked. I'd only joined *because of him*, and there I was playing drinking games with my new "pledge brothers," horrified to discover I had nothing in common with any of them. I was trapped and knew without Eliot I couldn't stay, so when the pledges were plastered, I took off for the Lambda Chi house. From the front stoop, with trembling hands I removed the Sigma Chi pin, but before I could get through the door, Eliot and an exuberant gang of pledges came barreling out. My eyes went straight to the Lambda Chi pin on Eliot's starched Oxford. "So you made a decision? Just like that?" I said, my chest tightening.

"This was a better fit for me."

"But, I don't know. I thought we would, we'd be . . .?"

"I thought you liked Sigma Chi? You seemed to—" he started, but was interrupted by his new "bros" honking their horns and calling for him. "Look, I got to go. We'll catch up later."

He left me standing on the front stoop of Lambda Chi with a Sigma Chi pledge pin in my pocket. *What do I do now?* I'd been to a few functions and knew some of the brothers, so I made it my mission to secure a spot, and in the eleventh hour when Lambda Chi offered me a bid, I accepted. But when I shared the news with Eliot, he seemed indifferent. *Was he mad I accepted a Sigma Chi bid before him? Does he know that sometimes when I'm alone in my dorm room I secretly listen to Elton John's song "Sacrifice" and think of him? Does he know...?*

After leaving me high and dry at Sigma Chi, I did yell at him in front of Reiber Hall; sneaking off and pledging a different fraternity felt like a betrayal. It was the last conversation we would ever have. We went from spending all our time together to not even making eye contact, despite the fact we were pledge brothers. And through all the blindfolds, candle-lit rituals, and secret handshakes, Eliot carried on as though I was invisible, and I carried on as if I didn't care. But I did care; my unrequited love was a brutal secret to hide. The frat house had become my prison, and I'd become a hostage to my own heart.

Eliot had become the college version of my high school friend, Luke. I'd fallen into the same hole in the same sidewalk—a damning realization to have from a basement single in a frat house. I'd become a bro-mo, and on a gray day in June, I broke out the Yellow Pages and looked under "P" for psychologists. And as I settled into the leather club chair across from Dr. Kaufman, a Hungarian Jewish psychoanalyst, I prayed he'd be able to navigate the labyrinth of my psyche, rewire my desires, and free me from these godforsaken bro-curious longings.

With therapy underway to address the glitches in my psyche, I focused on my female immersion program, finding the frat house to be fertile ground. Not two weeks later, on the Fourth of July, I was in Will Forte's room with a sorority co-ed named Hillary, or Heather, or maybe Holly. I didn't know, but she was on top, straddling me in the dark and clawing at my zipper. She was driving, and I was just a passenger. It was all happening so fast my head was spinning. (Actually, the head spinning started an hour prior when they broke out the ridiculous beer bong, a delivery system involving a funnel and a tube.) And when she had successfully unzipped me, I knew, even in my inebriation, I was about to lose my virginity.

This girl wasn't a nervous virgin, but a vociferous vixen.

I remember trying to focus my blurry eyes on her silhouette, but there were three of her. They all slipped off their panties. They all feverishly hiked their dresses. But only one, the real one, straddled me. It was slippery—and I was so beer-bonged that it didn't register what I was doing, or that I was doing it unsafely—and within a minute it ended with a fertile blemish on her blue dress. She yelled something about her dress, but the room was spinning so fast I couldn't stop it as the gallons of beer in my belly churned like a washing machine on the spin cycle. With the urgency one has escaping a burning building, I stumbled buck naked down two flights of stairs, only to hurl in the hallway outside my door. Not wanting to be found basted in my own barf, I belly crawled into my frat den, and instead of climbing into bed, I passed out on the floor.

The next morning I woke, and in a head-splitting moment of sobriety, I realized I had just lost my virginity to a stranger. As a zealous Crusader at Penn State, my commitment to celibacy was often mocked by my teammates. "I don't want to drag memories of the women I've had sex with into my marriage," I'd say, dreamily. "I want to be able tell my wife that *she's the first. That I waited for her.*" They would simultaneously roll their eyes, seemingly queasy from my gushy ideals. When renowned Christian apologist Josh McDowell came to Penn State to give his *"Why Wait?"* seminar based on his pro-abstinence book, I was asked to emcee the event and to introduce Josh. I was flattered, but balked at the idea of advocating abstinence on a stage in front of five thousand Penn State students when I was "waiting" for entirely different reasons. "Sex is a gift from God. God created sex!" I'd say. "But it's for the *covenant of marriage!*"

Lying in a pool of my own vomit, my spirit sank at the realization I'd waited twenty-one years for *this*.

And I didn't even know her name. *Holly?*

§ § §

A few months later, I was sitting at a café table in Westwood Village across from Kate, a girl I affectionately scooped ice cream with at Baskin Robbins in Hurst, Texas when we were sweet sixteen. She'd heard I'd transferred to UCLA and got my number from a mutual high school friend. We'd been living only a few blocks from one another and didn't even know.

In a city like Los Angeles, there's comfort in friendships that have a history.

"Yours was Rocky Road," I said, recalling her favorite flavor.

"Actually mine changed every week, yours was…what, chocolate chip?"

"Jamoca Almond Fudge. You don't know me at all!" I said, our rapport easy and familiar.

She smiled her smile, a marketable one. "I can't believe I found you! You look great!"

"You look great, too," I said. And she really did.

After high school, I learned she went to college briefly in San Diego before landing a modeling contract in Tokyo. She had just returned to LA with lots of yen and a dream of an acting career. I had no doubt she'd make it. She had innate sex appeal, long chestnut brown hair, almond eyes, and a raspy, sensuous voice. And when she picked me up at the apartment I had recently moved into with three frat brothers, Brock, the obnoxious stoner one, started salivating.

During our reunion filled with laughter and affection, the waiter commented we made a "great couple," prompting me to clarify we were old friends—a definition of the relationship soon to be refined. We were bonded by our history, and I needed a date for my fraternity parties.

After our first date, a good night kiss led to her bedroom where she lit candles, dimmed the lights, and explored my body with her tongue, navigating to my nether region in a way that proved effective. The next night she broke out the Trojans and even though we were the same age, it felt like *The Graduate*—she the older, experienced woman and me the boy, coming of age. As we descended into the post-coital decompression chamber that first time, I noticed something: I didn't feel guilty. I felt relieved.

"That was amazing!" she said, promptly removing the prophylactic and discarding it in the bathroom. She'd done this before, and I was still trying to clear my ears. At twenty-one years old, my copulatory credentials were limited to ninety seconds with a sorority girl whose name started with an "H". This was different. Not only did I know her name, I knew her favorite flavor of ice cream.

Over the next several weeks, I stayed at Kate's almost every night. And every morning while brushing my teeth—with *my* toothbrush she kept in the drawer next to hers—I thought *the waiter might be right.* I still had evangelical voices screaming in my head about the importance of honoring God by *waiting until marriage for sex,* but I quelled them with the fact that *at least* I was having sex with a woman. And if Kate's sexual healing turned me around, it could all be justified. In my head, we had all the ingredients of a great relationship except for two things: she had a lingering long-distance, on-again, off-again boyfriend. And my attraction to guys wasn't going away despite having a toothbrush at her place. I had toured Virginia and was fine wearing a tourist T-shirt, but it was a destination I wished I could just cross off the list—*been there, done that, and thanks for the memories!* But to succeed in my mission to change, I'd need to establish full-time residency. With Kate, it was more than all that. Beyond the tourist visa, I was consumed with a romantic affection for her. While my libido lagged, my heart was involved.

For Halloween, I dressed as a cowboy, and Kate was to be Daisy Duke. But when I called to tell her I was on my way, a scary snag in our plans led to the premature shedding of her short shorts. Her out-of-state boyfriend was in state, surprising her by showing up on her doorstep.

"He's here," she whispered into the phone. "I had no idea, so I'm not going to be able—"

"I take it you didn't tell him about us?"

"No, but he knows something is wrong. We've been fighting since he got here. Apparently he's counting condoms, which is just crazy. He's convinced I'm cheating on him."

"If he thinks you're cheating then you are! You said y'all weren't exclusive or whatever."

"I can't talk about this right now. I'm sorry," she snapped, hanging up the phone abruptly.

On the way to the party, I drove by Kate's place, and since her room was directly above the carport, I could see two shadowy figures though the billowy drapes, and they were definitely not breaking up. In the tandem parking space behind her car—where *I* usually parked—was the sporty BMW of her chronic out-of-town—on-again, off-again—boyfriend.

From where I was sitting across the street, he was in town and it was on again—a visual that initially provoked anger and a cruel reminder that I'd been playing second fiddle. But when I pondered the prospect of not having Kate in my life, the anger dissolved into sadness.

At the Halloween Party, the frat house had become a "Haunted House," so I had to maneuver through all sorts of bloody serial-killer nonsense just to get to the keg. And since one of the brothers was a cast member on MTV's *Real World: Los Angeles*, there were camera crews around every corner filming everything. It was annoying. I didn't want anyone to see me, and definitely didn't want to be on national television, so once I made it through the obstacle course of cameras and corpses, I poured a beer and watched all the stupid couples: Raggedy Ann and Andy, Superman and Lois Lane, Tarzan and Jane. And then there was me, the lone Cowboy.

My stoner roommate, Brock, approached dressed in a skeleton outfit. He was my least favorite roommate. He had failed out of school the previous semester but still went to frat parties, smoked pot all day, and partied all night. When he returned from his late night liaisons, he ate my food in the fridge. After one of the parties he hosted at our apartment, he set up a voyeuristic sex trap in his room where he'd have sex with some wasted sorority girl, or as he called them "bushpigs," while guys hid out and watched, the girls unaware of the Peeping Toms.

"You're such a fag!" he said, checking me up and down, scrutinizing and smirking.

And with these words, my ego deflated like a balloon pricked with a pin. "I'm, uh, a cowboy."

"A gayboy is more like it," he said. And although he teased that way with everyone, it wounded me in a way that took me back to elementary school.

I had to get out of there. It was as if he saw what I'd been trying to hide from my fraternity. *Was it the cowboy outfit?*

I suddenly became paranoid. I felt paralyzed. Or maybe without Kate, I felt more exposed. For weeks she had been my armor, my beard.

"Where's your hottie?" he asked, downing his beer, burping and blowing it my way.

"She's . . . uh, she couldn't—you're disgusting," I said, turning and walking away.

On the way out, I passed Eliot dressed as Dracula and bobbing for apples from a barrel with his bride, fake blood all over her neck and face. He resurfaced with an apple stuck to his fake vampire teeth. She took a bite, before it devolved into a bloody and sensuous make out—a visual confirming that I was still afflicted with unrequited desire. There'd been a crushing weight sitting on my chest since he walked away mid-spot, leaving me benching more than I could press on my own. Burning with shame, I slipped out, trying my best to hold back the tears.

While doing time on Greek Row, I resolved to find a love connection with a sorority girl and get on with the program. I drank from the ever-flowing keg and grinded with drunken coeds on beer-soaked dance floors in a desperate attempt to ignite the kindling of desire. Despite intoxicated sexual liaisons with nameless sorority girls, and a fanciful fling with Kate, I was still yearning to meet guys like me—guys who might look away when "Marilyn" bent over.

Frustrated with my frat-boy life, I returned to Campus Crusade for Christ, knowing that for me to change, I'd definitely need a *miracle*. I took comfort in the familiar fold of Campus Crusade at UCLA. And now on the streets of San Francisco, I'm officially back in the salvation business, walking the straight and narrow, hoping once again it will make me straight.

The door opens to reveal a short, round, middle-aged man wearing a chef's apron. He's a chef's hat away from being a stunt double for Chef Boyardee. He wipes his plump hands on his apron, scratches his bushy graying mustache and eyes us suspiciously. "Can I help you?"

"Hi, sir. Sorry to bother you, but we're going door to door doing spiritual surveys and wondering if we could ask you a couple questions?" I say, trying not to sound too preachy.

"Are you Mormons?" he asks, guessing as if on a quiz show.

"No," I reply, chuckling at his assumption that we're like *them*.

"Jehovah's Witnesses?"

"No. Getting colder," I say, smiling, doing my best to play the charming Christian role.

"Okay, what's the survey? Hold on. Let me get my partner. He loves this. He's a religion professor at S.F.U.," he says, singing toward the back. "Tim-aaahh-theee, we have guests!"

He eyes us with an unashamed smile as we all shift uncomfortably. Especially me.

Earlier this morning we'd attended a seminar given by a "former lesbian" who "came out of homosexuality," her testimony affirming that homosexuality is a brokenness that can be healed.

When Leanne Payne spoke of "ex-gay" testimonies of real change, a seed was planted.

Shortly after the seminar, I teamed with Monica and Heather, incidentally driving through the Castro, the infamous gay-borhood of San Francisco, all of us wide-eyed—the rainbow flags, the guys holding hands, the drag queens. I'd never seen anything like it. During my youth under the blinding Friday-night lights, when people said the word "San Francisco," they spit it out like a dirty word. It was where all the "fags" and "queers" migrated. And when they said "fags" and "queers," it was always delivered with venom. The images were enough to propel holy Heather into prayer. *"Dear God, send your Holy Spirit and convict these lost people of their sin. Use us, baby Jesus, as a light in the darkness, let*—" she stopped mid-prayer when she noticed two girls kissing at the bus stop. "Oh. My. God! Gah-ross! Those girls were totally—"

"Not here to judge, Heather," Monica jumped in. "Just to love and share the Good News."

"I know, but I just feel it. Can't you feel it, the *evil*? It's in the air."

Now, prepped to preach on a porch in the Castro, the three of us watch as a tall, slender, fifty-something man, dressed in corduroy pants and sweater, joins Chef Boyardee at the door, removing his reading glasses and looking at us with a warm smile.

"They're going door to door doing spiritual surveys," the Chef explains to Timothy.

Timothy notices the Bible I'm holding and then studies each of our faces. I'm unable to look him in the eye because I'm afraid he'll know. Heather is already pulling out the pamphlets.

"So, we're gay," says the Chef.

"I think they got that," Timothy jests.

"Timothy is the love of my life and since you're knocking on our door, I think it's only fair that we get to ask the first question."

"Okay," I say, wishing I could just disappear. I glance over and notice Heather is biting her tongue, doing everything she can to hold in the sermon brewing inside.

"How does your God view us and our loving commitment of twenty years?" asks the Chef.

"It's immoral," Heather blurts out, without skipping a beat.

I wish we had put a muzzle on her. Monica and I share a horrified look, speechless.

"And it's an abomination according to the Bible," Heather continues. "But I have good news: God loves you both and He can save you from all this sinniness and help you *change!*"

They both just look at her, not knowing what to make of her. It's an awkward silence.

"We have pamphlets we can leave with you so when you're ready to repent," Heather says.

She pushes the pamphlets; Chef reacts to the tracts as if they're serpents, while Professor Timothy politely takes one. "The Four Spiritual Laws?" Timothy reads aloud.

"It's easy. You can be saved in four easy steps!" Heather pitches, trying to make the sale.

"I'm not sure how to respond," Timothy says. "I appreciate your fervor, but it strikes me as odd: you knock on our door, you don't know us, and yet you're passing judgment."

"I'm not passing judgment," Heather says. "It's in the Bible, y'all."

"Where?" the Chef asks, more indignant and less patient than Timothy. "Can you point out the part that calls our relationship—based on love, commitment and respect—immoral?"

"It's in here," she says, holding up the Bible, as if it will speak for itself.

"Where?" the Chef demands.

"I'll have to get back to you, but it's definitely an abomination."

"So is wearing clothes made of two fibers and eating shellfish," Chef says. "So why aren't you picketing the Gap or Red Lobster?"

Heather turns to us for backup, but she's opened a can of worms we're not touching.

"Since you're subjectively interpreting writings written over two thousand years ago in a language that has been translated," Timothy says, "how do you deal with Apostle Paul's writings that women should submit to men, keep their heads covered, and are unfit to preach?"

Heather doesn't have a ready response so she dodges. "Maybe we should pray. Do you want to pray? Step four of the Four Spiritual Laws—" Heather pushes, but Monica interrupts.

"Why don't we just leave the literature, and if they want to discuss, there's a number on the back. Thanks for your time," Monica says politely, physically pulling Heather from the porch.

"But they need the Lord!" she whispers aggressively to Monica. "I'm not losing another one. If they go to Hell, it's not on me!" She turns to the guys. "Would you like to pray?"

They both just look at her speechless. Even I'm horrified, caught in the middle.

"I'm thinking . . . no. But thanks for the offer," the Chef responds, sarcasm unchecked.

"Again. We're sorry to bother you," Monica says, backing away.

"If you flip to step four of the Four Spiritual—" Heather starts, but Monica grips her arm, taking control of her much like a dog trainer correcting a misbehaving puppy.

At the end of the *Four Spiritual Laws*, there is a question whether the unsaved soul wants to invite Jesus into their heart, and if they say the prayer, it's like closing the deal: *Chalk one more for the Kingdom!* These numbers are used as statistics in measuring our ability as holy salespeople: *How many souls you save today? How many souls you save? I asked you first!*

Being a Campus Crusade Christian is all about signing others up for Heaven, and on the gray, gloomy streets of San Francisco, I'm struck by my own desperation. I have become *that guy*—the one ringing doorbells for Jesus in the Castro of San Francisco, as if God is handing out heterosexuality and a bride as a prize to the pushiest proselytizer, my life path curiously leading me to the front lines of a culture war I fear will never have clear winners and losers.

As I straddle the line in the sand that separates the gay couple and the evangelical Christians, since I'm the one holding a Bible, I realize this conflict defines my existence and my spirit will never be at ease until I'm able to reconcile the two sides. Since I'm a born-again Christian, I *can't* be gay. Not only that, I don't *want* to be gay. I've seen what happens to gay people.

If change is an option, then I choose change. And with God as my witness, I *will* change!

And I won't rest until I have.

CHAPTER 2:

HUGH HEFNER'S CLOSET

I'm in Hugh Hefner's closet, drowning in a sea of silk pajamas. My degree in psychology from UCLA is crowning and I'm wondering: If everything supposedly happens *for a reason*, then how did I end up *here*? Obviously, I have rebelled against God and have taken a wrong turn.

Or maybe the Lord does work in mysterious ways...

After returning from selling Jesus Christ like Girl Scout cookies on the streets of San Francisco, I began the year discouraged that my crusade for the Holy Grail of heterosexuality was still a bust. I didn't have a clue where to look next. Throughout the year, I continued to pray for Divine Intervention, all the while plagued with an aching sense of loneliness. Even in the company of goody-goody Crusaders and debased fraternity brothers, I'd become isolated, my secret forcing me to keep all of humanity at arm's length—all except Dr. Kaufman, my oasis in the desert. During our weekly sessions I continued to dig through my psyche, trying to unearth the root of my abnormal psychology, while he worked tirelessly to defuse the damage of my internalized judgment. In the twilight of my college years, I was going through the motions, half-heartedly attending Crusade meetings and church, and only sporadically showing up at fraternity functions, lacking the zeal to fraternize. Or see Eliot. I was hiding in plain sight.

And *then*, on the last eve of the year, a ray of heavenly light seemingly pierced through the darkness as I timidly approached the pearly gates of the Playboy Mansion. Through a fraternity brother with a connection, my name was on the list for the New Year's Eve Bash! While I might have rang in 1992 at an airport Best Western in San Fran with a banquet hall of born-agains, I'd be ringing in 1993 at the Playboy Mansion with Hugh Hefner and friends!

Of course I was entering through the servant's entrance, but you had to start somewhere, and in my mind, I was exactly where I needed to be. If there was any hope of ever making it in the Bunny business, the Playboy Mansion promised to be the ideal training ground and Hugh Hefner the ultimate mentor. Once through security, and after being issued my black vest and bowtie, I stumbled past the Gothic-Tudor-style mansion to the back lawn where a big tent sheltered a disco ball-studded dance floor and candle-lit tables of white linen. As a tuxedoed jazz band warmed up—flamingos and peacocks roaming freely on the lush and manicured 5.3 acres—even I was seduced by the intoxicating mystique, marveling at the infamous grotto glowing with lights and opportunities. As Bunnies and celebs arrived, the magical grounds transformed into a playground of grown-up boys (over sixty) parading around with peroxide blonde girls (young enough to be their granddaughters) with swollen breasts on the verge of bursting.

"Are you finished with your plate," I asked Tony Curtis, playing the role of Playboy butler, a springboard to bigger and better things. I was hoping if I aimed for excellence, someone would see beyond the butler disguise and spot my star quality. *Who's the new butler? Promote him! Did you see the way he cleared the plates off that table? He's a keeper!*

And that's what happened. I did such a stellar job whisking through the crowd of Hollywood elite, cleaning up empty plates and glasses, I kept getting asked back to work more parties. It's 1993, and Mr. Playboy is inconceivably *married*. Kimberly, a former Playmate, shed her clothes in 1988 and has become "the one" to usher in the Ice Age at the Playboy Mansion. They have two children, both under the age of three, four nannies and a staff fit for a royal family. The Mansion has mostly become a family playground, the infamous grotto a kiddy pool. Kimberly runs the mansion like a wicked queen, scaring off all the Bunnies and keeping us butlers on our toes. Sure there are parties, but not like the good ole days. The more senior butlers are full of stories; back in the day (a.k.a. "B.K."), there were enough Bunnies to go around. Or so they claim. The full-timers are guys whose odds of getting laid plummet as soon as they walk off the property. But at the Playboy Mansion, getting some tail is just one of the perks.

And that's why I'm here, my life path curiously leading to the Playboy Mansion. In my mind, Hugh Hefner is the keeper of the Holy Grail, and if *he* can't help me, then really who can?

In my circle of Campus Crusade friends, working for Hugh Hefner has meant one thing: I've crossed over to the dark side and working in the Lion's Den. *"How do you deal with all the temptation? How do you get any work done with all the—see, just talking about it is gonna make me stumble!"* But that's exactly my objective at the Playboy Mansion: to be tempted and to stumble would be a *miracle*. Hefner doesn't know I'm a furtive fundamentalist born-again on yet another detour from the straight and narrow and desperately in need of him to save me.

I didn't have to list that on my application.

Since I've been angling for an apprenticeship, I've elbowed my way into butler duties that give me the most one-on-one exposure. I want Hef to notice me, so I've set out to raise the standards of butler excellence to soaring new heights. When I prep his dinner tray (for a more senior butler to deliver), I am meticulous, double-checking the laminated diagram to ensure the plates, silver, and condiments are all in the right place. My first month, the head chef went ballistic when I placed the salt and peppershaker to the left of the appetizer plate and not to the right of the entrée plate. It was as if the entire foundation of the Playboy enterprise might topple if everything wasn't perfect. I'm not sure if it's Hef with the obsessive need for order, but the staff are used to things being a certain way, and as a rookie butler, I must meet their strict standards or else. Since I'm already a perfectionist, I'm perfect for the job—a part-time gig until I graduate from UCLA in June, or until the fire in my belly is burning for bunnies.

By the end of February, I learned I was being groomed, maybe tested. The rumor was that management believed I had "full-time" potential, which had me climbing the grand staircase balancing Hef's dinner tray *all by myself*. Since it would be our first one-on-one encounter, I was brainstorming the best way to solicit his support when his voice startled me back to reality, granting me entry into his chambers. I entered timidly, the tray heavier than I thought and shaking as though in an earthquake. I found him alone, sitting up in his majestic bed—a millwork miracle of English brown oak intricately carved with exotic images of naked women. Since he was writing his memoirs, the bed was strewn with

51

notebooks, photographs, and memorabilia. It's clearly the command center, the cockpit of the entire enterprise.

It's where *everything* happens.

Strangely, he eats all his meals alone and in bed. Even if he's hosting a party at 8:00 p.m. with a full buffet, he eats before, usually fried chicken and an appetizer of celery hearts. Teetering toward him with the trembling tray, I realized I hadn't been briefed as to the proper technique for the pass-off, so as I approached the landing pad on his lap, the tray began to shake—and to my horror, *tilt!* I braced for a crash, but then out of the corner of my eye I saw the sleeves of his trademark maroon smoking jacket, miraculously catching the tray and guiding it in for a safe, albeit bumpy, landing. When he smiled, I resumed breathing. As he settled in, I noticed his wrinkled hands—the hands of a sixty-seven-year-old man, the same age as my *grandfather*.

After a couple weeks of successful pass-offs, during our brief alone times, I've noticed he seems distracted, maybe sad. He just doesn't seem like himself, or rather the *image* he has created. The more senior butlers confide that he hasn't been off the property in years. People come to see him, but he never leaves the gates of the Mansion. I'm not sure if he's depressed, or just *married*. It shocked the world when he walked the aisle, and since then the Playboy lifestyle—the smoking jackets, pipe hanging from his mouth, scantily clad babes in bunny ears—has been in hibernation. The whole birth of *Playboy* was in response to the puritanical atmosphere of the 1950s, and now that he's married, he just seems like a caged animal.

Kimberly has him on a short leash, maybe a choke collar. Since I've been here, the eye candy has stayed in their wrappers. The Playboy Mansion is kid friendly and mostly Bunny-free.

Even to me it's weird.

Initially I figured it only a matter of time before Hef would see beyond my vest and bowtie and take me under his wing, showing me the down-and-dirty tricks of the trade. I imagined him bragging to the Bunnies about how far I'd come, telling the story about the time I dropped a tray of drinks on his backgammon table or that cursed day I brought the wrong cookies to Kimberly.

I'd be Mr. Playboy, Jr., skinny-dipping with centerfolds in the grotto in no time!

After three months of serving Mr. Hefner—on a mad afternoon in March—instead of bopping Bunnies, I'm mopping the floor of his closet with my tears: a Playboy butler with a Cinderella complex. It wasn't my intention to choke up in his closet, but as I held up a purple pair of adult PJs, I was sideswiped by how desperate I'd become: I'm sorting through Hugh Hefner's dirty laundry for eight bucks an hour, hoping some of his hetero might rub off on me? It's pathetic. And *what if* he were to walk in to find me crying in his closet? That'd be weird.

As I peer into the cavernous depths, I realize that in this cold, cruel world, Hugh Hefner's closet has become my safe place. It's larger than the bedroom of my apartment and unlike any closet I've ever experienced. It's not like I've gone around the world and conducted an independent study of people's closets, I just know there are few like this one.

I could live full time in this closet.

The walls aren't plaster with layers of old peeling paint like mine. These are lined majestically with antique wood intricately carved with details that hark back to the 1920s when the Mansion was originally built. The current resident seemingly has a silk fetish—hundreds of silk pajamas, in a diversity of colors, hang on a rod that extends for eternity, creating a sweeping silk pajama rainbow. As my fingers flirt with the silk, I marvel that I'm holding in my hand the potent signature of the Playboy lifestyle. *Pajamas.* And they do look comfortable... For a moment, I'm tempted to try a pair on, just to test the magic, but quickly abort the notion because it's... *creepy.* If there exists a heterosexual vortex in the universe, my theory has been I'd find it here. But after months of using Hugh Hefner's closet as base camp for my hetero-expedition, I'm beginning to doubt the pajamas have actual powers as I'd hoped. I just know I can't keep doing this—this hiding out in Hef's closet. Sooner or later, someone is going to find me.

I hear the master suite door open, springing me back into action. As I do my best not to sniffle on the silk, I feel a suffocating dark cloud hanging. I don't know if it's the senior year blues, the reality that I'm a Bunny-intolerant butler, or that two nights ago I had my first experience.

With a *dude*.

It all started last Saturday morning as I was tossing out the *LA Times* and inadvertently noticed the "male seeking male" section of the personals. With my bro-mates in the next room consumed with March Madness on TV, I began desperately scanning the ads, my curiosity heightened by my sense of isolation. I was looking for a guy who might fit in at my frat—a prophetic wish that would soon come to fruition in ways I could never have imagined.

Of all the ads, one took hold and wouldn't let go. It featured superficial buzzwords such as *"discreet, masculine, college jock."* When my roommates left to play basketball, I called the personals hotline and left a voice mail message for him. I made my situation clear: "I'm not *gay*. Definitely. Not. Gay. Just...curious. Bi-curious, I guess. No one knows, so..."

When he called back that night, he seemed normal, and

equally nervous. No one knew about him, either. That was a requirement. Doug was willing to meet sight unseen, but I wanted to see a picture first, which he agreed to mail. This was the tricky part. I live with two fraternity brothers. Doug is a stranger through a personal ad. What if the envelope rips, they check the mail and find pics of another dude addressed to me? Could be kind of awkward.

After a couple days of stalking the mailman, I intercepted the parcel on my way out the door to Kate's new apartment in Beverly Hills. After our spooky split, we didn't speak. And that winter—while I was sharing Christ in the Castro—she married an actor she'd met on a Bud Light commercial shoot, the marriage lasting less than two months. Like sand through an hourglass, so are the days of our lives. We reconnected a few weeks ago and went back to being friends—the way it should be. I never asked about a certain on-again, off-again boyfriend.

When we worked at Baskin Robbins as teens, customers often mistook us for brother and sister, and all these years later she is the closest thing to a sister I've ever had. In *Star Wars* terms, she is Princess Leia and I am Luke Skywalker. To restore our friendship, I've had to accept two things: I'm not Han Solo, and Princess Leia, though pretty, is really my twin sister.

We don't talk about the sex part.

Clutching the mysterious parcel, I jumped in my car, drove around the block and parked on a different street before opening it up. No way could I take the envelope inside the apartment.

I didn't want any evidence.

He told me he wasn't a model, but had dabbled. Glancing through the tinted windows, paranoid someone would catch me, I tore open the envelope to find a modeling ZED card: a 5x7 business card for models. On the front, a *GQ* shot of an athletic guy in a sporty suit. On the back, four shots showing four different looks. And they all looked good to me.

The ball was now in my court.

"You don't like it," Kate yelled from the kitchen where she was moving boxes around her new small, but swanky, one-bedroom apartment. She recently booked a television pilot, a big deal for an aspiring actress, and I'd been summoned over to watch the pilot episode.

"It's good!" I yelled back. "You look great," I assured her.

"You're not laughing," she said, moving into the room. "It's supposed to be a comedy."

"I am laughing," I said, but the truth was I was distracted by the package I'd received.

Since Kate was my first experience with a woman, nameless sorority girls notwithstanding, it felt odd to think I was a phone call away from having my first experience with a dude. Although physically present, I was in anguish, still reeling that I'd actually gone so far acting on impulses I'd repressed since puberty. I was hoping being with her might pull me from the edge.

"You don't have to watch the whole thing," Kate said, catching me daydreaming.

Since she's always been so supportive of me, I was there to support her. In high school, she once came to my gymnastics practice after school just to watch. And then we went to Pizza Hut and talked for hours about everything (well, almost everything). When I set the state record in men's gymnastics and received a scholarship, none of my friends were more proud than Kate.

She collapsed onto the sofa next to me, her mocha brown eyes full of uncertainty.

"I think it's good," I said, images of the mysterious guy playing in my brain, making my heart swell in a way it never had, even with Kate. "When will you know if it's picked up?"

"Tomorrow," she said, biting her lip anxiously. "Let's go rollerblading. I'm so sick of watching myself." As we rollerbladed through the streets of Beverly Hills into the early morning hours, talking and laughing, I felt like I was hiding something from her. And I was.

And not just photos of a stranger.

We stayed up all night, rollerblading to the corner newsstand at 7 a.m. to catch delivery of the Hollywood trade magazine *Variety* to learn her destiny: her show wasn't on the list. She deflated in my arms on the corner of Beverly as I assured her there would be other opportunities.

I would be proven right.

When I got back to my apartment, I darted to my room, hiding the pictures of Doug in the darkest recesses of my closet. No way could I go through with it. That's just so . . . *gay*.

But he was all I could think about.

The next day at the Mansion I was polishing silver with Tony, a new butler on the temp staff, and he asked if I'd seen the latest *Playboy* issue. I replied I hadn't, which absolutely shocked him. He wanted me to drop the forks and go check it out. Tony is one of the butlers who must continuously wipe the drool from his chin. The issue featured a new college co-ed named Jenny McCarthy, and she had all the butlers slobbering—all except me, it would seem.

"Smokin' hot," Tony said, salivating over the silver. "Rocket body. Nice tits. Pretty face. I'd do her."

During my break, I grabbed the issue, locked myself in one of the grotto bathrooms, and opened to Jenny McCarthy in full glory. On the backdrop of my imagination, I entertained a fantasy where she stripped me of my clothes and did all the things her pictures suggested.

Nothing. Not even a spark.

This wasn't a new ritual. I've been trying to force a sexual response to Playboy Bunnies since puberty, but now at twenty-three years old, I'm still no closer to understanding their allure.

I'm left feeling ashamed and paranoid, and in this heterosexual playground, I didn't want anyone to know Jenny McCarthy leaves me limp. Later on, when Tony asked if I'd checked out her spread, I covered as I had so many times before. "Yeah, man. Hot. *Smokin'* hot!"

"She'd turn even a gay guy straight," he said, unexpectedly.

No comment.

He was clearly getting hot and bothered just thinking about her, and I questioned if he was fit to even work here. "You know she's coming here tomorrow?"

"Really?" I replied.

"For real. She's coming for a photo shoot."

A seed was planted, and I looked now to Jenny McCarthy to save me.

* * *

The next night I was working the late shift. While outside by the grotto pool, Jenny and another Playmate approached, taking a seat at one of the poolside tables. My first thought was that she looked different with clothes, but pretty nonetheless, and maybe slightly intimidated to be at the Mansion. Perhaps it was Kimberly, the evil queen of the Playboy Mansion, that caused her discomfort, or maybe she wasn't used to all the new attention that comes when you pose nude for a magazine like *Playboy*. Or maybe she was nervous about meeting Hugh Hefner.

There wasn't a social event that night, and since I was the only butler stationed outside, I approached their table plotting how I might go about getting her to fall in love with me.

One night with Jenny McCarthy might do the trick.

I rehearsed a few introductions, quickly dismissing the "Coffee, Tea, or Me?" intro that initially popped into my brain. I decided to play it safe. "Hey, can I bring y'all something to drink?" but delivered as suave and sexy as I could possibly be wearing a butler uniform.

Jenny looked up and smiled. "Do you have hot tea? Maybe something herbal?" She was gracious, seemingly down to earth and beautiful, but not stirring my loins as I hoped.

"We do," I replied, projecting all the sex appeal I could muster.

"With lemon and honey if you have it."

"Oh, I got some honey baby," I said without words. At this point Tony would have had to change his boxers, and yet here I was inches away from the Playmate of the Month *in the flesh* and she wasn't even registering on my radar. "You got it," I said with a wink, holding the eye contact, trying to subliminally communicate with her that I desperately needed her help.

She turned to the other Playmate, a brunette with a bitchy attitude who couldn't care less about anyone but her. "Club soda. Dash of lime," she barked, as if I was the servant that I was.

"I'll be right back," I said, being as charming as I could be.

When I returned with the drinks, I stalled as Hef approached the table, bringing both girls to their feet. As they shook hands with Mr. Playboy himself, I worked around them, setting up their beverages and listening to the awkward exchange they had with Hef, who didn't join them, but simply welcomed them before returning upstairs to his wicked queen.

Once Hef was gone, I cruised back by to check on them. "Do you girls need anything else?" I asked, in a slightly seductive way directed toward Jenny.

Jenny looked to the bitchy Playmate, who was staring at herself in a pocket mirror, which I could only guess she did for hours every day. Without looking up, she shook her head, indicating that she needed nothing more from me. "I think we're fine. Thanks!" Jenny said, graciously.

I walked away and immediately began trying to eroticize my encounter with Jenny in my imagination, turning it into a Playboy video where instead of saying they were fine, Jenny said something like, *"There is one more thing we need,"* as my fantasy cued the porn music.

I watched them leave, hoping I didn't give off a creepy vibe because I was creeping myself out. She had a photo shoot the next morning, an erotic encore to her first outing. She'd become a leading lady in the fantasy life of countless men, and yet in my imagination, she wasn't even a featured extra. Even a fantasy inspired by the Playboy Playmate of the Year *in the flesh* failed to get a rise out of me, deflating my hope of ever acquiring a taste for bunny tail.

When I got home that night, I broke down and called Doug, telling him I'd like to meet.

Since he lived in Orange County, he agreed to meet me on my turf the following night at Stratton's, my *Cheers*-like college bar. Since my fraternity was having a social with Kappa in downtown, I figured the likelihood of someone knowing my name was minimal. But after I arrived,

I realized it was an egregious threat to my anonymity. I had instructed him to find a booth upstairs and I'd find him. As I climbed the stairs, I noticed a tall, athletic guy sprawled out in a booth that sort of looked like the guy in the pics—same square jaw, same bushy eyebrows, but blonde highlights replaced with a buzz cut, his overall appearance more college jock than male model.

Since he had no idea what I looked like, I walked past him a few times, trying to summon the nerve as a frenzied swarm of butterflies fluttered in my gut. I'd spent the day in the stacks of the UCLA library, comfort-reading the Kinsey Reports. The 1948 study by Alfred Kinsey documented in *Sexual Behavior in the Human Male* was controversial and contradicted conventional beliefs, but gave me more wiggle room: *46% of male subjects had "reacted" sexually to persons of both sexes in the course of their adult lives, and 37% had at least one "homosexual experience."* Translation: I'm not alone, and closer to normal than I thought.

The Kinsey Scale, a sliding scale of human sexuality, was introduced to account for the finding that a majority of males didn't fit neatly into exclusive hetero (0) or homo categories (6), and instead fell somewhere in between. The scale was genius. It allowed me to be a little bit gay, but not totally gay, and as long as I was never gayer than a 4, I'd be fine. The Kinsey Report was like chicken soup for my soul, nourishing my normalcy. As I circled the strapping stud waiting for me, I finally took the plunge, sliding across the scale and into the dimly lit booth. "I was looking for *GQ* dude or the '*look how cool I am in a leather jacket*' guy."

"I almost wore the bathing suit so you could pick me out of the crowd, but I thought I'd be discreet," he replied with a cocky grin, putting me immediately at ease.

He poured me a beer from his half-empty pitcher while I threw paranoid glances around the bar, absolutely terrified I'd see someone I knew.

"I noticed you circling," he said slyly, as I gulped my beer. "I was hoping it was you."

After two hours and two pitchers, I was showing him which tree to climb to access the balcony to my room in the apartment I shared with two fraternity brothers. I had wanted my first encounter to be anonymous, so I never told him my last name. Having him scale the ficus to my bedroom wasn't exactly an "anonymous" maneuver.

Once safely in my room, the gravity of the situation hit me: I'm twenty-three years old, and this is the first time I've ever acted on my same-gender gravitations. The fact that two of my fraternity brothers were sleeping in adjoining rooms was a reality that required certain precautions. I had already prepped Doug before he shimmied the tree that there could be no talking. With us both on mute, the doors locked, and the lights off, I began to hesitantly explore his clothed body much like a blind person trying to determine the physical attributes of a new person. At first it was clinical; my hands started at his face, which was chiseled and angular, his shoulders and chest firm and athletic, his abs defined and tight. As my hand breached below the belt, I felt like a doctor performing a hernia test. I didn't ask him to cough as I cupped him, but knew I was officially out of bounds. And when it started to feel less clinical, I withdrew. My hands had explored a fair share of sorority girls, familiar with the curves and intricacies of the female form.

This was entirely different.

It's like using your right hand your entire life while secretly knowing you're left-handed. With it being the first time I'd ever used my left hand, it felt clumsy and awkward, so I ended my exam, all the while reassuring myself that on the Kinsey scale, that was mild, no more than a 3.

His hands were larger than mine, athletic and strong, as if made to palm a basketball. And as they began exploring my body, the dormant parts of me began stirring to life, which was frightening and exhilarating. *I shouldn't be doing this! This is wrong! You're sinning against God!* Since he's probably six-foot-five, he craned down to kiss me, which was really just *gay;* I mean, it was all gay, but the intimacy of the kiss was something that just seemed *more gay,* or maybe just intimate. And to this point, my intimacy had involved the delicate lips of females. Doug's lips were not delicate and his tongue was wild and caught me off guard, so I turned my head away. His man lips took the cue and moved down my neck—not in a gentle, tender way—but in a raw, uninhibited way that was stimulating to my body but troubling to my brain. As his hands worked to unbutton my jeans, it felt as though there was a Pandora's Box in my briefs, and once it was opened, I feared there was no turning back.

Am I really doing this? What does this mean? This is really, really gay!

Just as he unzipped my package, we both froze at the sound of a door opening to the bathroom I share with Colin, a pledge brother and one of my closest friends. Colin knew I had gone out, although I was vague with the details. *Did he hear me return ten minutes prior?* I frantically began orchestrating an evacuation plan in my head should he knock on my door. It wouldn't have been uncharacteristic of him to check in, and since the walls were thin, I stopped breathing. Even Doug was holding his breath. Any signs of life might have solicited a knock.

The toilet finally flushed, his door shut, and we both gasped for air.

At that point, I was thinking maybe I wasn't gay after all. This was my one experience that I just needed to get out of my system—the reality was not the fantasy after all—and now I could get on with my life as a fully-functioning, Bunny-chasing, stripper-loving hetero.

Doug turned the heat back on, but my fear had already extinguished the flame. Just the thought of Colin finding out, or any of my fraternity brothers, *or my family*, was enough to throw cold water on this whole sexperiment. As he leaned into me, consumed with a desire I had already put back in its cage, I pulled away abruptly. "I'm sorry. I can't do this."

He stopped suddenly, and neither one of us moved. And although it was dark—the streetlight and alarm clock casting a shadow on his chiseled face—I could see, and feel, he was thrown off.

"This is what I've always fantasized about," I whispered. "But now that I'm—well, I just can't. I'm sorry." With the stealth of a ninja, I ushered him through the darkened living room, past the closed doors of my sleeping roommates, out the front door, down the stairs, through the courtyard, and out the gate. "It was nice to meet you, though," I offered. "Good luck!"

He was definitely stunned by the sudden change of direction. I went back to my room, thankful I didn't go through with it. I knew I would've felt worse about myself the next day if we actually had a full-fledged sexual encounter. This one didn't count. This one didn't mean *anything*. And it certainly didn't mean I was *gay*. No way. This was simply a college experiment, an experience that only confirmed what I was hoping: *I'm not gay after all!*

* * *

The next day, yesterday, I called him. I had to see him again.

It wasn't sex that fueled my drive to Orange County last night. It was to talk. There was comfort knowing there was another human being living a similar existence. He was definitely surprised to hear from me but invited me down to his place, an apartment I knew he shared with two team-mates. I cringed at the idea. "Are you kidding? Can't we meet down the street? How about this: I'll honk three times and that'll be your cue to come out and meet me?"

He insisted I ring the doorbell like a normal person. I couldn't believe he was going to just introduce me to his roommates. After an hour drive, I finally found the address scribbled on a Post-it and parked in front of a ratty apartment building near UC Irvine. It was already dark, past nine o'clock. Pacing at the complex gate, I skittishly scanned for his name on the directory. When I buzzed his apartment, a voice answered, and I couldn't tell if it was Doug or not.

"Uh...hey, I'm here to see Doug," I said, talking macho, which I know sounded lame.

"Yo, Bryan. Doug's in the shower but come on up," the voice said, and then a buzz.

Shower? I opened the gate, entered the courtyard and walked up the stairs to apartment 206. Standing in front of the door, I raised my hand but couldn't knock. It wasn't too late to make a run for it. I'd let the gay genie out of the bottle, which felt safe with Doug, but with his jock roommates, what if they see through our charade? What if they out me? What if—

The door suddenly opened to reveal a real-life giant. He was so colossal that my head was at his waist. He was wearing a UC Irvine basketball jersey and sweatpants, and eating a bowl of cereal. He extended his mammoth hand, which swallowed mine. "Bryan. Kyle. Come in, bro."

I followed the mutant into the living room—a typical bachelor jock pad. Dishes were piled in the sink, a laundry basket had exploded on the floor next to the door, posters of basketball players were tacked crooked on the wall, and the TV tuned to ESPN. Kyle was glued to the basketball game in progress, the sounds of which filled the entire apartment. I felt like I was at the game, with the roars of the crowd, the announcers talking excitedly, and the sound of shoes squeaking across the court. Kyle, without taking his eyes off the action, cleared some dirty clothes and a pizza box from the tattered sofa. "Have a seat, bro. Doug'll be right out. Beer?"

"Sure, bro. I'll take a beer." Being in a fraternity, I knew bro-speech.

As I examined the sofa, my eyes went to a pizza sauce stain that definitely pre-dated the box, and other disturbing stains I didn't want to think about. I had little doubt there were things growing underneath the cushions, but I decided to take my chances and sat down on the bro-fa.

Kyle took two giant steps to the kitchen and opened the fridge, his eyes trained on the game. "USC at Stanford. Stanford is down four," he said, as if I was on pins and needles. I don't give a rat's ass about basketball but acted absolutely obsessed. He handed me a beer, collapsing on a recliner that didn't exactly accommodate his girth. He looked like an adult sitting in a chair for toddlers. I took a long nervous gulp of Keystone Light. I've never actually tasted urine, but I think if it was chilled and canned, it would taste like this. At every fraternity party for the last two years, it was always Keystone Light for one simple reason: it was cheap. The favorite method of delivery was a beer bong, and really, if you're going to drink it, it's better to get it over with. The heinous taste tormenting my tongue triggered the part of my brain in charge of memories and sitting on a grubby sofa in Irvine waiting for a stranger through a personal ad, I recalled all of my Keystone Light-soaked sexcapades with sorority girls. I wasn't keeping score, but figured I'd met my heterosexual quota.

Doug entered looking like he just popped out of the game on TV—Adidas sweatpants, Nike court shoes, UCLA jersey, and palming a basketball. His short hair was spiky wet. He approached me, extending his hand for a bro-shake. "Hey man," he said. "You found it."

"Yeah, man. Traffic was a bitch."

We acted like we were just two guys about to hit the town to chase some tail.

"You gotta be kidding me! Call it!" Kyle yelled at the TV. "I can't believe—did you see that shit?" Kyle asked Doug. Doug turned his attention from me to the TV and reacted.

"Are you serious?" Doug said. "What happened? I left and Stanford was up eight!"

"They lost Miller. Pulled his hamstring. Again. Plus the referees are fucking blind!"

I shook my head as if I was also disgusted, and then downed the rest of the putrid beer.

"I can't watch this shit!" Doug said, looking at me and nodding toward the door.

Kyle slurped the milk from his cereal bowl, scratched his balls, and unapologetically let out a burp that made the walls shake. He looked over at us and said, "What's up for tonight?"

"Mellow. Gonna shoot some hoops," Doug replied, grabbing his keys. "What about you?"

"Mary's on her way over. We have a Bio test tomorrow."

I took my empty can to the kitchen to find the trash, but really I could have left it anywhere.

"Cool. We're out," Doug said.

"Good to meet you, bro," Kyle said to me.

"Same, man. Thanks for the beer," I said, walking to the door with a stupid swagger.

Once we escaped the apartment, I began to breathe again. I followed Doug out to the street.

"I'm glad you called. I didn't think I was ever going to see you again," he said, eying me with a grin as he spun the basketball on his finger like a Harlem Globetrotter.

"Was that not just weird for you?" I asked, looking around to make sure we were alone.

"What?"

"Introducing me to your roommate. And I thought you had two?"

"I do. Tom's at his girlfriend's place—and no, it wasn't weird. Why would it be weird?"

"Uh...I don't know. We met through a *personal ad!*"

"Yeah, but they don't know that."

"Do they have any idea"?

"None. About me, or you, for that matter. You've got nothing to worry about. Let's go."

He turned and led me down a path to a park behind his apartment complex.

An hour later we were on a basketball court playing P-I-G. Since my skills were less than stellar, he offered a handicap: he'd shoot with his eyes closed. I set up for a granny shot from half court. The park was empty, just Doug and me, and it all felt strangely comfortable.

"Ernie and Bert are not gay," I said, laughing as I lobbed the shot, which at least hit the rim.

He grabbed the ball, dribbling across the court until he found a spot. "You've got grown up men taking baths together," he said, effortlessly making the shot with a swish. "And Peppermint Patty. Doing Marcie for sure. She calls her 'sir'. Definitely something going on there."

I laughed as I joined him at the spot where he just made the shot. I set up and shot, but as soon as the ball left my hands, the lights on the court went out. "What the—" I started.

"And he makes it! *In the dark.* Nice one!" I heard him say, and could see his shadowy figure at the net. "Just as you were getting your groove on."

"What happened to the lights?"

"On a timer. They go off at ten every night," he said, dribbling toward me and leading me over to the bench. I made sure to sit with plenty of space in between us. He leaned back, putting his long, lanky arms on the back of the bench and stretching out his massive legs. His hand accidentally touched my shoulder. *Or was that on purpose?* I scanned the dark edges of the park and wondered if we were being watched. Nothing gay was going down, but still.

"That was fun," I said. "And you play for UC Irvine?"

"Yeah, but I'm transferring to UCLA this fall."

"What? You're kidding me. You're transferring? You didn't mention that last night."

"I didn't want to give you any reason to bolt. I know how you want to keep things private."

"And anonymous," I said, reminding him.

"And anonymous. Right. And for what it's worth, I still don't know your last name. *And* you're graduating, so you've got nothing to worry about. But fair warning: I am moving up to your neck of the woods this summer, so if our paths cross, I promise to pretend I don't know you," he said. "Although I may grab your ass when no one's looking."

I smiled, but had to look away because when he looked at me, it turned me on. I shifted uncomfortably on the bench. "So your family has no idea?" I asked.

"Are you kidding me? No way. It's not even a question. They're conservative. And religious. They'd never accept it. Plus, I'm my dad's only son. Three sisters. Not a day goes by my old man doesn't tell some stranger that his son is an all-American basketball player. He's always been so proud of me. It would destroy him. I know the role he wants me to play, and I play it well. Coming out isn't an option. I come out and I lose my family, my friends, my scholarship, and any hopes of going pro. I keep silent and I lose myself. Either way, I lose."

I looked away, considering the stakes for him. And me.

I noticed his profile was stoic and handsome. He looked like a basketball star. It was easy for me to imagine him leading a team across the court. I was tempted to reach over and touch him, but had to remind myself of the boundaries I'd drawn. I was just there *to talk.*

"So, besides me, does anyone know?" he asked.

"You're the third."

"Who was the first?"

"My Campus Crusade for Christ Bible study leader. Brett."

"Are you serious? How'd he take it?" he asked.

"Actually he came to me. About him."

"Get out of here!"

"Yeah. I'd never studied the Bible before; he was knowledgeable and a great teacher, and so I was like a sponge. I'd been going to Bible study in his dorm room for almost a year, and one week he asked if we could meet to talk. I could tell it was serious. He was stumbling for words before finally blurting out that he wasn't gay, but struggled with same-sex attractions."

"Which is kind of, I don't know, *gay.*"

"He just didn't plan on staying that way."

"So you told him about you?"

"No way. I couldn't even admit it to myself. I waited another year before I trekked in the snow to his dorm and shared my struggle."

"What happened to him?"

"I transferred to UCLA and we lost touch, but last time I saw him he was going into full-time ministry work with Campus Crusade for Christ and had a girlfriend."

"If I'm the third and he's the first, who's the second?"

"Dr. Kaufman. My Hungarian Jewish psychoanalyst."

"A shrink? When did you start seeing a shrink?" he asked, seemingly amused.

"The summer I pledged a fraternity and moved into the frat house."

"Did something happen?"

"I was experiencing same-sex attractions for my best friend, Eliot. He had no idea. He's the only reason why I joined a frat. That summer, in my single room in the dungeon of the frat house, I hit bottom. I was a prisoner at the frat house and a hostage to my own stupid heart."

"Wow," he said, passing the basketball from hand to hand.

"Dr. Kaufman saved my life, I think. I don't know how I would have made it. It was months before I shared the shameful secret that I sometimes broke down and yanked the chain. He assured me I was normal. It was still another few months before I told him the object of my affection."

"How'd he respond?"

"Took it in stride. Not an ounce of judgment. When it comes to homosexuality, he's neutral, which is in direct conflict with my training as a fundamentalist Christian where I've learned to judge this part of me as a sickness and a sin."

"A belief that has put you at war with yourself," he said, summing it all up succinctly.

I looked away, unsolicited emotions stirring.

Doug reached over and put his massive hand on my knee and looked at me tenderly, in a way that made me feel like we were connected. Like prisoners inside the same cell, a bond was forming. "I'm glad I've found you," he said. "You have the honor of being the first I've told."

And when he reached in to kiss me, I didn't turn away.

This morning, before my Playboy shift, I was in Dr. Kaufman's office for an emergency session. He's a tall, lanky man in his late-forties with a warm smile and a calm energy. His sophisticated psycho-den on the 17th floor of a high rise in Westwood has floor-to-ceiling windows that cinematically frame Beverly Hills all the way to the Hollywood Hills. Every week he reclines in a leather Eames chair, smokes a cigar, and listens to me patiently for an hour, sparsely dispensing wisdom in a thick Hungarian accent. I've found verbally vomiting my issues once a week, even if I am paying someone to listen, to be a calming activity. But this morning I was manic, trying to convince him, and me, that it was my *first* and *last* "experience." It didn't *mean* anything!

"I'm glad I got it out of my system. I've never felt so straight. It was lumbering and awkward and not something I'll need to do again. I'm definitely *not gay*, that's for sure!"

Silence. He didn't say anything, just listened intently to the silence. I hated that.

"Why aren't you saying anything? You're supposed to say something!"

"I think this experience has really shaken you up. It's undeniable you've had an experience with a man, and that's a homosexual encounter," he said. "If you could only stop judging yourself, you could begin processing what that means for you. The trouble is you can't stay out of your judgment, so you dismiss it—like you're doing now—so it doesn't really get processed. It gets put in the same awful place. Judging is not the same as processing. Did you enjoy it?"

"I told you. It didn't really even count. It's not like we had sex. It was minor sleight of hand and mostly—you know what, it doesn't matter if I *enjoyed* it. The point is: *it's wrong!*"

He took a slow drag of his cigar, blowing smoke in the

air and shaking his head.

"I know that's all judgey and everything, but . . ."

"As I tell you every week, I think you have so many great qualities. You're handsome, smart, talented, but you can't see any of that because you're obsessed with this one part of you."

"This one part is a big deal."

"To you, yes, it is."

"Not just to me, to the rest of friggin' society! I don't know how it is in Hungary, but here a majority believes being gay is either a *mental illness* or an *immoral lifestyle choice*. And under sodomy laws, it's *illegal* in the state of Texas! I know the psych field is all loosey liberal—*let's just love and accept ourselves*—but it's not realistic! Not in the world I live in."

Welling with empathy, he took a long puff, disappearing in a cloud of smoke.

I'm a tough nut to crack.

And now, as I hang Hef's pajamas, trying not to snot the silk, I'm of course thinking about Doug. I don't want to think about him. I've gone to obsessive means not to think about him, but I'm thinking about him—and how comforting it is to finally feel connected to another human being.

This part of me that I've denied, repressed, and spent

my life trying to alter has been given slack, and I'm not sure how to reign it back in. *What am I doing?* I can't believe I groped a dude. I've fallen away from God. I can't call Doug again. I definitely can't see him again.

I refuse to go down a path that will lead me away from God's will.

Usually I have Hef's closet to myself, but suddenly he enters, prompting me to turn my head and discreetly wipe the tears. He's so accustomed to having staff around 24/7 that a butler in his closet or a maid in his bathroom is normal. He acknowledges me and I respond with a fake, teary smile, but I don't think he notices. Although he's courteous to the help, there is an upstairs and a downstairs. He doesn't seem to notice my meltdown but I feel transparent, as if he were to look closely enough, he'd know I kissed a dude the night before. It would undoubtedly upset him. It happened on his watch. But he's on a mission to find something in his sock drawer, and as he digs, I quickly finish hanging his pajamas and then turn to leave, but can't. Not yet...

Being in the closet with Hugh Hefner is bringing up all my "issues."

As I fiddle with the silk, I rehearse my plea, stealing glances of him fumbling through his sock drawer for something other than socks, reminding me of my dad. If my dad was hiding *Playboys* in his closet, what might Hefner be hiding? Is there a hidden stash of *Hustler* or *Penthouse* tucked behind the dress socks? *"So, Hef,"* I imagine saying, looking for the right way to solicit his help. Maybe I'll just shoot straight. *"I found your magazine in elementary school. It was the worst day of my life. Bo Derek in all her glory and the only emotion I felt was shame. And that's when it began: the hiding. No one can ever know and I have to change! And that's why I'm here. Still hiding, only now I'm in your closet. And since you're Hugh Hefner, I'm hoping you can help with the change part. A spark of Bunny lust is all I need, some assurance when I walk down the aisle with my future wife, I'll actually want to see her naked on our wedding night. For her sake, I'll obviously need to get over my indifference to her anatomy."*

If I've made it this far and he hasn't called security, I'll beg. *"Look, I'll make a deal with you. I'll gladly slave away for your family for $8.25 an hour, warmly greet your guests, graciously pick up their dirty plates and gleefully sort through your dirty silk laundry. I'll be the best servant you've ever had. With one condition: let me be your apprentice. I'll come in early and I'll stay late. I'll do whatever you say, just take me under your wing and show me the way. For the love of God, I beg of you, help me cultivate a taste for Bunny!"*

He finds what he's looking for: a picture frame with a black-and-white photograph of a woman. I can't make it out from where I'm standing, but it looks like Marilyn Monroe. His mind seems to be chasing the past, and I wonder what's going through his head. He looks up at me, catches me watching, but doesn't seem to mind. He smiles—a content, emotional smile—and I swear I see tears welling in his eyes. I wonder if he sees the tears forming in mine.

He turns and walks out with Marilyn, leaving me alone in his closet, suffocating on silk.

And from inside Hugh Hefner's closet, I do the unthinkable: I start praying.

CHAPTER 3:

LEAVING LAS VEGAS

After praying in Hef's closet, I go home and flush Doug's number, not because I don't like him, but because I do. It was a wrong turn and a dead end, and as the Post-it floats—the Sharpie ink of Doug's name and digits slowly dissolving—I pray for forgiveness before flushing.

And then watch sadly as it swirls dizzily in the inky toilet water.

And then *whoosh*, he's gone.

Because the world keeps turning and I have to keep living, I focus my time and energy on more pressing matters, like graduation in June and *what the hell I'm going to do with my life*.

I've spent my senior year working as a college intern in the psychiatric ward of the LA County General Hospital, a.k.a. "The Zoo." A career caring for the insane sounded sane: I'd be making a difference *and* getting paid for it. But my do-goody career path has been taking its toll, losing its luster completely a mere week before graduation when I'm head-butted by a patient. The abrupt blow to my brain either knocks a screw loose, or makes everything fall into place, I'm not sure, but in this moment my mind goes to Plan B: *I will become an actor in Hollywood!*

With a door opened by a fraternity brother with an agent, I'd been dabbling on the down low with acting during my last year at UCLA. Since my only experience was a semester of Drama Club in 7th grade, I typed up a less than truthful (fake) acting resume, auditioned for and was actually cast as the lead in two student films: one at BIOLA, a Christian college, and one at the University of California Long Beach. I even scored the coveted Screen Actors Guild (SAG) union card after being cast in an episode of *Unsolved Mysteries*, mysteriously airing one day in the dayroom at the psych ward. I was playing checkers with Doris, a three-hundred-pound bundle of mania. "That kid looks like you," she said, jumping two of my checkers and crowning hers.

I noticed a few other patients look from the TV to me, not sure if it was actually me or their meds simply needed tweaking. "That's weird. He does look a lot like me," I dismissed.

With the ink still drying on my college diploma, I abandon the future for which I have studied and prepared, and take the road less traveled—which proves, nevertheless, crowded.

The week after graduation, with Kate's referral, I enroll in acting school with the preeminent Hollywood guru acting coach, Howard. His studio is like a secret society: you have to *know someone* and be *referred*. He's the acting coach to the stars, and everyone knows celebs have him on speed dial. On the first day of class, trembling on a small stage in Beverly Hills, I observe the other actors arriving, a diversity of types with one common trait: a narcissistic belief that they're going to be huge stars. I just don't feel like an actor. I feel like a normal person acting like an actor, an imposter infiltrating a cult. *What am I doing? What if I actually have to act? I have no training!* When I acted in a student film earlier in the year and my character was required to cry at the grave of his dead brother, I wasn't feeling it, so in between takes I slipped into the bathroom and put Dial soap in my eyes. My eyes were red for two days. Even in the scenes when the brother was still alive, there I was with bloodshot eyes, looking on the verge of tears throughout the entire movie. I would soon learn this soap-in-the-eyes trick is an acting abomination and Howard's technique requires the actor to probe the psyche to uncover authentic emotions.

When Howard enters, a hush sweeps the studio as if royalty has graced us. There are no trumpets or anything. He doesn't need them. I already know he's gay and Jewish, but he's younger than I expected, maybe late-thirties, with a manicured goatee, round face, and dark-rimmed glasses. He has a commanding presence and instantly scares the shit out of me.

"If there's anything else you can imagine yourself doing, if there's a career that will provide you with some degree of satisfaction, then my advice: you should get up now and go do it."

This should've been my cue to run for the hills.

But I stay, stepping onto the Hollywood treadmill and running madly after my destiny.

With plan B in action, I also move out of my college apartment and into a Hollywood Hills mansion with Maria, an actress I met on a student film, and two other aspiring actresses (a living arrangement I don't recommend.) I say mansion—it has three-and-a-half bedrooms—but the bragging right is that Robert Downey, Jr. is our next-door neighbor. It sounds good and makes the girls feel more like actresses than waitresses, but we're renters. The girls have the upstairs rooms with views; I have, appropriately enough, the downstairs butler's quarters. To avoid being charged for a fourth person, my name isn't on the lease, so whenever Bud, the dirty old landlord comes around to collect the rent or "fix the sink," I play the role of Maria's boyfriend.

With graduation, the move to Hollywood, the hours slaving away at the Playboy Mansion, acting classes and auditions, I've successfully distracted myself from the whole sinful charade with Doug. Although I've dismissed it as an "experience" that didn't *mean* anything and flushed his number, before I moved out of the college "bro pad" in June, I was secretly scouring the March phone records. When I found Doug's number, I scribbled it down. Just in case.

By September, I still haven't called, but on a night I have off from playing butler, I find myself alone in an empty Hollywood house with Jimmy the cat, gazing out at the twinkling city lights and fumbling with the sweaty piece of paper with Doug's number.

An hour later, Doug and I are sitting in an empty over-grown residential lot at the summit of Kings Road that boasts panoramic views of all of Los Angeles, from down-town to the ocean, a giant urban sprawl of city lights. It's a magical spot, and if it weren't the building pad for a future celebrity dream home, it would be called Lover's Point. But on this night I'm hoping to name it Platonic Peak and not Devil's Bluff. I haven't seen him since March Madness.

"That's Beverly Hills," I say, pointing out the landmarks that dot the landscape. "And see those tall buildings next to it? That's Century City—"

"And Westwood," he says. "I see the Fox Theatre. Where's the Playboy Mansion?"

"Follow Sunset Boulevard down through Beverly Hills," I point. "And right before UCLA, see that neighborhood cloaked in darkness and depravity south of Sunset? It's in there."

The last time I saw him in March he was sporting basketball shorts and palming a basketball, but tonight he's dressed sharply in jeans and a sporty black sweater.

"How's that going?" he asks, peering at me, a palpable tension stirring.

"Since I went full time after graduation in June it's been stressful."

"Stressful? I'd like to hear an example of butler stress," he says, amused.

"Okay. Well, in the butler pantry there's a red phone with a button that has Hef's little face on it. It's called the Hef Line, and when he calls from his bedroom his face lights up."

"Is that what he goes by? Hef?"

"By everyone who knows him personally. Call him Hugh and you're just a moron. Now, only the most senior butlers are qualified to answer the Hef Line. I'd just gone full-time and hadn't even been trained, but one night, it was close to midnight and my shift was almost over. Before I could leave, the senior butler needed to do a quick perimeter check. As he left I asked him, 'What do I do if the phone rings?' He assured me it wouldn't, that Hef and Kimberly were tucked away for the night. And no sooner had he left—"

"Hef's face started lighting up? Did you shit?"

"Panicked! I mean, I was frozen—the red light flashing ominously. 'Answer it!' the head chef yelled. I hesitated. 'Answer it!' he screamed, bringing all the staff in to judge the new full-time butler. I answered, 'Uh . . . butler's place, I mean, pantry. How can I help you?'"

"Butler's Place?"

"I know, even the chef mocked that one, mouthing 'Butler's Place?' to his staff, who looked at me like I was an idiot. Hef started rattling off an order, something about a sundae for him, with caramel, not chocolate, or the other way around, and one scoop of vanilla and one scoop of strawberry, or chocolate, I don't know, and then Kimberly wanted her special cookies, the ones she keeps hidden in a special place, and on and on—all going in one ear and out the other."

"You didn't write it down?" he asks, eying me with a steamy spark in his eye.

"No. With the staff awaiting orders, I started throwing out clues like we were on a game show, the chef furiously trying to guess the answer. It was awful. The head butler returned to utter mayhem. And no way was I taking *that* tray up! Kimberly would have bitten my head off, so the head butler did. Within a minute he was scurrying back down with the full tray, the Hef Line ringing again. This time I answered promptly with pen and paper ready and Hef politely repeated the order. But the anxiety generated around two scoops of ice cream and Kimberly getting the wrong cookies was crazy. I mean, I busted my ass in college—five years clawing to keep my GPA above average—all so I could be a butler, stressing over cookies and ice cream!"

"But you're a butler for *Hugh Hefner*. That's pretty cool."

"Until you get your paycheck, then it's not so cool. But enough about you, let's talk more about me," I say, jokingly. "How's UCLA?"

"It's alright. Not the dream scenario I was hoping. First week of scrimmage I developed a stress fracture in my ankle so it's kept me from really doing...well, it all just sort of sucks."

"I'm sorry," I say, watching as he chases dreams that are fading.

"Yeah, it's been rough. Be better if you were still around. It bummed me out when you didn't call. I thought we had a connection and then...radio silence. It's the—"

I nod, ushering in a silence steeped with longing.

He looks out at the city lights, his brows furrowed and eyes intense. Finally, he looks over at me with a coltish grin. "What if we were just *intimate*, without being *sexual*?"

"What, we take turns holding each other?"

"In one-minute intervals," he adds, both of us laughing. "I'm okay, not loving it, but okay with just being friends. And I promise to do my best to keep my hands off you."

"The temptation is overwhelming, I'm sure," I joke.

"You have no idea the restraint I'm exercising right now. I deserve a trophy."

"I knew it. I could tell you were thinking about something other than my words—"

"True. My thoughts went carnal thinking of you in a butler uniform. But see, I was able to control it and move on. It's a sacrifice I'll make if it means having you in my life."

We gaze out at the City of Angels, our bond deepening— in a confusing way.

"Do you want to be held first, or can I go first?" he asks.

We both laugh—a way of expelling the tension, sexual and otherwise.

The next weekend I'm stumbling upstream on the Las Vegas Strip, dodging schools of tourists whizzing by me completely unaware my life just reached rock bottom. I thought I was scraping the bottom in Hef's closet, but I had no idea that when you're spiraling out of control, you never know when you'll hit bottom. And the minute you think you have, things can always get worse.

And usually do.

My head is down, and I'm scurrying in a hurry with no destination in mind—just away, away from Caesar's Palace, that godforsaken part of the earth where I just gambled away my life, as I know it. The Camel Lights I began smoking two days ago at the blackjack table have left an offensive taste in my mouth, and the "free" Jack Daniels and Coke that were refilled—I have no idea how many times—have impaired more than just my judgment. I'm just focusing on putting one foot in front of the other as my mind explores the consequences of my gamble.

I just wagered my future.

And lost.

What began as a weekend getaway to Vegas with new friends from acting class has taken a turn for the tragic. In June, I was a cautiously optimistic college grad with a bright future; by September, a butler burnout stranded on the Strip with empty pockets and no ride home.

It's how tragedies begin. Or promising careers in prostitution.

If I could turn back time, I would have gotten up from the beastly blackjack table when Lauren and Eva came to my rescue. The fact I'd come to Vegas with them, and Lauren was sort of my date, but I wasn't leaving with them, or her—well, it set the stage for my downfall. Lauren is pretty and smart and we have much in common, but she's not Doug. This awareness, in no small way, contributed to my demise as I attempted to distract and numb the god-forsaken longings I've been harboring for a basketball player. Not to mention the destabilizing realization that after nine months of working intimately with Hugh Hefner, I've become nothing but a moneyless minion with a chronic Bunny allergy. When the cocktail waitress came around: *Sure, I'll have another!* When the wasted woman with yellow teeth at the blackjack table offered a cigarette: *I don't smoke, but sure, I'll take one!* And when the dealer asked if I was in: *Of course, I'm in! Double down, why not?*

I've been scrambling all weekend to anesthetize these intolerable realities.

By Sunday, playing a role had taken its toll. When Lauren and Eva found me, I was wagering my future at a black jack table, a drowning victim refusing to grab the life preserver.

And now here I am, alone, and skipping toward insanity in Sin City.

I stop at the Mirage to take a full inventory of my wallet. *Maybe I missed a credit card, a measly twenty a ticket back in the game!* Nothing: Credit cards maxed, and bank account drained. I'm tempted to call Doug, but what would I say? I'm clinical.

The Mirage "volcano" rumbles, inciting tourists to go ape-shit, flocking to the fake lava and cheering at the fiery spurts. *It's water with red lights, people!* Swarmed by bugging tourists, I'm rethinking the, *"Everything is for a reason!"* philosophy people chirp when horrific things happen, as if there's some cosmic agenda that justifies plane crashes, tsunamis, and gambling.

No. There's not a *reason* for this. Not *everything* is for a reason.

And then I find a chink in my new philosophy: Doug.

Of course everything is for a reason. There is a reason I answered his ad. There is a reason we met. I'm not sure what it is yet, but maybe God wants me to—and before I can finish the thought, my brain clamps down on the rose-colored deception, redirecting my attention to the pressing question of getting back to LA without a penny in my pocket.

As lava spews, I remember the emergency $100 bill stashed in my bag that's *still* at Harrah's! With the haste of a crack addict in search of a fix, I sprint down the Strip, weaving in and out of tourists. When I approach the girl at the baggage claim, I am breathless, sweating, and chasing the silver lining.

"Hi," I spew, my dirty ashtray breath engulfing her.

When she returns with my bag, I liberate the Ben Franklin and make a beeline for the blackjack tables, all the while brokering deals with God, Jesus, and the Holy Ghost: *If you help resurrect my bank account, I promise to donate half to charity and never to gamble again!* As I hunt for a table, I try tuning into the Holy Spirit to make sure I'm being led to the *right* table. But when this leads to a $100-minimum table, I pause. *Really, Holy Spirit? We're starting at a $100 table?* Just as I register my doubt, the Holy Spirit whispers: *If you have the faith of a mustard seed, you can move mountains!* Since a mustard seed is minuscule and my faith is at least the size of a raisin, I decide to bet my last buck, trusting God will not only replenish my bank account, but I'll have enough to quit the Playboy Mansion and pay cash for a small, comfortable beach bungalow in Santa Monica. I sit down beaming with faith and joy, and just as I'm about to play my blessed hand, Lauren and Eva appear like guardian angels. They hadn't left after all!

"But I just—" I start, defending my insanity, but the looks on their faces silence me.

Before they were begging; now it's an intervention, and they are not leaving without me.

I surrender, stuffing the sweaty C-note in my pocket and tailing them into the circular drive where Ralph is impatiently waiting, sunglasses on, and as I suspected, Sinatra blaring. Like a puppy rescued from the gutter, I join Lauren in the back seat; Ralph is so inconvenienced he can't even look at me. Although the sun has set, I put my sunglasses on, a tear slipping from behind the tinted lenses. As we cruise west on the Vegas Strip, I know nothing will ever be the same. Lauren takes my shaky hand, an empathic gesture, moving my tear ducts into overdrive.

I turn to her, sunglasses leaking, and ask for a breath mint.

When I return from Vegas, it's clear working full time at the Playboy Mansion for $8.25 an hour with no tips or benefits is not a living wage. On Monday morning I march to management and ask for what I deserve. If they don't give me a raise, I'll start a union! "I think I'm an asset to the butler team, and since I'm coming up to the one-year mark, I'd like to ask for a raise."

They agree, offering twenty-five cents more an hour. "A *quarter* more an hour? I quit! But you haven't seen the last of me. Just wait. One of these days I'll be back. *As a guest!*"

I don't even get to say goodbye to Hef, and I'm left wondering if he'll even notice I'm gone.

To keep my sinking boat afloat, I even hustle the trendy Sunset Strip restaurants, but waiter jobs in LA are as difficult to land as acting gigs. Within weeks of leaving Las Vegas, my Hollywood house of cards collapses, forcing the curtain on Act One of my lame, but true, Hollywood story and sending me packing my bags and placing my belongings in storage. I'd seen the writing on the wall in Vegas, even calling my mom collect to apologize for being born and ask if I could move in with her until I could get back on my feet again. She was happy to clear out my old room, graciously sending some money to help me get by, as she's prone to do.

On my last session with Dr. Kaufman, I'm quieter than I've ever been.

"What are you thinking?" he asks, which startles me. He's never had to ask before.

"I was thinking about how crazy I am. You should've seen me in Vegas. I was out of control in a way that was self-destructive and.... Do you think maybe I need medication?"

"I have a psychiatrist colleague I can refer," he says, exhaling smoke while thoughtfully considering. "I think your issues are psychological. But your symptoms—the depression, the obsessive-compulsive ways you try to control and defend against your innermost desires, and the paranoia that the boogie man is waiting around every corner to 'smear the queer' as you say—those symptoms do seem psychiatric and medications might provide some relief."

I stare at the print on the rug, an African tribal warrior slaying an animal, thinking about all the hours I've spent in this room and how I'm that warrior trying to slay the beast inside me.

"You are a case study of what happens when we cut ourselves off from feeling our true feelings. As I've said many times before, the judgment of your innate impulses and the way you punish yourself for not being able to live up to the expectations of your family, friends, and church are leaving scars. And until you learn to accept yourself, and all the parts, without this awful judgment you attach, you will continue to suffer and self-destruct, even with a pill."

Psychology would point to my theology as the root of my pathology.

I'm thinking about Doug, and even if I were to accept us, the world, our friends, and our families never would. "If there's a Psychotherapist of the Year Award, I'll write a letter because you've been nothing but affirming and patient, and I want to thank you because I don't think I would've..." I start, but choke. It's the first time raw emotions have escaped in front of him. I've approached our sessions in a clinical, detached way, much like reporting the weather. But at this moment, it hits me: the person we've been talking about for two-and-a-half years is *me*.

"No one can live your life. No one can be in your skin, and no one can tell you what's best for you. Only you know that. It's your life, and you're the only one that can be in charge of it."

When my time is up, we agree to phone sessions from Texas on an as-needed basis. As I extend my hand to shake as custom, he unexpectedly draws me closer for a hug. With the door closing on our last session, I recall our first: what began with an Eliot is ending with a Doug.

The issue hasn't changed, just the name.

A few nights later I'm with Doug in my cramped quarters of the Hollywood house. I'm lifting one side of my desk, he the other, and together we are maneuvering slowly past the grand entry, down the front steps, and into the tiny cave-like garage already stuffed with boxes.

"Should we put the desk where those boxes are and——" I start.

"I still don't get why you didn't call me. I would have come and gotten you," he persists, as we move all of my earthly belongings into the depths of this dingy Hollywood garage.

"Las Vegas is four hours away! You're seriously gonna get in your car and drive all the——"

"Or course! Are you kidding?"

"You'd do that for me?"

"I'd drive a lot farther than that if it meant saving you——"

"From myself?"

"Yes. Hell, yes," he says, looking at me in a raw, vulnerable way that's jolting.

"I appreciate it, but I don't think you would have been able to—"

"Keep you from going to the ATM thirteen times in one hour? Yes, I think I could have been of some assistance in that area. I mean, what were you thinking? Why would you—"

"I obviously *wasn't* thinking! Look, I don't want to talk about it. What's done is done."

Silence, as we place the desk at the back of the garage and begin stacking boxes on top.

"I just can't believe you're moving," he finally says, steeped with melancholy.

"Yeah, well, don't get your hopes up, but I may call you from time to time."

"You better," he says, as we finish the last of the boxes. I begin labeling and taping them up while Doug sits in my desk chair, looking at me in a way that makes me feel transparent.

"I'm worried about you," he says, his eyes hearing my restless body language.

I continue my organizing, trying to control the boxes since I can't control my mind.

"Dr. Kaufman referred me to a psychiatrist. And I met with him yesterday."

"What's the verdict?" he asks, doing a swivel in the chair like a kid.

"He prescribed a med to help with depression and the obsessive-compulsive tendencies I have which stem from trying to control..." I say, gesturing to him and me. "This."

He stops spinning, caught unaware at the depth of my disturbance. He pulls the string on the garage door until we are standing alone in the darkness, a single bulb illuminating.

Towering above me, I feel him looking at me, but my eyes can't meet his because I'm afraid he'll see my unguarded longing for him. His massive hand, the one that is normally palming a basketball, gently and tenderly rests on my shoulder, forcing me to look up at him.

When I look into his eyes, it's a startling reminder that this isn't all about me. His eyes are teary, forcing me to recognize that standing before me is another human being going through similar emotions and trials. I can see it in his eyes. I can also see keeping his own secret inside the brutal locker room culture of collegiate athletics hasn't been easy for him. I'm the first he's trusted behind the curtain. Then I disappear for six months without a trace, not once considering how it might affect him. Since we've reconnected, I've been taken aback by how much I care for him. It's like going through your whole life thinking you are the only one, and then finding someone who has not only been going through the same thing, but actually *understands.*

As he looks into my eyes, I feel vulnerable. And known.

It's the most intimate I've ever been with another human. And we aren't even touching. And maybe that's why I can't stop thinking about him. When I'm around him, I feel free.

He pulls me close, a tender embrace, nothing sexual, just an unguarded moment that serves as an affirming reminder I'm no longer alone. It's a comforting embrace that scratches an itch.

It's an embrace I wish didn't have to end. But know it will. And has to.

In Vegas I had developed a stress fracture as well.

Just not in my ankle.

CHAPTER 4:

BACK IN THE NEST

One month after finding solace in the stable embrace of a college ballplayer in a Hollywood garage, I'm lying listlessly in my childhood bed in the suburbs of Dallas/Fort Worth, Texas.

Living with my mom.

Once you leave the nest, the hope is that you'll fly away and do great things. Instead, I'm a twenty-three-year-old college graduate—wings clipped, future cloudy, and nesting with my mother.

As I stare at a vintage booger I flicked on the cottage cheese ceiling in 7th grade, it's unsettling to be living under the same roof as my mom while secretly pining over a point guard, still stricken with March Madness. I've been away five years out of state for college, so to be back in the bedroom of my youth feels regressive. I feel heavy, overmedicated, and under-motivated. Since I packed up and left California last month, it's been hard to get out of bed in the morning. I'm still on California time and have a feeling I will always be.

With my brother at college and my dad remarried six years ago, my mom has an empty nest. Since my collect call from Vegas, she has been busy clearing out my old room, which had become her craft room. She's even put up my old car posters from high school to make it feel like *my* room. But it doesn't. I don't give a rat's ass about Lamborghinis and Ferraris anymore.

As I lie in the bed of my past, contemplating my future, I replay the conversation I had with Howard, my acting coach, before I left. When I told him I was moving back to Texas for a while, he asked me to come by the studio before I left town. On the day of my appointment, I had to wait as a photographer from the *Los Angeles Times* finished a photo shoot of him for their annual Oscar edition where they publish his thoughts on the acting performances. As I shyly waited in the corner, I realized Howard is the first openly gay person I've known. Aspiring actors love him because he's nurturing; celebrities worship him because he makes them better; and industry professionals respect him because his name means something on a resume.

The fact he's gay is irrelevant to his professional life. He's gay *and* respected.

"Bryan," he said, leaning back in his chair, a look of concern washing over his face.

I was nervous; we'd never had a one-on-one conversation. And since he's highly skilled at reading human behavior, I figured he'd noticed my unstable psyche and might refer a shrink.

"How serious are you about acting?" he asked, seriously.

"How serious am I? Well, I don't know. I've been dabbling, I guess."

"You could have a major career," he said, unexpectedly.

"I'm sorry," I said, thunderstruck by his endorsement.

"You have all the qualities to be a working actor, but you can't dabble, and you'll have to commit and do the work. It's a crazy business and two-plus-two doesn't equal four. It'll take discipline and devotion, much like you had with gymnastics. So when you've finished dabbling, I want to help you get there. I'm prepared to offer you a scholarship to my studio."

"Are you serious?" I asked, his affirming words chipping away at the walls of my insecurity.

"While you're in Texas, figure it out—do theatre, develop your craft. In class, you're always interesting to watch, but as I've told you, your main acting challenge is being an observer instead of a participant in your scene work. I see you watching yourself, judging every move. Being self-critical might have made you a better gymnast, but in acting, being self-conscious is the enemy to creativity and good acting. You have to let go of all the control and the judgment."

It was unnerving to hear him say things that concurred with Dr. Kaufman, that my psychological issues were not only driving me crazy, but also short-circuiting my potential.

"Keep in touch with me, and when you're ready to return, the doors are open."

As I rehearse my Oscar acceptance speech in my childhood bed, it hits me: the Obsession/Aqua Net bomb my mom sets off every morning before work. Since my brother left for college, my mom has been working 9 to 5 at a travel agency inside the *Stripling & Cox* department store in the North Hills Mall. It takes about ten minutes for the maternal perfumigation to reach my room, sparking a recurring dream I'm being gassed, jarring my slumber, and leaving me gasping for air.

Moving in with my mom hasn't been so bad.

Not only do I have the mom all the other kids called "Mom," at my brother's soccer games she yelled the loudest, and at my gymnastics meets she was the one with the camera, signs, and cheering squad. She's always been so supportive. Once I get back on my feet again, get a job and all that, she told me yesterday morning she wanted to show her support by setting me up on a blind date with the daughter of one of the women at the travel agency where she works. We were in her bathroom; she was holding a Diet Coke in one hand and a curling iron in the other.

"She's pretty, independent, and from what I can tell *very* funny," my mom pitched, sticking the curling iron into her permed and frosted Texas hairdo. "She was in student council in high school just like you *and* Young Life," she said, taking a comb to her hair and teasing.

My mom doesn't wear clothes; she wears "outfits," all the accessories creatively coming together to create her flashy style. She doesn't like to blend. When I was in junior high, while most kids were being picked up in Toyota Corollas and Dodge Caravans, my mom was zipping up in her 1984 little red Corvette, mouths collectively gasping at the number of kids she could cram into the hatchback. When my parents divorced in 1988, my dad bought her a fancy Mercedes, a parting gift for seventeen years of marriage, although she would've rather kept my father. Since it wasn't candy-apple red, and more burgundy, it was always "the wrong red."

"So, what do you think?" she eyed me in the mirror, moving on to the application of the makeup, a morning ritual that keeps Merle Norman Cosmetics in business.

"I don't know, Mom. We'll see. In case you haven't noticed, I don't have a penny to my name and I'm living with my mother. I don't really have the cash reserves to be taking—"

"I'll give you the money," she said, putting on eyeliner, her eyes looking at me expectantly in the mirror. I looked away, wishing I could be honest, but knowing I couldn't.

And never will. She'd never be able to accept it. I know because in 1983, Phil Donahue had two *gay dudes* on his couch. In was the summer before 8th grade, the day seared into my brain: my mom was scrap-booking, pictures of our childhood blanketing the den like a detonated memory-bomb, when my best friend Sean, my little brother and I were coming inside from swimming. The image on TV stopped me in my tracks, dripping on the carpet. My mom had one eye on them and one eye on us, making sure we didn't drip on her Kodak moments.

"Are y'all dry?" she asked, eyes glued to the TV, her face not hiding her dismay.

"We're dry," I said, also fixated on the TV. They were like two aliens that had just landed and Phil was probing to see just how much they had in common with humans. They didn't fit the flamboyant stereotypes. I wouldn't have known they were gay if they weren't on national television talking about it. And they were in a long-term *relationship*. I didn't know that was even possible. Or legal. In the conservative suburbs of the Bible Belt, I didn't know one *openly* gay person. A "fag" in Texas was about as safe as a black person at a Ku Klux Klan meeting.

"And they're so *good looking*," my mom tsk-tsked, apply-ing glue to the back of a photo of me on the first place stand at a gymnastics meet. And then she spat the words: "*What a waste!*" It was a comment that sliced into my psyche with the precision of a razor blade. I didn't identify as gay, but knew on some level—based on the way my compass was pointing since hitting puberty—that I had something in common with them. And from my immediate inquiry, by "waste" she meant their "good-looking genes" would be wasted, since no children would be produced. There was something about watching them with my mother, brother, and best friend that made me feel strangely vulnerable, as if whatever disparaging remarks the show might elicit, those words—although not directed at me—would somehow hurt me. "Why don't we all go to Circuit City? They're having a Father's Day sale and Dad wants a new VCR!"

When we arrived at Circuit City, we entered to find Donahue and the gayliens projecting from every TV screen in the place. From the RCA 15-inch to the Sony big screen, Donahue and the attractive but "wasteful" gay couple sur-rounded us. There was no escaping them!

To make up for being a waste, I knew I would have to be perfect.

§ § §

I'm sitting in a quaint Italian restaurant in Fort Worth across from Mindy, the woman my mom thinks I'll fall madly in love with, marry, and give her tons of grandchildren. We're on a blind date set up by both of our mothers who are convinced we are perfect for each other.

"I just don't think guys should drink fruity drinks out of Martini glasses. It's very feminine. I like my guys to drink beer. Out of mugs," she says, pontificating as to her perfect man.

When the waiter comes by, I order a beer and she orders a Cosmo.

"I like beer. My favorite is Guinness," I say, a manly option sure to impress her.

"Oh, I'm not into foreign beer. I like my beer American, just like my men," she says, catching her reflection in the window, prompting a quick hair appraisal. "Ughhh! I so hate the humidity," she says, examining her shimmering black, chin length bob. Mindy graduated from beauty school last year and works in a salon where all the wealthy women of Fort Worth go to get their hair and nails done. With her immaculate makeup, parlor-perfect hair and glamour nails, she has the look of someone who spends all her waking hours inside a salon looking at herself in the mirror.

"You'd like California weather. It's pretty dry compared to here," I say, trying to make conversation, but I'm gathering that if it's not about her then she's not interested.

"I don't see how you lived there. All the liberals would drive me crazy. My dad always says California is the land of the fruits and nuts. I bet you're glad to be back in Texas."

"Yeah, well, I'm not sure yet. I liked California."

As the waiter serves her Cosmo and my beer, I notice all the waiters are staring at her, a fact not lost on her. In high school, I'd guess she was the pretty girl, the one who knew she was pretty and used it to her advantage to get and do whatever, and whomever, she wanted.

As we peruse the menu, she asks me her first question of the night, but I'm sure she'll find a way to pull the attention back to her. "So what do you do?"

"Uh...well, I just graduated from college. I got a job a few weeks ago waiting tables."

She sips her Cosmo, her eyes examining me up and down, judging. "You went to college so you could be a *waiter*?" And when she says waiter, she might as well be saying janitor.

"For now, until I find something more steady."

"What did you major in?"

"Psychology."

"And what exactly were you planning to do with *that?*" she asks, eyeing me like I'm retarded.

"Become a psychologist; make a living listening to people's problems. I'd already taken on that role with friends and thought I might as well start getting paid for it. I saw myself empathizing with maladjusted normal people for a hundred and twenty dollars per hour from my home office in Malibu, offering my homegrown wisdom with complimentary organic coffee and tea. Instead I found myself playing the Christ role on ward four of the LA County Psychiatric ward, a.k.a. The Zoo."

"You worked in a *psychiatric* hospital?" she asks, as if on par with shoveling manure.

"I started as an intern my senior year at the state hospital. Since employees aren't paid enough to care, I was this eager intern, a beacon of light. I had patients swarming me like bugs circling the light of a bug whacker. But I quickly learned my popularity wasn't about me. They simply saw me as naïve and a potential source for cigarettes."

"So what happened? Why aren't you still working there?" she asks, sipping her Cosmo, ever so delicately, so as not to smudge the layers caked upon layers of frosted red lipstick.

"I was head-butted by a patient, and it sort of deflated all my career aspirations."

"Head-butted? That's hilarious," she says, her head tilting back and delivering a delirious cackle. It's as if she's acting, her response an attempt to solicit attention, which works.

"Yeah? Well, it wasn't your head," I say, forcing a smile.

"So what happened?" she asks, with a tinge of interest, licking the rim of her glass.

"Well, I'm not sure if you've been inside a psychiatric ward?"

"Uh...no. Do I *look* crazy?" she replies, surprisingly defensive.

No comment. "Well, every ward has a dayroom where patients take their meals, fight over the remote, or pace like caged animals. This common area leads to two separate corridors: one for men and the other for women. It was often my role to play hall monitor to keep each hallway gender-specific. The primary concern was separating the sexes to prevent any sort of illicit behavior. You know, God forbid the crazy people start mating."

I take another gulp as she scans the restaurant to make sure she's still the center of attention.

"And so there I was sitting in the little hall monitor desk, and here comes Alice, one of the normal ones. I often wondered why she was even there. When we played backgammon, she talked about how much she missed her kids and how her placement in the loony bin was a mistake her family was sorting out. But on this day, she was walking toward me with the intensity of a bloodthirsty pit bull that had escaped its cage. I tried to defuse her fragile state by saying cheerfully, 'Hi Alice? How are you today?' But she was in no mood for small talk. She stopped in front of me, her demonic gaze piercing through my thinning psycho-shield, and with a big smile says, 'I'm *so* sorry to do this,' before flipping up my baseball cap and butting her crazy head against mine, hard enough to bring about an entire constellation of stars."

"Oh my gawd. What a bitch. What happened?"

"Everything went blurry. After my brain rebooted, I watched as security lurched for the raving lunatic, a Tasmanian devil of legs, arms and teeth. She wasn't going down without a fight. It took three large security guards to restrain her in a straitjacket, and all the while she howled like a beast. As they dragged her writhing body across the shiny sanitarium floor to the padded isolation chamber, the nurses examined the goose egg on my forehead. As an intern, I didn't have access to the charts, so I asked one of the nurses why Alice was there. When the nurse replied flatly that Alice had tried throwing her three-year-old son out of a fifth-story window, I instantly plotted out a new career path in my head—a mere week before graduation."

"So if you're not going to be a psychologist, what are you doing to do?"

"Well, I've decided to pursue an acting career," I say, cringing as I say the words.

She rolls her eyes. "So you've moved back to Texas to *pursue acting?*"

"Well, no, not exactly. After graduation I sort of...well, I wagered my future and bank account at a blackjack table in Vegas. And lost. So, I've come back to Texas—"

"To live with your mom?"

"Just until I get back on my feet, so to speak. I plan on returning to LA within the year. But I've been working. I had the lead in a play in Dallas last month and just landed the role of John Boy in a theatre production of *The Waltons* at the Kimball. It opens next month."

"Exciting," she says, completely unexcited. "I'll be sure to bring all my friends."

And the conversation loses all its air. I down the rest of my beer and browse the menu.

"So, basically you're a waiter that lives with his mom," she says, snobbier by the second.

"Yeah, what a catch I am, huh?" I say, attempting to be charming.

She looks at me flatly. No emotion. "Where do you wait tables?"

"Uh...Pappadeaux. The Seafood Rest—"

"I know Pappadeaux. I love their crayfish. Which one?"

"One of the locations over in Dallas."

"Dallas? Which one?"

"Uh...the one over near Oak Lawn." And when I say the words "Oak Lawn," the look on her face is amused and even expectant, as if I'm suddenly going to say, *just kidding!*

"In *fag*-town?" she says, in a lower decibel, emphasizing the word fag.

"I'm sorry?" I play naïve, although I know where she's going with this. Oak Lawn is known as the gay part of Dallas, and when I was looking for a restaurant job, I thought the tips might be better in Dallas. And there was something about being in "that" part of town that piqued my curiosity—a way for me to spy on the gay community, without actually having to be in it. Although I had never been in a gay bar, or anywhere near Oak Lawn, I was curious.

"I guess you've noticed it's *totally gay* over there," she says.

"It's come to my attention, yes."

"All the fags at my salon go there every night, and of course, we have to hear all the faggy details every morning. Those fags are worse than the girls. Gossip, gossip, gossip."

And this is when I just draw a blank. I have no idea how to respond to her. "Do you know what you want to eat?" I ask, staring at my empty beer mug and checking my watch.

"I'm not really hungry, so maybe just a Caesar salad."

For the entire dinner, I listen as she talks incessantly about her ex-boyfriend who plays for the Dallas Cowboys. She doesn't want to mention his name, so I don't ask, but she's dying to drop it, and it bugs her that I haven't asked. I can't wait to drop her off. All I can think is that my mom doesn't know me well, obviously. And if I were to reproduce with this woman, our children would be bratty. If we had a daughter, she'd be wearing makeup to kindergarten.

After dinner, she excuses herself for the ladies' room, clutching her designer purse. She's made it an entire hour without looking at herself, so I'm sure she's going through withdrawals. As she struts to the back of the restaurant—with her ultra-high heels and tight, black dress—she takes small steps, giving her hips more time to shake and allowing her tits to get a good bounce. The waiters, busboys, even the chefs in the kitchen, stop to watch her strut by. Our waiter, an Italian man in his fifties, comes by, and the look on his face indicates he needs a cold shower.

"You lucky man. She beautiful," he says, with a thick Italian accent. He even does the Italian, finger to the lips, "Mwaaa," gesture usually reserved for savory spaghetti sauce.

I don't readily respond, but my face communicates that I'm not as lucky as he thinks.

"Can I bring you and the lady anything else? Cappucino, Tiramisu?"

"Just the check."

After gleefully dropping her off, I pull into the driveway, rehearsing what I'll tell my mom.

One of the drawbacks of living at home is that her room is right off the garage, so I have to pass by it every time I come in at night. I tell her not to wait up—I've been away five years and I made it home safely every night—but it's in her nature. She can't sleep until she knows I've made it home. She's a light sleeper so there's no sneaking past her door. Tonight, when I get to her door, her TV is still on and she's lying in bed, and I know I'm obligated to give a report.

"You're home early," she says, the light of the TV flickering across her face slathered with night cream. She sits up, patting her bed so I'll come sit. "So, how'd it go?"

For my mom, romance is a *Lifetime* movie where people live happily ever after. She grew up Southern Baptist, marriage until death do you part. So my dad wanting to part before death turned her world upside down. She was so worried about the stigma of divorce; her greatest fear was that other mothers might not let their kids play with us because our parents were *divorced*.

"You didn't like her?" she says, crushed, as though the wedding invitations had been sent.

"The lasagna was good."

"That's it? That's all you're going to say about it?"

"I appreciate you trying. So, what did you do tonight?" I ask, changing the topic.

"Well, I had a long talk with Patty White," she says, her tone indicating a story.

The Whites had two sons: one my age, one my brother's age, and were the first family on the block to get a pool. Growing up, our families were inseparable, until the father became a Southern Baptist preacher and moved the family off to small, rural Texas towns to start churches. I hadn't seen them in years. The son my age became a Baptist preacher as well. I ran into him at the Southern Baptist Convention in Dallas the summer after my first year at Penn State.

"How are they?" I ask.

"Well, I think they've been—I didn't want to tell your brother because I didn't want to upset him—but apparently, and don't repeat this, but Bobby is...well, he's *gay*."

Bobby is the son my brother's age—over-functioning and studious—the one everyone picked on, and currently on a full academic scholarship at a university in Boston.

"It's such a shame. I just feel so sorry for her," she says, considering the horror of it all.

I don't say anything, but I don't feel sorry for the mother. I feel sorry for Bobby—to have a father and a brother and both Southern Baptist preachers. I thought my situation was thorny.

"They're all devastated. Can you imagine?" she poses, shaking her head.

"Uh...no," I say awkwardly, turning my attention to the news on TV: a reporter on location at an apartment fire in Arlington, a fireman descending a ladder with a kitten.

"*Ohhh*, would you look at that? *Poor thing*," my mom gushes.

"It's late. I'm going to bed," I say, giving her the obligatory kiss goodnight.

"Love you," she says.

"Love you, too" I say back, walking out of the room, sadness hitting me like a tidal wave.

I'm not sure if it's an innate need in every child to please the woman who brought them into the world, or just me, but in light of all the sacrifices she made for us, I still have a need to make her proud—a need being complicated by the fact that she finds the news of her friend's son coming out as gay too upsetting to share with my brother.

If *that's* upsetting, I wonder how she would respond to the fact that after she's gone to bed, I've been calling Doug, careful to use a calling card so she doesn't know I'm calling long distance to a dude I met in the LA personals.

It would destroy her. There's no question.

§ § §

Six months later I'm sitting in a booth at Chili's with Henry, a familiar stranger in high school, who has strangely become my closest friend since returning to Texas. We spent the morning at Texas Stadium, home to the Dallas Cowboys, but on this chilly weekend in October, Mecca for Bible-toting men from all over the Lone Star state and beyond, collectively migrating for a two-day Christian conference packed with preaching, praying, and praising—*just for men*.

Although he played football in high school, Henry is a handsome Hispanic about the size of a horse jockey. And though small in stature, he was always big with the ladies—a righteous Rico Suave who didn't drink, didn't cuss, and didn't date girls who did. He's now a varsity football coach/Spanish teacher at an inner-city high school in Dallas and one of the handful I know actually raised as a fundamentalist Christian. His mom works for *The 700 Club* with Pat Robertson, and his family attends a charismatic church. When he told me about a Christian "men's movement" sweeping the nation and packing football stadiums, I was on board.

According to registration materials, Promise Keepers is *"a Christ-centered ministry dedicated to uniting men through vital relationships to become godly influences in their world."*

"Homosexuals can't be *real men* biblically," Henry spews, mouth full of hickory burger.

Sunburned and shamefaced, I take a skittish sip of iced tea and thumb through my Bible.

"They pervert what God intended our relationship should be as brothers in Christ."

It's only the first day of the conference, but with all the "wife" talk, I get the sense Promise Keepers might be on the opposing side in the tug-of-war for the rights of gay people.

I almost let the "real men" comment go, but open my Bible to 1 Samuel 18:1.4 and read: *"And it came to pass...that the soul of Jonathan was knit with the soul of David, and Jonathan loved him as his own soul... And Jonathan stripped himself of the robe that was upon him and gave it to David, and his garments, even to his sword and to his bow and to his girdle."*

"Dude, that doesn't mean they had a sexual relationship!"

I flip to 1 Samuel 20:41: *"...they [David and Jonathan] kissed one another, and wept one with another..."* And then to 2 Samuel 1:26: *"I grieve for you, Jonathan my brother; you were very dear to me. Your love for me was wonderful, more wonderful than that of women."*

He just looks at me shaking his head. "You're not defend-ing homosexuality, are you?"

"I'm just playing the Devil's advocate."

"Yeah. Literally. I bet you saw tons in California. I went to visit my brother in San Diego last summer, and they were everywhere, in their Speedo's checking me out as I walked by."

"That's what you get for wearing a thong," I joke, but knowing why they looked. He's handsome; it's all I can do to keep my constant cravings behind the iron curtain of my denial.

With Henry there's a dueling dichotomy. On the one hand we're Christian brothers strengthening one another in our faith, but I also like him in a way that I know will never be reciprocated, but nevertheless drives me to want to spend more time with him, even if it is two days at a Texas stadium learning how to be godly husbands to our future wives.

But something unexpected happened this morning in the stadium.

Just before lunch, I had one of those spiritual epiphanies where it felt like God was speaking to me directly. It's hap-pened only a few times, most significantly my senior-year rebirth in Lake Tahoe, but while listening to Pastor Jack Hayford preach, he said words that resonated: *"God's not interested in our perfection, but our direction."* After two years of futile fanaticism at Penn State, the major stumbling block in my mission was that I was operating under the naive notion I could curry favor with the Creator by being perfect. Pastor Hayford spoke about shifting the focus from perfection to direction, essentially replanting the seed of fundamentalism uprooted during my last years of college. My secular shenanigans on Greek row and at the Playboy Mansion—desperate attempts to spark hetero-desire—backfired. If God is going to work a miracle, and I believe He will, I need to *change my direction* and get right with God again.

While on holy halftime at Chili's, I'm actually looking forward to six more hours of sermons because in my quest to be the man I believe God wants me to be, it's a spiritual oasis.

"What's up with the name Promise Keepers? Sounds kind of weird," I ask Henry, flipping through the PK handbook, noticing a smidgeon of hickory sauce on his lips.

"According to the dictionary," he says, referring to the handbook, "*integrity is defined as 'a strict adherence to a moral set of values: (1) utter sincerity (2) honesty (3) candor (4) not artificial (5) not shallow (6) no empty promises.'* A man of integrity is a *Promise Keeper.*"

And that leaves me silent. To be sincere, honest, and candid with Henry seems impossible.

"How can I pray for you?" Henry asks me, his winsome brown eyes reading my face.

"What do you mean?" I ask, stalling because I know exactly what he means.

"As brothers, we need each other, to keep each other accountable. I need to know your weakness so I can help keep you strong. I pray for you every day, but it's good to be specific."

"Well, you know, just…" And this is when I just want to tell him the truth.

"Women? Is that a weakness for you?" he asks, pen poised to record my prayer requests. "It's okay if it is. It is for me. I mean, sexual purity is a challenge for all of us men, but by holding off sex until we're married, we honor God with our commitment and our future wives."

He looks at me expectantly, and if I was a real Promise Keeper, and not artificial and shallow, I would say: "*I met a dude through the personals, a basketball player. No one knows about him. Or me. We've fooled around only twice, sort of, but we talk all the time…*"

Instead, I simply say, "Sure. You can pray for my sexual purity."

In a desperate need to talk to someone who can truly appreciate my holy tug-of-war, I track down Brett, my Bible study leader at Penn State. I find him in Florida, enrolled in seminary, still walking the straight and narrow, although not without a few bumps in the road.

"You're in seminary? I thought you went on staff with Campus Crusade for Christ?"

"I did. I was staffed in Florida, but after three years, I felt God was calling me to seminary. Plus, I became sort of depressed. There was a fellow staffer, a male, that I had become good friends with and I started having feelings that...I don't know, it was rough."

"So you moved off to seminary to get away from a dude you were having feelings for?"

"Sometimes you have to flee temptation," he says. "That's why it's probably good you moved away from Doug. You have to be careful, Bryan. All this dilly-dallying with Doug can be dangerous. Any time you spend with him, you're sowing the seed of sin. I have a book you should read that I'd like to send you. It's written by Joe Dallas, president of *Exodus*."

"The ex-gay movement?"

"Exactly. We're not alone. *Exodus* is a great resource; church-based and rooted in the theology and psychology that homosexuality is treatable. Joe's book, *Desires in Conflict* has been instrumental in my own healing. What's your address and I'll send you a copy?"

For the next few days, I camp out at the mailbox every afternoon waiting for the postman, my heart rate quickening just at the mere sight of the mail truck coming up the block. It's as if I'm dying from a fatal snakebite, and the anti-venom serum that will save my life had to be mailed and every second counts. On the day the anti-gay serum arrives, the book is out of the package and I'm already on page three in the time it takes to walk the thirty feet from the mailbox to the front door, and for the rest of the night, I don't put it down. After finishing, I'm led to believe change is definitely possible since the author was *way* more gay than me. Joe was *gay* gay—the kind of gay that had *lovers* and went to *gay bars*. And now he has a wife and kids!

I jump on the ex-gay bandwagon, the curtain to my destiny opening just enough to give me a glimpse of my calling as an ex-gay leader. I imagine writing my own ex-gay book someday and sharing Oprah's couch with my hot wife and adorable kids. I'll wheel out a big ol' bucket of gay onto the stage as the audience gasps, inspired by my significant gay loss. Oprah will coo at my kids and gush at my wife and me: the portrait of Biblical marital bliss.

To prepare for my destiny, I order every ex-gay book ever written, with titles such as, *You Don't Have to Be Gay: Hope and Freedom for Males Struggling with Homosexuality*, and *Coming Out of Homosexuality: New Freedom for Men and Women*. I read them at night by the pool, but I cloak them inside the jacket of another book so my mom doesn't see what I'm reading. I'm doing this for her, to spare her the shame of having a wasteful gay son.

And for me, so I can be the man God wants be to be.

And for my future wife.

For spiritual sustenance on my journey down the yellow-bricked straight-and-narrow, I begin listening to Dr. James Dobson, founder and chairman of Focus on the Family. More than 220 million listen to his show daily and I proudly become one of them, even supporting his ministry financially with a portion of the peasant pittance I receive in the form of tips at the restaurant.

My favorite program on Christian radio is called *"New Life Live!"* hosted by Steven Arterburn, founder of New Life Ministries—the largest faith-based broadcast, counseling, and treatment ministry in the nation. I find the program compelling because it fuses my education in psychology with my evangelical faith, so I tune in daily to listen to the dream team of Christian psychologists offering Bible-based anecdotes to maladjusted Christians calling in with every issue under the sun: depression, substance abuse, marital infidelity—or what to do if your child might be *"that way,"* as one disgruntled mother put it.

I'm pulling into the YMCA in the family van the morning the host announces the topic of the week will be "Homosexuality: the Biblical Perspective." I skip my workout and instead sit in the parking lot of the YMCA, enraptured as they kick off the series with a disgraced preacher caught having an affair with another preacher, both with wives and kids. The truth came out, but he didn't. The scandal-scorched reverend had repented of his depravity and was working to restore his relationship with his wife. Although still in the midst of "recovery"—attending a men's prayer group *daily* to help thwart the ongoing attacks of Satan and his dominion—he gives listeners hope for change.

The rest of the week features similar stories of redemption and hope.

On the last day, the show is devoted to Jerry, the gay brother of the New Life founder, who died of AIDS shortly before the book they co-wrote together, *How Will I Tell My Mother? A True Story of One Man's Battle with Homosexuality and AIDS*, hit bookstores. James Dobson trumpeted the book to his flock of millions and sales skyrocketed. At the end of the week, I send in a $35 check for the "homosexuality" package that includes the book, cassettes of the weeklong series, and a tragic VHS bonus video filmed while Jerry was wasting away with AIDS, sending an eerie message: this is what happens when you "choose the homosexual lifestyle."

In the final analysis, the message is clear: homosexuality is a *sin*, therefore a *spiritual* problem, but has *psychological* roots which can be *treated* and *healed*. Change *is* possible.

Although contrary to everything I learned at UCLA and from Dr. Kaufman—and despite warnings from the American Psychological Association that such methodology is harmful—my understanding of the Bible sides me with the New Lifers, trumping ungodly secular studies on the topic. All the research in the world doesn't change the fact that when you get right down to it, homosexuality is an immoral psychological condition that needs to be cured, not celebrated.

§ § §

"The flight gets in at 5:00 p.m.," I tell Doug, over the phone. "If you're late, that's fine."

I received a call the day before from the Los Angeles Police Impound that the car I'd left in LA, discreetly parked on a cul-de-sac in Hollywood, had been impounded. So I started making plans for a return trip and asked Doug to pick me up at LAX. He agreed, but has just informed me that he'll be coming straight from a scrimmage—*and will have a buddy with him.*

"What do you mean, buddy?"

"A teammate. He's cool, so don't start freaking."

He assures me repeatedly that everything is cool, but the idea of meeting a stranger is just strange. Besides, I'm flying in to tie up some loose ends. Doug's actually one of them. My plan is to make it clear to him that he doesn't fit into God's plan for my life. If I am going to succeed in *changing* my sexual orientation, it means I can't see Doug again. He is "temptation" and will only lead me away from God's will. But the truth is he's been occupying a fair amount of my headspace. I miss him in a way that casts an ominous shadow on my newfound identity as a Promise Keeper and an "ex-gay." But I'm living in the *spirit*, not the *flesh*.

On the plane, I start to panic. The idea of hanging out with a third party is distressing, and as I exit the baggage claim, my heart is beating so fast I feel the blood pumping through my brain. *Why am I dragging this out? Why didn't I just tell him over the phone? Just end it, move on, and get over yourself!* Just as I consider hailing a taxi to avoid being with Doug and a stranger, I watch his little white Corvette pull up to the curb, the hatchback release, and to my horror, the passenger door opens to reveal the former president of my UCLA fraternity.

Suddenly my worlds collide, leaving me mashed in the middle.

"Bryan?" Bradford says.

"Bradford?"

We both look at Doug; the unmistakable emotion on Doug's face mirrors mine: fear.

"What's up, man?" Bradford asks, reaching out for a fraternal handshake that sends my mind scrambling for the proper finger code. I fumble through the fraternal gestures, my bro skills rusty. I'm wearing a jacket and tie; they sport basketball shorts and jerseys, the poster boys of collegiate basketball. Since there's no back seat, I throw my bag and myself into the hatchback and look up as Doug closes the hatch over me, giving me a wink that betrays the awkwardness of the situation. I suddenly feel trapped and claustrophobic, wrapping myself around my suitcase like a pretzel, my senses swelling with the salacious musky stench of sweat and Right Guard Sport scent.

Bradford is genuinely surprised to see me: "Good to see you, man. How you been?"

"Pretty good," I lie. I've always liked him. He has a natural charisma that made him well suited for leading a rowdy bunch of drunken college frat boys.

Doug looks at me in the rearview, giving me the sense he's glad to see me. He has a laid-back personality, so even in stressful situations, he comes across calm, cool, and collected. My brain races for an explanation to the inevitable question marinating in Bradford's brain.

"How was the flight?" Doug asks.

"Bumpy. I'm a little nauseous," I reply, my tie constricting around my neck like a snake.

"Why are you all decked out?" he asks, referring to the jacket and tie.

"My dad's wife works for American, so I fly standby and there's a dress code," I say, realizing I don't fit as well in the back hatch of a Corvette as I did in junior high.

"So, how do you two know each other?" comes the question from Bradford.

Suddenly the small, small world feels cramped.

"We met through some mutual friends," Doug lies, and I play along.

And that's why I'm here: I can no longer play along.

We play our designated roles through pizza and beer at Shakey's in Westwood, and I'm grateful for my acting training because I'm doing my best to act like Doug and I are "bros" and not "mos." Bradford seemingly buys into our charade, but I am so nervous, I can't eat.

"It's all you can eat, bro," Bradford says, noticing me nibbling.

"I ate on the plane," I say, picking at a cold slice of pepperoni pizza.

Since the Lakers are playing on the TV, conversations can only happen during commercial breaks. They are both so consumed in the game, it's as if we are front row, courtside. As they whoop and holler, I realize that the only thing I have in common with Doug is the love that dare not speak its name. Doug lives and breathes sports; when he's not playing sports, he's watching sports, betting on sports, reading about sports, and talking about sports. When he and Bradford talk wildly about the Lakers, it's as if they are speaking another language, and I'm illiterate.

"You still seeing Kate?" Bradford asks me during a commercial.

"Kate?" I repeat, surprised he remembers her. "You remember Kate?"

"Dude, how can anyone ever forget Kate?"

"Who's Kate?" Doug asks.

"You don't know Kate?" Bradford asks.

Doug shakes his head, eying me with one eyebrow raised.

"She's a friend from high school. I took her to a few frat parties. That's it."

"Where is she now?" Bradford asks, but before I can answer, the game is back on and within seconds a score brings all the Lakers fans uproariously to their feet—all except me, it seems.

As they act like fanatics, I withdraw inside, realizing it was a mistake to ask Doug to pick me up. Inexplicably, I had even planned on staying with him, in a separate room since his roommate is out of town. *What was I thinking? I can never see you again, but do you mind if I crash here for the night?* While they cheer, I slip out and call Ralph, a friend from acting class.

An hour later, instead of being alone with Doug in an empty apartment, I'm sitting in his Corvette outside Ralph's apartment in Hollywood. After we dropped Bradford, I panicked.

"You graduated," Doug says, forcefully. "I play basketball. They play basketball. We met playing basketball. They encouraged me to rush. I rushed. They offered me a bid. I accepted. How was I supposed to know it was your fraternity? You never once told me the name."

He has a point. I guarded my privacy with an iron fist, which in this case, didn't exactly work to my advantage. He's on the verge of losing his cool, and I've become paranoid.

"Who else do you know?" I ask.

"What do you mean? You want me to name our fraternity brothers?"

"Who are you friends with?" I demand.

"I'm friends with everyone in the house. What do you mean?"

"Colin? Are you friends with Colin?"

"McCarthy?"

"Oh my god," I react, twisted by this strange twist.

"Why is that weird for you?"

"He was my roommate. It was his door you sneaked past that first night!"

He looks out the window, resigning to the sidelines of this argument. I look at him and consider all the soul spilling talks on the phone since I moved to Texas. Out of all the people on the planet, besides Dr. Kaufman, he probably knows me the best. And being this physically close to him—his athletic body, lips, basketball shorts (all things I've fantasized about)—I have an overwhelming need to break my solitary confinement. Instead I put my hand on the door.

"I can't believe you're not going to stay with me. My roommate is out of town," he says.

Over the last few months, our phone conversations had become sterile. Shortly after I went to Promise Keepers and started reading ex-gay books, we both knew things would be different.

"In light of what's been going on with me, it wouldn't be right to stay with you," I say.

"So, you're really serious about the ex-gay stuff?"

I nod, grabbing my bag and retrieving a Promise Keepers Bible devotional that I brought for him. He looks at it suspiciously, as though it may bite. It's dark, so he angles it toward the streetlight and reads the title, *"Promises to Keep: Daily Devotions for Men of Integrity."*

"It's really helpful. And healing," I pitch, as if I've just given him a prescription.

"Read once a day and pray every night, and this will heal my nasty gay disease?"

"I wish it were that easy. Healing is a process. It's like recovery."

He looks at me, seemingly processing the changes that have taken root in me after almost a year in Texas. It must be strange for him to see me so zealous, so convinced that God not only wants us to change, but will help us change if we submit to His will for our lives.

"Why would God create us this way only to suffer because of it?" he asks.

"I don't think God created us this way. It's simply an expression of our sinful nature."

"So this is it, huh?" he asks, his stoic demeanor melting in front of my eyes.

"Just know, you'll be in my prayers," I say, strong with conviction.

I open the door, grab my luggage, and look at him one last time. His eyes are teary. I feel strong, unemotional, and absolutely confident I'm doing God's will.

But two days later on the flight back to Texas, from seat 23B, I have to run to the lavatory because all the unwanted emotions resurface like a big ol' turd after several flushes.

§ § §

A few weeks later, I'm lying in a hospital bed on the outskirts of Dallas wearing a hospital gown. There's an I.V. in my arm and my eyes fixate on the steady blip of my heartbeat on the monitor.

Blip, blip. Blip, blip. Blip, blip.

And then Chuck Norris approaches my bedside, peering down at me. I've heard he's a Christian and I'm tempted to ask if he will pray for me. Surely God listens to Chuck Norris. Just as I'm about to spill my special prayer request, a booming voice interrupts, "Places everyone!"

Chuck backs away out of sight.

Another voice yells, "Rolling!" which is my cue to close my eyes and play dead. Not dead, but in a coma. And then another voice screams, "Action!" sending me into a melo-dramatic blackout. I hear Chuck and his sidekick console my "mother" while attempting to get the details that led to my apparent drug-induced coma. Walker, Texas Ranger is on a mission to find who's behind my overdose! "And Cut!" a voice yells impatiently, cutting right in the middle of Chuck's lines. "Bryan, settle your eyes. They're going back and forth, and it's distracting."

I almost go into my justification for my choice. *Don't people in comas have rapid eye movement with eyeballs going back and forth?* I thought I was making a clever acting choice, but apparently I'm upstaging Chuck, which honestly doesn't take much. We do another take, I relax my eyeballs, and we make it to the end, the director giving my cue to die.

I begin convulsing, feel the cold paddles on my chest, and hear the nurse yelling, "Clear!" And because it's not a real shock, I have to *act* shocked, which is really an opportunity for my acting skills to shine. A couple of unsuccessful chest shocks, I flatline beautifully, dying like a pro. My character mother goes nuts as Chuck consoles her, vowing to seek justice for my death.

When we wrap, Chuck compliments me on how well I died, and before I can ask his advice on standing up for Biblical values in Hollywood, he's ushered away for the next scene. As I hand in my wardrobe, I'm doing my best to not allow the fact that I've worked with Chuck Norris go to my head. I don't want to be conceited; I mean really, it's not my style, but I have worked with Chuck Norris. And this is when I know, almost as if God is speaking to me directly through Chuck, that *I am ready* for my second act in Hollywood!

My first act I did it my way. This time I'm doing it God's way.

A few days after Christmas, a full year since returning to the nest, I'm in the driveway saddling up the 1987 Cadillac Sedan Deville I bought from grandma. Burgundy with a white-canvas top, dark-tinted windows, and glitzy gold trim, it's the car you expect to find an old lady driving. Or a pimp. While it's not the chariot I imagined to deliver me to my destiny in Hollywood, I got the "grandson rate," and it does have luxurious leather seats, power windows and street cred.

My mom, dad, brother, and Henry have gathered to see me off, but as I stretch my wings, their attention isn't on me but on the rear bumper of the pimpmobile dragging the pavement.

"The automatic suspension isn't kicking in," my twenty-year-old brother, J.T. diagnoses. He's a senior frat-boy at the University of North Texas and the little brother I bossed around until I left for college, and he grew and joined the wrestling team. At one of his frat parties this past year, I learned that although Lambda Chi might be cool at UCLA, at UNT they're a bunch of "fags."

"It usually kicks in. I don't get it," I say, sitting in the driver's seat, turning the key on and off, an action that usually trips the computer-generated suspension. *Did I pack too much stuff? Did Mawmaw sell me a lemon? Is God trying to communicate His will?*

My dad has taken off work to see me off and is smoking a cigarette and flipping through the Owner's Manual while my mom surveys the cabin. "Now, is there anything you don't need?" she asks, sipping her Diet Coke and culling through my personal belongings.

Although my parents have been divorced for almost seven years, they're still friends, baffling most everyone. They'd grown up together, and had two sons together, always putting my brother and me first. They're both here to see their oldest son return to Hollywood.

My mom emerges with two Sam's Club-sized boxes of Grape Nuts. "Do you need sixteen pounds of Grape Nuts? I'll give you some cash, and you can buy smaller boxes along the way."

"No. I need my Grape Nuts," I say, walking to the back of the Cadi to investigate.

"I don't know how you eat that stuff," Henry says.

"I don't either," my brother adds, surveying the engine. "It's like eating small pebbles."

I'm standing next to Henry, flanked by my mom and dad, all of us staring at the mopey rear-end, while I admire my newly minted Promise Keepers bumper sticker with the words: *"Seize the Moment"*—a recurrent theme at PK events, encouraging men to make decisions *now* to become godly influences in the world. I have made the decision, and I am ready to seize!

If only I can make it out of the driveway. Is this a sign? I thought I was ready.

My year in Texas has been like basic training, and now I'm ready to return to Hollywood for my second tour of duty to carry out God's will for my life and the world—the infectious Promise Keepers mantra connecting me to the Bigger Picture. I'll use my platform as an actor to stand up for godly virtues and spirit-affirming, family-friendly TV programming. Not since Kirk Cameron has an evangelical

Christian rocked Hollywood; my return hailed as the Second Coming in my *True Hollywood Story*. And when they uncover Doug, I'll simply cite God's Amazing Grace when I explain how I went from him to a wife and three kids in the suburbs.

"I say we unload everything and see if it's the weight," my brother says, joining us at the bumper, all of us staring at the Cadi, a promising thoroughbred that has become a mule.

"Maybe you're meant to stay longer," my mom says smiling. It's a joke, but not really.

There's an anti-climactic moment of silence before my dad jokingly says, "Welcome home son!" as the rest act like I've just returned from a long absence. It's endearing.

"Let me check one more time," I say, moving to the driver's seat, fiddling with the ignition. *Maybe going to Hollywood to become an actor isn't really a part of His plan.* I watch my family and my best friend in the rearview mirror, noticing I am as close to each as my secret allows, which is still too far to feel connected. When they say they love me, it never takes root, because I know once I take off the mask, their love will be revoked.

And then *click*—the rear suspension miraculously lifts, giving a lift to my farewell party.

I am cleared for takeoff.

"No stopping in Vegas," my dad jokes.

143

After a fond farewell filled with "I love you's," I flap my wings and prepare for another leap from the nest of my youth, praying this time my wings work.

PART II

CHAPTER 5:

1 (800) NEW-LIFE

When I roll into Hollywood for my Second Act, I'm high on the Holy Spirit, singing praise songs from my pimped-out granny-Deville. After prayerfully scanning the "roommate wanted" classifieds, I move in with a twenty-six-year-old Mormon investment banker in Westwood, land a waiter job in Marina Del Rey (strangely at the same Polynesian-themed restaurant I took Kate for our first frat date), and accept the acting scholarship at Howard's studio, launching myself into the starry orbit. I even sign with a talent agent, so it feels like God is handling the situational details.

But the messier details of the heart, mind, and body—those are killing me softly.

It doesn't happen overnight, but I notice my sunny repression escalating into a myopic depression, descending like a suffocating gray fog that won't break despite the brilliant

California sunshine. Reality eclipses my faith on Valentine's Day, a day that starts like any other, but ends with me on the wrong end of Cupid's bow. When I arrive at the restaurant for my V-Day shift and cross over the Koi pond where Kate and I first kissed, I don't sink reminiscing about our futile fauxmance, rather it buoys my spirits, reminding me how much I miss her. While on hiatus in Texas, we'd kept in touch; I told her once I got settled I'd call. But something has been keeping me from reaching out to her, or anyone. Like a caterpillar in a cocoon, I'm just not ready. Once I finish molting into the man God created me to be, then I'll reemerge, flutter my ethereal wings, and become social. Until then, I need to focus on my heteromorphosis.

The restaurant is open range for Cupid and his amorous arrows; one sappy couple after another camping out in my section of the moonstruck marina deck, slurping Mai Tais and getting fresh al fresco, several belligerently disregarding the rules of common decency. (If your waiter has to do a courtesy fake cough, more than once, to break your slutty embrace to serve your surf 'n turf, then you really should get a room.) In the wake of the lovey-dovey skullduggery, my own latent longings for intimacy begin gathering like storm clouds on the horizon. Refusing to become ensnared by petty emotions or bogged down by bitterness, I chase after the moonlight. When customers ask if I have a special Valentine waiting, I don't cringe and lament my singleness.

No, I keep my head high, celebrating my solitude, proud to be a party of one. *I don't need anyone to complete me. I'm doing just fine on my own.*

And then, while opening a bottle of champagne for an adorable couple celebrating sixty-five years of marriage, the sprightly elder woman asks if a special lady has my heart, and just as the cork pops, one of Cupid's abominable arrows pierces the chink in my godly armor, sending bottled up thoughts of Doug bubbling into my consciousness. The last time I saw him I was giving him a Bible devotional—he has no idea I'm even back—but in an instant, my heart is effervescent thinking about him. I've been hoping the "out of sight, out of mind" proverb might hold true, but in this moment, "absence makes a heart grow fonder" is proving more accurate.

"No, ma'am. No special lady, yet," I say, bashfully pouring the bubbly.

"Oh, don't you worry, my dear boy. She'll come along when you're ready. You'll see," she says, like a doting grandma. "I tell you, if I was a half-century younger, I'd just eat you up!"

Her laughter is infectious; the good-natured husband joining in, their time-tested love giving me goose bumps. They insist I join their toast, and as I clink glasses with the enchanting octogenarian couple, she toasts the "special gal" who will one day steal my heart.

After my shift, dizzy with heart-shaped delusions, I drive into the Hollywood hills to walk, think, and pray. With its quiet streets and panoramic vistas, this plush neighborhood of multi-million dollar homes perched high above the insanity of the city makes my Top 5 for Best Places to Loathe Oneself in LA. I drive past the old Hollywood pad; the girls moved out after the year lease so strange cars are parked outside, and the house has been painted an ugly beige color. I continue to the top of Kings Road, parking where Doug and I once communed cliff-side, but the empty lot has been bulldozed and sealed off by a chain link fence and a "No Trespassing" sign.

As I prayer-walk through LaLa Land, I spot the Hollywood sign shining like a beacon on the distant horizon. As if under its spell, I begin jogging toward it like a moth to a flame.

But the closer I get, the farther it becomes.

It's a beautiful night; the City of Angels sparkles in the backdrop like a scene in a movie, the neighborhood is calm and serene and all is well in my fairy tale—until I see the edge of the cliff on the horizon—and the sprint of my life becomes a mad dash to my death.

It's weird. With each fateful step toward the jagged edge, the rational part of my brain that's supposed to signal danger and order my legs to stop fails to give fair warning, and as I get closer and closer, I know it will be the end of me. And it's a relief.

As I race toward my fade out, I can hear the hum of traffic on Sunset Boulevard below, and not wanting to see what happens when my body plunges into the Hollywood abyss, I close my eyes, and just when I expect to hear the celestial choir, I trip on my stupid shoelace, sending me tumbling over what, upon closer inspection, isn't an edge after all, but a gentle slope into someone's ridiculous backyard rose garden, into which I crash and burn, a flurry of roses and thorns, flesh and blood. I sit up, my breathing shallow and rapid like prey narrowly escaping the jaws of a predator—except I'm the predator. And the prey.

Safely back at the Mormon-pad, I tweeze thorns and swab scratches, the brunt of the damage inside, in places I can't reach with the antiseptic. I turn to the phone, my lifeline, and my mind races. I want to call my family, but it would force the facts and I'd rather die with my lies than spread the shame of my truth. The thought of taking my own life is so messy and melodramatic; I begin begging God to do it, to just beam me up. I even count to three, plenty of time for my Maker to save me from myself, but when I open my eyes and I'm still breathing, I grab the phone, instinctively dialing a number ingrained in my brain from the *New Life* radio show.

The number: 1 (800) NEW-LIFE. *"Are you suicidal? Have you lost hope?"*—a suicide hotline for maladjusted fundamentalist Christians. If longing for a bro is a *sickness* and a *sin*, then a Christian psych ward promises to be the answer to my prayers.

Oh, the boundaries of love… They really are killing me.

"I'm just going in for some tests. A look under the hood," I whisper to Doug, the dawn following my near Valentine's Day massacre. After dialing for a new life, I called him.

"Dude, it looks like you had a brawl with a herd of cats. And lost," he says, tenderly applying Neosporin to the scratches on my back I can't reach on my own. We are sitting on the edge of my bed, my shirt pulled up in the back as he operates. "There's two gnarly thorns back here," he says, as I hand him the tweezers. "How do you trip into a rose garden?"

"I told you. I was running and my shoelace——" I stop, wincing as he pulls the thorns.

"I got 'em," he says, gently applying healing balm to my back, an intimate act that arouses.

"That's fine. Thanks," I say, abruptly standing and pulling my shirt down, my back burning as if lashed with a barbed whip. I tiptoe to my closet, pulling out my battered and bruised Samsonite; one of the wheels fell off its axle, so the exposed metal shaft leaves a trailing scar wherever I roll. I'll get it fixed one day when I'm not living hand-to-mouth.

As I pack for my new life, Doug sprawls out on my bed, tossing a basketball above his head and catching it with the dexterity of a pro. At six-foot-five, he doesn't fit on my queen-size mattress. He also doesn't fit into my life, a fact blurred with every toss of the ball in my bed. I wanted to see him *one last time*, but as soon as I opened the door and saw his intoxicating smile, I felt like a recovering alcoholic returning to the bar just to say goodbye to everyone.

"Are you crazy?" he asks, a decibel above my comfort zone. The Mormon is in the next room, and I don't want him to know I sneaked a dude in our apartment. I figure if caffeine is a sin, and their family values don't exactly celebrate gay people, I should be discreet.

"Obviously," I deflect. I don't want him to know how scared I am, so I focus on packing: *What do you pack for a visit to a holy insane asylum? Do they give us robes?* It's just for a couple days; however long it takes Jesus to wash that gay right out of my hair.

I'm hesitant to put a timeline on miracles—God knows I've been praying for one since puberty—but from the hopeful, uppity tone of the intake counselor, it sounds like Jesus Christ is not only on staff, but his miracles will be fully covered under my COBRA plan.

"What's wrong? I thought God was fixing you," Doug presses, palming the basketball as though it's an extension of his hands and looking at me in a way that confirms our connection.

"I'm just..." I stumble, stuck on the fact that this isn't the first time I've been unable to tether the desires of my heart. "I told you. It's nothing. It's like having a mental health physical."

"What if they don't let you out?" he asks with a grin.

"Then you can come visit."

"Yeah, right. I don't think so. You've made that much clear," he quips.

"What do you mean?"

"I'm not naive. You've called me over because this is the big, dramatic final goodbye. You start your 'new life' today, and your new life definitely doesn't include me."

"That's not true," I say. "We can still be friends."

"Friends? That's funny. You've been back—what, six weeks?—and living a few blocks from me *and I had no idea*! What kind of friend is that?" he says, not hiding his frustration.

"I was going to call, I've just—"

"Bullshit!"

"I've just been busy," I weasel, trying not to let on that I've avoided him like the plague.

"Whatever. Let's just say it out loud: you have no interest in being my friend. You're too hung up someone in our frat is going to find out about us!"

153

"There is no 'us'!"

"*Exactly!* So what's the problem, 'bro'? We're 'just friends,' remember?"

I close my suitcase, peering at him sitting on the edge of my mattress spinning the basketball on his finger. His eyes are focused and intense, his mind spinning with the ball.

"They don't have to know how we really met," he says. "Come on, they're *your* friends."

"And now they're *your* friends!"

"You can't avoid them because of me."

Since I've been back in LA, I've made no effort to contact my friends from college. They're all friends with Doug, which is just awkward. So, I've closed the chapter. "I'll make new friends," I say, voice quivering and spirit crumbling thinking about how isolated I've become.

Not to mention the fact I am checking myself into a mental hospital!

He gently tosses me the ball, and I catch it, fumbling with it clumsily. I look at him fighting the feelings that flood my being—warm, loving, tender—feelings that I hope to put a stop to, feelings that remain despite my zealous efforts to reprogram, heal, and change.

I toss the ball back.

He catches it, staring at it pensively. He'll never tell

the truth. From his perspective, there's too much at stake. How many gay college basketball players are there? He had hoped to play professionally, his chronic tendonitis not his only Achilles heel. He'll marry a woman, have a family, and play the game. The truth isn't an option, so he's resigned to living with his secret.

My secret; however, is gnawing on my soul like a rabid dog, and now that Doug's been branded with the same Greek letters, I feel like a traitor, terrified by what might happen if someone gets a peek behind our Greek masks. You can't fool all the people all the time.

"Do you think anyone suspects?" I ask, seeking assurance one last time, my imagination setting the stage for the secret ritual reserved for banishing bromosexuals from the brotherhood: Doug and I chained back-to-back, surrounded by spooky hooded figures reading by candlelight from the Code of Ethics, their voices ominous and condemning, as the angry crowd of bros spit and seethe, taunt and mock— *and then the goats, for the love of God, not the goats! No!*

"Would you stop?" he says, interrupting my frat-mare. "You've got no worries. Besides, *our secret* is safe with me."

But secrets are cancer, and I am sick.

He tosses me the ball, but this time I make no effort to catch it.

§ § §

"I'm not suicidal, lady!" I bark at the psychiatric troll posing as a nurse at the nurse's station.

"I'm sorry," she says, glancing at my chart, "Mr. Christopher, but as I told you, all new patients are placed on a seventy-two-hour suicide watch."

This part of committing myself must have been in the fine print. "But, I'm not suicidal. Look at my chart. I just want to go for a jog around the property. I need some fresh air," I say, calmly and sanely, certain that she's simply confused me for a crazy person.

"Policy is policy," she says, with an almost snobbish authority, giving me the impression she takes pleasure in making sure none of us *crazies* get loose.

"I understand," I say, attempting to reason with her. "But I'm not like the other patients. I came here on my own free will. I checked myself in yesterday. I was a psychology major at UCLA. I did my internship at the LA County psychiatric hospital. Now, I'm simply on the other side having a mental health checkup. That's all. I'm not crazy!"

She looks at me like I'm crazy.

I know the look—a similar look I'm sure formed on my face when I had patients at the LA County psychiatric ward testify to their sanity. And now I'm the crazy one.

The nuthouse nag is not budging, and I'm not giving up. "A seventy-two-hour suicide watch makes sense for patients with a history of suicidal behavior. I'm not suicidal, therefore, a seventy-two-hour hold is unfair, unnecessary, and a violation of my patient rights!" I testify.

She refers to my chart, finding ammunition: "You told the hotline counselor that you were passively suicidal."

"*Passively* being the key word. I'd never actually *do something*. If my life were to end by circumstances beyond my control, I'd be okay with that. I just need some fresh air," I plead. The idea of being trapped in here for the next seventy-two hours is making me crazy. "You're not the boss of me, lady! You can't keep me against my will. I'm not crazy!" I vent, sounding crazier by the second. "You have to let me out. Please! I'll come back, I promise. Please, just let me go!"

"Mr. Christopher, I don't how to be more clear. I can't let you out."

"Yes. *You can.* You just push the little button and the door opens. It's very simple!"

Since she's used to dealing with the insane, her body language changes, as if transitioning to lunatic-aversion mode. I notice her finger discreetly moving toward the button for security.

"Oh, great! You're going to call security? What are they going to do, come and put me in a straitjacket?" I snap.

"Suppose I let you out and you passively walk the double yellow lines on Interstate 5?"

"But I would never do that!"

"How do I know that? You've only just checked in. If you want an exemption from the seventy-two-hour hold, then you'll need to get a doctor's permission," she says with finality.

The phone rings, but her eyes hold on me until she sees that I've surrendered.

I storm to my room and draw the curtain around my bed, careful not to wake my roommate slumbering in the next bed who actually did try to commit suicide. He's still breathing, which was not part of the plan. They take the suicide business seriously: razor blades, scissors, or any object that could be used to harm is confiscated upon entry. (A girl tried hanging herself in the shower the week prior with a bed sheet.) For the first seventy-two hours, nurses check every few hours just to make sure—even in the middle of the night. Last night I was awakened three times by the nightshift nurse poking me until I showed signs of life, each time leaving me with a disrupted REM cycle and a head full of questions all pointing to a fundamental truth: *I'd rather die than be gay.* As I sit on a cold hospital bed, suicidal and psychotic Christians milling through the hallways, reality settles: *I've just checked myself into a psychiatric ward in Orange County.*

I didn't tell anyone. Not even my parents. Only Doug.

"What're you here for?" my roommate, Samuel, whispers hoarsely from behind the curtain.

For a moment I consider pretending I'm asleep, but I pull the curtain to find him propped on his side. My eyes go directly to his heavily bandaged wrists; his palms forced up and open as if begging. "I've been a bit depressed, I guess," I say.

He looks to be in his late twenties, has short military hair, pale skin, and sickly bags under his eyes. He's sedated and disoriented, and his eyes are barely able to focus on me, as if any minute he might expire. It's the first time he's uttered intelligible words since I arrived yesterday, although the curtain separating us was unable to cloak his muffled sobs that haunted me all night.

"You try to kill yourself?" he asks, matter-of-factly.

"Not exactly. But my care factor is pretty low," I say, trying not to stare at the tiny blotches of blood seeping through the bandages on his wrists.

"I know what you mean," he says, lying back in his bed, raising his wrists so gravity helps keep the blood inside his body. "My five-year-old boy found me. My wife was supposed to be at work, but Nicholas called in sick from school. I never take baths but…" He breaks down.

My instinct is to comfort and console. You want to assure the suffering human being that there is hope and time heals and all that. My degree in psychology trained me for this. But today my bed is one curtain away from his in a mental ward—the blind leading the blind.

The nurse enters to inform me it's my time to see the doctor and notices my suffering roommate, quickly consoling him with a shot and tending to his bloody bandages.

With a drowsy slur, he wishes me luck as I exit and venture out into the ward.

Surveying the ward, the vibe is similar to any other psychiatric ward: patients shuffling, nurses pushing pills, doctors making rounds, but social activities are imbued with church-camp camaraderie. After you've taken your meds, you're free to join the others for "Kumbaya" and praise songs in the dayroom. Some of the diagnoses are not difficult to diagnose.

Earlier at breakfast I sat with two twenty-something females: Marge, a dreadlocked hippie chick insisted the transmitter in her tooth planted by aliens that allowed her to communicate with Jimi Hendrix didn't make her schizophrenic. It's so tiny she's yet to find a dentist able to remove it, so she's learned to live with it, occasionally interrupting herself mid-sentence to tell Jimi to pipe down.

"He's annoying that way," she said. "Whenever he catches me talking to a cute guy, he gets so jealous, sometimes lighting his guitar on fire just to get my attention."

"Well you do seem like a *Wild Thing*," I joked. And at that, I became the only one who truly understood her.

"My parents are the crazy ones," she said. "Totally cuckoo for Christ. I mean, they think I'm demon-possessed. Now that's crazy! I'm just a gypsy at heart. It's what Jimi likes about me."

Then there was Alicia, a skeleton with skin, the poster child for eating disorders. At seventy-nine pounds, she confided that when she looks in the mirror she sees a fat girl, and when I didn't say anything, she pushed away her tray of untouched pancakes and stared at me expectantly, finally saying, "You think I'm fat, too, don't you?"

Most patients are suicidal, my roommate not the only failed attempt. If slicing the wrists, swallowing the pills, or pulling the trigger doesn't do the trick, this is where you're brought and given a second chance—whether you like it or not.

During orientation, I'd been given the *New Life* New Patient Manual, their treatment philosophy stated on page one: *"We believe that the Bible is the word of God...It is the source of greatest wisdom we can know here on Earth. Everything we do is based on principles taken from the Bible."* The *New Life* approach is designed to meet the *psychological* and *psychiatric* needs of patients, while acknowledging their *spiritual* needs. (All group therapy sessions are mandatory, but devotions and Bible study are optional.) From the manual I read: *"New Life Clinic is a 'boot camp for recovery'. If you came through the door to be 'fixed,' you are mistaken. You came to us with an empty toolbox for coping with life—we give you the encouragement and the tools to fill your empty toolbox. It is up to you to meet us halfway."*

As I wait for the Christ-approved psychiatrist in a Christian insane asylum, I pray this doctor will be in possession of the golden de-gaying tool still missing from my empty toolbox.

The doctor is Pakistani, has a thick accent and bushy moustache and is dressed like a doctor: white lab coat, stethoscope hanging around his neck, and intense dark eyes scrutinizing my chart filled with unsettling blanks. He puts the stethoscope to my still-beating heart, checks the glands around my neck, and shines a light into both of my eyes. As he stares into my corneas, I become curious as to his faith since he's working in a Christian institution. During the checkup, he doesn't once speak in tongues, cast out stubborn demons, or even pray. He examines me as though I'm a lab rat, his bedside manner uncultivated or simply culturally irrelevant.

He transitions to the standard psychiatrist script: "What made you call?"

"Well, I guess I've been a little depressed," I answer, timidly.

"Do you know why you're depressed?"

Although my inability to comprehend heterosexuality is at the core of my misery, in this Bible-based bedlam, I'm not sure how that will fly, so I lie. "I'm not sure why I'm depressed."

"How long have you been depressed?"

"Off and on since puberty."

He looks up from his clipboard. "In that case, we'll need to run some tests."

As a student of psychology, I am familiar with all of the psychological tests. I just have never taken any of them. First is the boring and tedious Minnesota Multiphasic Personality Inventory, or MMPI, consisting of well over a million absurd true/false statements. Next is the Rorschach, or inkblot test, which seems about as scientific as interpreting dreams. I talk around the real issue all day until the Thematic Apperception Test, or TAT, finally forces my hand. In the TAT test, a subject is presented with a series of picture cards and asked to tell a story. The assumption is that we project our own drama onto the pictures. It works; the one most revealing is of a young man standing in a kitchen and facing an older woman staring out the kitchen sink window. When asked to describe this picture, my mouth opens before I can filter: "Easy. The man is telling his mother that he's gay," I say, without a doubt, as if completely obvious.

There you have it. In all my years of roaming the planet, this is only the fourth time I've shared my unvarnished humanity with another human. Within the hour I'm given their homosexuality recovery package consisting of tools I already have in my toolbox. It's the same *How Will I tell My Mother?* book, the same audiotapes of the *New Life* radio series I heard (and ordered) while in Texas, and the same tragic video of Jerry wasting away from AIDS.

Although it feels remedial, like going back to Kindergarten when you're ready for college, I revisit the book and tapes, hoping it might spark a breakthrough. When I cue the first audio tape, it takes me back to the parking lot of the YMCA, listening to evangelical parents calling into the radio show terrified their child might be *you know* (most unable to even utter the word). Without fail, the compassionate and well-intentioned *New Life* fundamentalogists ask the "father question," propagating the theory that if a boy isn't affirmed by his father, an emotional deficit can develop, increasing his "gay risk" since it may drive him to seek "father-affirmation" elsewhere, in ways that pervert the laws of nature. My interpretation of this theory: If a child doesn't have access to clean, pure drinking water, the child might resort to desperate means to quench his or her thirst, like drinking sewer water. Eventually the child might develop a taste for it, so even when presented with clean water, the child desires the sewage. Figuratively speaking, from the evangelical perspective, "choosing the homosexual lifestyle" is like choosing bottled disease-ridden poop water over the traditional *Eden* brand bottled fresh from the Garden.

Blaming a child's bent on a domineering mother and a weak or absent father is a theory discredited by all major medical and mental health organizations, but the *New Life* Biblio-therapists stand firm behind their dogma-inspired premise that a failure in nurture leads to hetero-deficiency in humans, rejecting the nature argument that anyone is "born this way."

The most disturbing part of my reparative redux is watching the propaganda video of Jerry, emaciated and ravaged with AIDS, denouncing the "homosexual lifestyle" on camera, stating "homosexuality is wrong" and there is "nothing good in it." When asked during his last days why he thought he was gay, without skipping a beat, he blamed being molested at church camp during elementary school. Steven, founder of the clinic in which I'm interned, believes that if his brother would've *talked* about the molestation while younger, he might not have been so susceptible to the deception of the "homosexual lifestyle." By placing blame, it made his brother Jerry a victim, not a homosexual, adding credence to the overall message that childhood molestation and/or relational/familial inadequacies can homo-fy if not addressed early enough.

The next morning, I'm fidgeting in a room with a forty-something female therapist. Her hair is pulled back into a perfect bun, schoolmarm glasses rest on her pointy nose and she's analyzing my chart, occasionally peering up at me with an icy look that sends shivers down my spine. It's been well over a year since my last session with my warm and compassionate Jewish psychoanalyst, so it's jarring to be a patient in a Christian madhouse meeting with Cruella.

So much has changed in my life, yet so much remains the same.

"So, how are you feeling?" she finally asks, armed with a clipboard and poised to take notes, a clinical act putting even more distance between us. Dr. Kaufman never took one note.

"Frustrated," I spew. "I told you I already have all the material you gave me yesterday. But I went through it again, and what's disturbing is this stupid assumption that a person is 'choosing a homosexual lifestyle.' Do you know how ridiculous that is? If it's as simple as 'choosing a heterosexual lifestyle,' do you really think I'd be sitting here across from you in a mental ward?"

I've caught her off guard and wait for her to catch up. Her quick little fix was a Band-Aid, and I'm looking for major surgery. She scribbles in my file, not listening, merely transcribing, and when finished, swats at a stubborn piece of lint on her pressed, navy-blue business skirt.

"They frame the so-called 'homosexual lifestyle' as this hedonistic way of living—one devoted to partying, drugs, and reckless sex. I've been in a fraternity, and I've worked at the Playboy Mansion, so I'm under no illusion that the 'heterosexual lifestyle,' when lived out irresponsibly, can be equally dangerous or destructive. My fraternity days were defined by debauchery and sexual immorality, yet I haven't seen James Dobson or any of my fellow fundamentalists cracking the whip up and down Greek row and warning of the dangers of the 'heterosexual lifestyle.' I've also attended far too many bachelor parties to take seriously the idea that homosexuals have somehow cornered the market on 'sexual immorality.'"

She looks completely thrown, her lips pursed together like she just sucked on a lemon.

"Even the co-founder of New Life makes it clear this clinic doesn't *treat homosexuality*. They refer 'strugglers' to *church* ministries like *Exodus* that specialize in the 'recovery' of homosexuals. For the last year I've been immersed in Exodus 'ex-gay' material and yet here I am! The 'ex-' part of 'ex-gay' isn't sticking, and the books and tapes don't offer solutions, only hope," I say, tugging at the hospital bracelet constricting around my wrist. "I'm dying of hope!"

She doesn't dare look up. She'd be forced to witness my pain, instead she scribbles away in my file. "Are you currently living a homosexual lifestyle?" she finally asks, peering at me above the rim of her glasses, her squinty eyes narrowing, preparing to judge.

"Are you not listening? I've never lived a *homosexual lifestyle*. That's not my problem. My problem is that I've been living a *heterosexual lifestyle* and there's nothing natural about it!"

"What about..." she says, referring to her notes. "Dale?"

"Doug," I correct her, resenting the way she seems to be belittling the feelings I have for him. "It's over. I'm just frustrated because I fear I could be in love with someone of my own gender and my 'tool box' is still missing the tool that is supposed to take that away!"

Because she's completely unqualified to get into the *how* I can change part, she puts down her clipboard and walks over to a file cabinet. I can't figure out if this is her office or where they keep all the self-help material because she returns with Xeroxed pamphlets on Codependency.

"Codependency?" I ask, suddenly nauseous from the new meds, which I've taken on an empty stomach because the food is inedible and I've barely eaten since being institutionalized.

"And here is a list of CODA groups in your area," she says, handing me a referral sheet.

"CODA?"

"Codependents Anonymous."

Apparently I'm not in love with Doug. I'm simply Codependent. *What does that mean?* From the handouts, I learn codependents are "cling-ons," having a tendency to obsess and "cling-on" to destructive, unhealthy relationships. I notice a photocopy from a book, *Doctor, Alcoholic, Addict,* and read the highlighted part aloud to Cruella: *"And acceptance is the answer to all my problems today. When I am disturbed, it is because I find some person, place, thing, or situation—some fact of my life—unacceptable to me, and I can find no serenity until I accept that person, place, thing, or situation as being exactly the way it is supposed to be at this moment."*

"It's an excellent book and quote," she says, not looking up from inking my file.

"Acceptance? Are you kidding? This is where I hit a brick wall with Dr. Kaufman. This is why I'm here! Don't you get it? It's been branded on my brain since birth that on the list of things that God detests, homosexuals are at the top. So how do I accept the *unacceptable?"*

"...exactly the way it is supposed to be at this moment," she emphasizes. "That doesn't preclude change. By overcoming our adversities, we honor God and can be a blessing to others."

I just stare at her, my mind going numb. My Middle-Eastern M.D. has me on two different anti-depressants, and I'm starting to feel dull, my emotions going into hibernation.

"There's a CODA group meeting in five minutes," she says sharply. "You should go."

"It's sink or swim, people, and we gotta swim!" Leon says. Leon is a dumpy, balding man with a comb-over, bubbling with Zig Zigler (*I'll see you at the top!*) energy, which is fine for about two-minutes. As our cruise director, he leads group therapy as well as the CODA meetings (and from what I can tell, we're all codependents).

"We can't wait for someone to rescue us! We gotta keep our heads above water! Move those legs and arms people!" he says, pantomiming swimming in the air. I get the sense that if he weren't giving peppy talks to Christian psychotics at the *New Life* clinic, he'd be selling used cars in Torrance. I scan the sullen faces of my fellow patients and most seem content to drown. We're a room full of depressed, suicidal, and psychotic Christians, so he needs to switch to decaf. I notice Alicia, the skeleton, diligently taking notes, while Marge talks to Jimi Hendrix, having way more fun than the rest of us. I sit in the back row next to my bandaged and damaged roommate, leaning back in his chair, arms crossed, unresponsive to the uppity psychobabble.

"It's okay to need others," Leon continues. "No man is meant to be an island unto themselves! God created us to be in fellowship. Stop isolating. Reach out! We need each other!" Leon paces, trying to connect with us loonies, but we're unresponsive to his feel-good tactics. None of us feel good. "Everybody repeat after me: We need each other, and it's okay."

Is he serious? I look around the room, most of us baffled. Is he really asking us to repeat after him? What is this, *Sesame Street?* "We need each other, and it's okay," I say out loud, sort of, noticing that everyone has about as much enthusiasm as me, which is negligible.

Samuel leans over and whispers, "If he calls for a group hug, I'm out of here."

We laugh—a first for both of us since our holy incarceration.

"I'm sorry, is there something you want to share with the rest of us?" Leon says to us.

I look to Samuel and back to Leon, all eyes burning into us, the rebels in the back row.

"It's bullshit," Samuel says, surprisingly, eliciting a collective Christian gasp.

"Okay, Samuel, I'm so glad you've chosen to share with us in group. It's been two weeks, and it's wonderful to see you engage. Would you like to share more about how you're feeling?"

"I feel like my head might explode if I have to listen to any more of your uppity psycho-bullshit. It's like nails on a chalkboard. And your tone... It's so...degrading. You're talking to us like we're five. You have no idea what it's like to be in our shoes, especially mine."

"You're right. I don't know," Leon concedes. "But I'm more than willing to listen. Since you have our attention, would you like to share more about how you're feeling?"

All eyes are glued to Samuel. He wants to talk, but he's being held back, as though what he might share, the words that might come out of his mouth are too much for any of us to handle.

"You people wouldn't understand," he says, dismissively.

"Try us," Leon challenges.

Samuel, still crossing his arms and covering his bandaged wrists, shakes his head.

"Are you depressed?" Leon pursues, as though he's on the verge of a breakthrough.

"I don't know," Samuel says, holding out his bloody, bandaged wrists. "You tell me!"

"So what exactly is depression, Samuel?" he asks, trying to lure him out of his shell.

"I don't know. You're the expert," Samuel replies, not playing into his psycho-trap.

"Depression is *anger* turned *inward.* The number one myth of depression is the belief that if we were loved enough by others, we wouldn't be depressed," Leon says. "God loves us and people love us, but we're still depressed. The problem is...*we don't love ourselves.*"

These words penetrate the fog.

"If we could learn to love ourselves, the way God loves us, we wouldn't be depressed."

This is where I fall into the hole in the sidewalk—the same hole in the same sidewalk, day after day, month and month, year after year: I can't love myself.

Not until I fix this "immoral, perverted, abhorrent" part of me that God detests.

"So which of these therapists have training with my *specific* issue?" I ask Cruella.

I've survived my seventy-two-hour holdup and have negotiated my release. Since it's our last session, she hypes the importance of attending my CODA meetings, as well as getting into therapy with a "spirit-filled Christian therapist." She's hands me a list of holy therapists in my area, and as I scan the list, she furiously pens notes in my file, words that I never, ever want to read.

"All are excellent, trained to treat a wide range of issues," she says, without looking up.

"That's not good enough. I already had two and a half years of therapy in college, and it didn't make a naked female any more alluring."

She actually stops defiling my file to look up at me, grimacing stiffly.

"I need an expert. I need a referral to a therapist that actually does 'reparative' or 'conversion' therapy. I need someone who can help unearth these so-called 'root' issues because no one molested me, and I have great parents! And frankly, I'm sick of talking about myself. So unless you think one of these doctors can help locate my hetero-switch, then this list is a big waste of time," I say, throwing the list of holy doctors on to the table in front of her.

She looks from the list to me, one eyebrow rising ominously. We're at an impasse.

"I'm sorry. That's our list," she says, with a sinister look that would petrify a puppy.

"Well, it's not good enough. I've been here for *three days,* and I'm leaving with more questions than I came here with. You can't help me. No one here can help me!"

"That's all I can offer you, Bryan," she says, cold as ice.

When I return to my quarters to collect my things, a janitor is mopping the floor around Samuel's empty bed. When I ask the nurse, I'm saddened to learn he'd ripped off his bandages. A nurse caught him trying to rehash the razor wounds in his wrists with a toothbrush. He'd been taken to an area (padded room) where he could be closely monitored. I never got to say goodbye.

When I hug Alicia goodbye, she's so fragile I fear I might break her. She reports that she's gained two pounds, so I congratulate her, but it sets her off: "I look like a heifer! Can't you see it in my cheeks?" She moans, tugging at the loose skin hanging from her gaunt face. I avoid the goodbye scene with Marge; in the last twenty-four hours she'd taken to following me around the asylum like a puppy, wildly making plans for our lives together once we "bust outta this Jesus joint." "We'd be so good for each other," she'd say. "And don't worry about Jimi. I'll talk to him."

As I make my escape, dragging my crippled suitcase toward the light at the end of the hallway, the hotline counselor, the one who answered my cry for help and negotiated my stay, intercepts me. He's an older black man with warm energy, a deep James Earl Jones voice, and striking green eyes. He invites me into his office for a debriefing before I reenter the so-called real world. After seventy-two hours of lamenting my "traditional values" impediment, I've taken off the filter, venting my grievance that I'm leaving without a contact for a therapist who actually specializes in homo-to-hetero mutations. While I talk, he's actually listening, empathizing with compassion. And when I finish, he pulls a business card from his desk drawer and offers.

"*Melvin Moon: Men's Mentor,*" I read aloud. "Does he have experience with my issue?"

"He does a lot of mentoring of men. He's one of the best out there."

He doesn't answer the question, a troubling sign. "I'll give him a call. Thanks."

Dragging my baggage out of his office, I exit into the parking lot, the axle of the missing wheel sparking against the concrete and leaving a trail all the way to my car. Crawling into the luxurious leather womb of the Cadillac, I collapse into the driver's seat and take a long, deep breath. I'm *finally* outside of the clinic, giving me the illusion that I'm free. My eyes go straight to the blinking red light of my pager the *New Life* policy required me to leave in the car.

There are nine pages from my mother.

CHAPTER 6:

HOW DO I TELL MY MOTHER?

On the drive from my divine internment, I agonize over how to tell my mother *without* telling my mother. How do I tell her I just spent three days in a mental hospital without telling her *why?*

When I cruise into the Mormon hood, I notice my roommate's Toyota, inspiring me to get my story straight. (I think I told him I went down to O.C. to visit old college friends.) He's a good roommate (he works day, I work nights), but since I've moved in, his wife-clock has been ticking. After graduation from BYU and completion of the mandatory two-year mission, a good Mormon boy is expected to marry (lest the tribe think he's gay, the streets of Salt Lake roaming with gay Mormon kids kicked to the curb). Although Jared is behind schedule, his orientation was clarified the day I caught him feverishly fishing a *Victoria's Secret* catalogue (addressed to him) from the kitchen garbage. Caked with eggshells and coffee grinds, he explained with a wink that it wasn't junk mail, but the Mormon's *Playboy*. As a twenty-six-year-old virgin, he's chomping at the bit to get married, if nothing else to know Victoria's Secret firsthand. In the Mormon faith, marriage is a big deal: after a man dies, he's granted his own planet where he will reside with his wife(s) and kids for *eternity*. Strangely, Jared recently met a *divorced* mother of two at the "Ward," a singles group held at the Temple on Friday nights—a Mormon breeding ground. They've been dating a few minutes and are already racing to the altar at a breakneck speed.

I walk in to find him and his refurbished, bleached-blonde, Mormon fiancée on the couch "watching" TV. Since they can't have sex until marriage, they dry hump a lot on the sofa.

When they see me falling in the front door with my baggage and that *New Life* glow, they quickly peel off one another, and I make a mental note to knock next time I enter the compound.

"Dude, your mom called like a hundred times," he says, tucking in his Mormon underpants.

"I know. I just found my pager. I'll call her. How are y'all?"

"Good. You have a wild weekend?" he inquires, soliciting lurid details, the kind allowing him to live vicariously.

The Mormon lifestyle is even more restrictive than the fundamentalist Christian one I'm living. We've had several faith discussions; he gave me a Book of Mormon as a "gift." I asked how many wives he'd have on his planet and if there were any black Mormons.

"Yeah, it was...*crazy*," I cover. Which is true.

Shortly after I moved in, he shared something that forever changed my perception of him. He proudly presented a Polaroid taken in South America during his two-year mission: the snapshot didn't highlight the country, showcase its people, or illustrate the positive impact Mormon missionaries were having in the world. No. The photo was of a foot-long turd sitting at the bottom of some third-world toilet. I wasn't expecting: *"Here, look at the giant crap I took in Bolivia!"* and so it caught me off guard, proving to be a photo with an aftereffect. Once you've been forced to cast your eyes on somebody else's shit, everything changes.

"Well, I'll let you two get back to whatever you were doing," I say, aborting any personal questions and keeping that roommate distance. I scurry to my room and shut the door. To drown any details that might surface after I pick up the phone, I turn on the fan and the radio.

I take a deep breath and dial my mother.

When my mom answers, the worry in her voice is palpable: *"Where* have you been? I've been worried sick!

You didn't return pages, and your roommate didn't know where you were."

I consider covering with the same story I told the Mormon. Instead, I tell her the truth—at least partly. "I'm fine, but I...well, I decided to check into the hospital for a checkup."

"You did *what?*" I can hear her gasp all the way from Texas.

"Since insurance covered it, I went down to Orange County and checked into a psychiatric clinic where I had a full mental health evaluation," I explain, as sanely as possible.

Silence, as she processes. "You checked yourself into a *mental ward* without telling your mother?" she says, in a way that makes it clear a kid just doesn't check into the loony bin without clearing it with the woman who brought him into the world. This is just a given, I guess.

"I didn't want you to worry," I say, trying to do damage control.

"You not returning pages is what had me worried—that, and a book I found while cleaning out the closets this past weekend. But are you okay?"

My heart sinks. "What book?" I ask, tentatively.

I can hear her walk over and pick it up, my heart skipping when she reads the title, "*How Will I Tell My Mother? A True*

Story of One Man's Battle With Homosexuality and AIDS."

I'm up against the wall, the irony hitting me like a ton of bricks. It's the copy I ordered last year. And in that same box, if she keeps digging, she'll find the tapes and Jerry's tragic video.

This is the perfect opportunity to share my suffering with the woman who gave birth to me, but I can't do it. During my voluntary confinement, I already answered the question posed by the book: I won't tell my mother. Not now. Not ever. *Why worry her with something I'm changing anyway?* My toolbox might still be missing the magic tool, but I'm not about to give up. And in this moment, the fear I hear in her voice solidifies my resolve so I won't ever have to have *that* conversation. Besides, she'll only blame herself, and if she reads the book, it'll only reinforce her guilt that she failed me in some fundamental way, which isn't true. So I deflect her fears by breaking into riotous laughter and giving an Oscar-worthy reply, "Oh, *that* book. That's *hilarious!* That was just research for a screenplay I was working on. No need to worry!"

She seems to buy the lie, but after the damage-control phone call, I'm trembling, prompting me to pull out my second copy of *How Will I Tell my Mother?* In the book, Jerry (now dead of AIDS) has a message to struggling homosexuals that I highlight, the same excerpt I highlighted in the copy my mom dug up in my musty childhood closet. I hope she doesn't read the book, notice the incriminating highlights, or try to decipher the cryptic notes jotted in the margins.

I believe you want to change. I hope you feel you must change. You have to try. There is a better way. God has a better plan. With the decision to seek God's will for your life, your life can be fulfilling. If you make a decision to leave the homosexual world behind, I want to suggest a plan that could be of help to you.

I'm not exactly in the "homosexual world" but I've had a chronic "experience," so I put pen to pad and begin outlining my New Life Action Plan. The dying author laments:

If I had been more involved with the church and Bible study, I probably would have been better able to handle the temptations of homosexuality. I would not have been so vulnerable. Therein lies the danger for all of us. When we stop growing, we allow Satan to move in and take control or at least lay the foundation for control.

Not only is my body afflicted with disordered lusts and my mind warped from supposed childhood deficiencies, but I also have to deal with Satan and his dominion as they wage a spiritual war for my soul, hell bent on keeping me gay. I don't want to give Satan any wiggle room, so I vow to find a church and Bible study; Jerry's admonishment to find support not unlike an AA sponsor encouraging a recovering alcoholic to attend meetings and work the twelve steps.

At the end of the book, an ex-gay group based in LA, *Desert Stream Ministries,* is listed under resources, so I jot down their contact info. To protect my mom from having a shameful gay son, I pledge to take advantage of every resource available, leaving no stone unturned. I will allow myself to become a human guinea pig, testing (and hopefully proving) the efficacy of ex-gay psycho-theology. If there are human beings on the planet who have truly changed, then *I will* follow them to the ends of the earth! But even as I re-script my fate on paper, blotting out the rainbows in black-and-white, I know the most challenging step in my plan will be Doug.

I've closed the door, but my heart is still gaping open.

Phone calls to let him know I'm "codependent" and won't ever be calling again go unreturned. And when I finally do catch him, he's withdrawn and "too busy to talk," but tells me after the game that night he'll be at Stratton's, the bar where we met, if I want to drop by.

That night, I walk to Westwood Village, knowing I won't be going inside. I've already said goodbye forever twice. Thankfully the rabbit I'd planned on boiling in a pot of water in his kitchen got away, so for closure, I'm just going to stalk him from a distance. With my NY baseball cap pulled down to shadow my face, I approach my old college bar to sneak one last peek into the world I left behind. They must have won the game, the bar packed to the rafters with hot-to-trot sorority babes and loosey-goosey b-ball groupies orbiting the virile nucleus of frat jocks and basketball studs. It's a familiar scene, but when I spot Doug in the midst of all the hoopla with a boozy sorority girl hanging on him like an accessory, it stops me cold, a chilling reminder of what's at stake for him. In this testosterone-fueled world of fraternal athletics, placing personal ads and dribbling on the down low with other dudes is officially out of bounds.

I feel woozy, everything going into slow-motion: I glance at the upstairs booth, recalling how nervous I was that night, pacing around until finally sliding in across from him, unaware it would one day lead me to this moment as a maladjusted college grad with a psychiatric file stained with the name of a certain basketball player, spying into my past as my fraternity brothers, now *his* fraternity brothers, laud him as one of their own. I feel like a member of an audience watching a Greek tragedy play out before me, thankful I've already made my exit from the stage.

I spot Eliot on this stage, the Newport Beach surfer whom I followed onto Greek row (my subsequent bro-dependence leading me to the Yellow Pages and to Dr. Kaufman). And the Kappa whom I was set up with for our annual Hawaiian-themed "Dress to get Lei'd" party. And although she rocked the hula skirt, pesky amorous longings for Eliot devalued the bountiful booty discovered when I popped off her coconut shells. Observing this den of depravity from the outside, and through the polarizing lenses of my New Life goggles, it's strange to think I spent two years in this world, and despite the shrink and the lei's, I still ended up in a bromance.

The slo-mo bromodrama cuts to real time when Doug looks my direction and I think spots me. I cut and run. About halfway down the block, I hear Doug's voice call after me: "Bryan!"

I don't stop, but keep walking, pretending I don't hear him.

"Bryan!" he yells, again, with that raw, vulnerable tone heard not with ears, but the heart.

As much as I want to turn, I keep walking, reminding myself that God is not interested in my perfection, but my direction—and every step away from Doug is one step closer to God.

Shedding the skin and the shackles of my old life, I walk faithfully into the new.

And despite the beckoning basketball player behind me, I don't once look back.

The next morning, I'm fidgeting in the waiting room of a Christian Counseling center in Van Nuys, waiting to meet Melvin the "Men's Mentor"—the referral from the New Life counselor. Except for the nature posters with Scripture quotes and the instrumental church hymns playing softly, it's like any other counseling office. When Melvin emerges—silver haired, handsome and sixty something—he greets me warmly with a firm handshake, leading me down a hallway to the empty closet he rents out twice a week. It's not a traditional office, no desk or couch, just a couple of rolling office chairs, a corded phone on the floor and bad florescent lighting.

"Do you mind if we pray first?" he asks, rolling toward me.

"Sure," I say, bowing my head.

He places one hand firmly on my shoulder, praying for me with the disposition of a grandfather praying for his grandson. It's disarmingly un-clinical. Dr. Kaufman never started our sessions with prayer. Melvin has a good, old-fashioned, *Waltons* vibe. I imagine one day we'll be drinking lemonade and fishing in some pond as he tells me all about the good ole days. When he finishes his heartfelt plea to the Almighty, he rolls back. *Let the mentoring begin!*

"Before I ask you about the events that led to calling the hotline, let me tell you a little about me. I've been married to the same woman for forty-five years, have four sons, and nine grandchildren—all boys, except one girl, God bless her. I've been working in men's ministry for over thirty years, helping churches to develop the tools necessary to help men be better men."

"Are you a Promise Keeper?"

"I am. I've spoken at several events and find their ministry a blessing."

"I am, too. I went last year for the first time," I say, relieved to find common ground.

"There's strength in locking arms with our brothers and fighting the good fight together. As men, we have a tendency to isolate, and that's when we get in trouble. Are you married?"

"Uh...no." *Did he not get the memo?*

"Well, when you do find a wife, you'll find that the Lord blesses the man who puts Him first. Promise Keepers deals with this on a large scale. I focus on one man at a time, helping that man mature and grow to be the man God wants him to be for his wife, his kids, his community."

After his sales pitch, I have a sudden urge to flee.

"So, what made you call the hotline?"

"Well..." I stutter. "Working off what you just said about finding a wife, and all that ... I'm not sure if you've dealt with my particular 'men's issue,' but the reason I called," I start, but for some reason I start to tremble. "The reason is... I seem to have an aversion. To women."

When I bring this fact into the light, he stops me, asking if we can pray again, at which point he calls on the Almighty with an intensity that makes me think he's trying to exorcise the stubborn gay demon trapped inside of me. I don't start

convulsing, or anything like that, but he begins commanding Satan to let go of his demonic grip *in the name of Jesus*.
When he finishes, brow sweaty, he studies my face as if to see
if anything has changed. I feel the same.

"Am I healed?" I ask, slightly joking. I even smile, but
he's gravely concerned.

"I believe you can be. Satan is very deceptive. But our
God is a God of miracles. As you know, acting out in a
homosexual way is not in God's design, but I believe with
every fiber of my being that with prayer and a commitment
to sexual purity, change is possible."

"But you're not a specialist in this area?"

"No. That's not my training, but I am familiar with the
work of Exodus International and the fine work being done
by the ex-gay ministries that are a tremendous resource
and blessing."

I also learn he's not even a licensed therapist, just a
"men's mentor" who believes in the healing power of Jesus
Christ, and since insurance won't cover our sessions, he's
willing to meet for $30 an hour. I'm barely making ends
meet waiting tables in Marina Del Rey, but I rationalize it
as an investment in my heterosexuality and worth the cash
advances on my credit card.

At the end of our first session, he refers to my therapy
with Dr. Kaufman as "abusive."

"He opened the door to the idea that acting out on unnatural urges was acceptable. Were you not under his supervision when you answered the ad and met Doug?"

"I was, but Dr. Kaufman was...well, I wouldn't have made it without him."

"He might have made you feel better about making a sinful lifestyle choice, but it was abusive. You have to remember that when you meet with a secular psychotherapist licensed with the American Psychological Association, they don't take into account God's Word and truth. Otherwise they wouldn't have declassified homosexuality as a mental disorder in 1973."

"So meeting Doug, you think, was a mistake?"

"A grave mistake. It led you down a dangerous path. But you've learned, and I trust now know that next time you're tempted to stray from God, it only leads to a dead end on Sin Street."

I look down at my feet, the feelings stirred just thinking of Doug are unsettling. And wrong.

"Shall we pray for your new life?" he asks, smiling warmly.

I bow my head.

When I call Desert Stream Ministries, I'm excited to learn they offer a complete conversion package entitled *Pursuing*

Sexual Wholeness: How Jesus Heals the Homosexual, which includes a book, workbook, and a twenty-cassette-tape series. To save on shipping, I drive to their office in Venice Beach and charge the $400 conversion combo to my credit card. Again, I don't have the money, but it's certainly worth the investment. I'll pay it off one day when I'm straight.

The ex-gay guru behind Desert Stream is Andy Comiskey, a former homosexual who testifies that "sexual brokenness" can be healed through a relationship with Jesus Christ. The tapes are a series of talks given by Andy as a part of the thirty-week *Living Waters* reorientation program.

After I leave the office, I can't wait to get started, so from the parking lot of a seedy strip mall, I insert the first tape and crack open the book. I listen and read for hours, until a security guard taps on my window. I find Andy's testimony compelling: from a promiscuous youth in the gay discos of LA circa 1970s to being "wooed by Jesus," Andy is now married (to a woman) with children, testimony that Jesus *can* heal the "homosexual struggler."

When I read his claim that God has spoken to him audibly, I'm of course envious, wondering what God's voice sounds like and why I've never heard it. He does cite possible deliverance from a tormenting spirit, so his approach assumes a charismatic theological persuasion. But I'm on board, eagerly listening to the tapes in my car, a wise use of time spent sitting in Los Angeles traffic. If I'm going to be trapped on the 405, I might as well be healing my "sexual brokenness" and getting to the root causes of my "sexual disorder."

With the *Living Waters* sexual healing tapes on heavy rotation in my Cadillac-degay-Deville—and meeting Melvin the Mentor weekly—I figure I'll be straight by Christmas.

CHAPTER 7:

PROMISE KEEPERS

Homosexuality is a relational problem (p.80). This process of change is dependent on relationships that are close and non-sexual…I can't overemphasize this point: All of the prayer, insight, and effort you can muster won't change your sexual desires one bit if you don't establish the kind of relationships you need (p.123). I am convinced that healthy, intimate relationships are the key to outgrowing homosexuality. And those relationships are best found among believers (p.80).

—Joe Dallas, *Desires in Conflict*

From my ex-gay studies, I learn it's not enough to simply pray away the gay.

Since the key to actually *changing sexual desires* and *outgrowing homosexuality* lies in developing non-sexual, intimate relationships with other believers, one day shortly after plotting out my new life, I begin feverishly praying for Christian brothers. And that day, Tyler calls.

I met Tyler my senior year at UCLA when I responded to a casting call for a student film being produced at BIOLA, the Bible Institute of Los Angeles. Based on the headshot/ resume I mailed, Tyler, a senior film major and director of the film, called me to set up an audition.

When I arrived for the audition, I found a stage with lights, cameras, and a room full of students waiting for the action. Before I could get through the door, Tyler, the all-American, clean-cut director, enthusiastically greeted me, handing me a script and giving a manic break down of the film, which I learned was a senior class project and a family drama.

As I crammed for the audition, Tyler interrupted, introducing me to Jake, the producer, and Wade, the writer. Jake had movie star looks, and I wondered why they hadn't cast him as the lead; while Wade looked like a college jock, his presence warm and reserved. Tyler was hyper, relishing being the director and the one calling all the shots—which seemed to set Jake and some of the others on edge. Within ten minutes of showing up, I was thrust into the spotlight, acting out a melodramatic scene in a graveyard where my "brother" was just buried, requiring emotions I did my best to summon. After my audition, they offered me the role on the spot, and over the next few months, we shot the film, working around my class schedule at UCLA.

During my hiatus in Texas after college, Tyler kept in touch, calling every few months to see when I was returning to LA. He had made the move to LA after graduating from BIOLA and was networking. Now that I've returned and am in the embryonic stages of my new life, the timing of his phone call seems divine. Since we're both looking for a church, we agree to meet at John MacArthur's Grace Community Church, an ultra-conservative, evangelical mega-church.

Fidgeting in the lobby of Grace, my sweaty hand clutching the Sunday program, I'm discouraged by the lack of people under the age of sixty. Amongst the sea of gray hair, I do a double take when I see Tyler strutting in wearing cowboy boots and jeans, his hair long and pulled back into a ponytail. He'd gone from all-American Bible college kid to slick Hollywood cowboy.

We attend the service, and then go to lunch afterward to catch up.

"Promise Keepers sounds great. I'm in," Tyler says, straw slurping his Sprite at Subway. I can't get over his tight black T-shirt, at least two sizes too small, and his long hair.

"You've rebelled, haven't you?" I ask, jokingly.

"What do you mean?"

"The long hair? The cowboy theme you have going.

You've been repressed by Bible school for so many years, you get out and then *this* happens," I say, gesturing to his look.

"You don't like the hair?"

"It's kind of Steven Seagall-ish. I don't know. Have you ever even been on a horse?"

"I grew up on a horse. Remember, I'm from Ohio."

Actually, I don't remember. During filming, we had a director/actor dynamic, not really a friendship. And now sitting across from him, I realize he's a stranger. I don't know him at all.

"You know, Jake and Wade will probably want to go to Promise Keepers as well."

And I know them even less.

"Where are they?" I ask. When we shot the film, I was a backsliding frat boy working for Hugh Hefner, so they probably had no way of knowing I even shared their faith.

"Venice Beach. They're both working at a Christian film studio in Santa Monica."

"Cool," I say, catching Tyler sneak a peek of his own bulky biceps.

"So, how's the acting going?" he asks.

"I saw that."

"You saw what?"

"You just checked yourself out."

"I did not!"

"You did. You've been working out. We all get it," I say, busting his chops.

"How's the acting going?" he asks, again.

"Going. Resumed my training with Howard. I've had a few auditions."

"What are you doing for money?" he asks.

"Waiting tables in Marina Del Rey. You?"

"Working as a film editor, doing trailers for movies. It pays the bills for now," he says. "I'm excited about Promise Keepers. Can't wait to tell Jake and Wade."

And that's how God works, I guess. Mysteriously.

Brought together on the set of a Bible college student film two years prior, on a warm May day, I am in the stands of the Los Angeles Coliseum, standing shoulder-to-shoulder with my new evangelical entourage: Tyler, Jake, and Wade. We're not cheering on a team, but rather praising God with 72,000 other dudes—all shapes, sizes, colors, generations, and denominations.

"Ahhmaaazing Grace, how sweet the sound, that saved a wretch like meeeee," I tearfully sing along in spirited unison, the harmony of male voices thundering and moving. *"I once was lost, but now am found, was blind, but now I seeeee."*

I *seeeee* a Coliseum packed as if there's a football game, but there's not a football in sight. Just a stadium filled with a multitude of men holding hands and singing church hymns.

It's weird. There's not a drop of estrogen in the place.

The football field—from goal post to goal post—is stacked with a sea of chairs, and except for the nosebleed section, there's a guy in every seat. In the end zone, a charismatic worship band leads the myriad of masculine souls, many with hands reaching toward the heavens. We are collectively calling on the Almighty to attend this year's Promise Keepers event.

Promise Keepers is like one big God pep rally, and judging from the energy in the place, you might think it's the Super Bowl or Jesus Christ is about to moonwalk across the stage. The pastors preach with fire and fervor, more like coaches giving pep talks to a team when the score is tied with seconds left on the clock. The worship band rocks the place out. And the attendees, many bussed in by their churches, are fired up to a fault: *"We love Jesus, yes we do, we love Jesus, how 'bout you?"* comes the thunderous challenge from the opposite side of the stadium.

Oh, no you didn't. Our side rises to the challenge, thousands of voices, mine one of them.

"We love Jesus, yes we do, we love Jesus, how 'bout you?"

I notice Tyler and Wade lending their voices, while Jake looks at us like we've gone mad.

He loves Jesus, but doing peppy cheers is just lame.

I had no idea when I was cast in their student film that God would one day use these guys to help heal me. They don't know it yet, but they are a part of God's plan.

I have no doubt.

Since this is my second Promise Keepers, much of it is déjà vu, as many of the pastors were on the speaking circuit last year when I attended at Texas Stadium. But it's still *ahh-mazing*.

"Single men," Coach Bill McCartney's voice echoes throughout the Coliseum. "Time to head now for one of the exits. Guys, listen up. You'll find PK ambassadors leading you to the Men of Integrity seminars, especially for you single men. And for you married guys, sit tight."

"Where are they sending us?" Wade asks, as we join the stampede of single men.

"We're being punished for not being married," Jake says, adjusting the ball cap on his head.

Thousands of mate-less men flood the aisles, descending in droves into the catacombs of the Coliseum for seminars designed to equip us single men for the woman God has for each of us.

"Or maybe being married is the punishment and really we're the lucky ones," Tyler chirps.

"Let's see: we're single and *celibate*. I'm pretty sure we're the unlucky ones," Jake says, highlighting the sexually frustrated sentiment that defines our evangelical existence. Not unlike my Mormon roommate, the fundamentalist Christians hold to the same standard—*no sex until marriage*—making marriage a *top priority* in the sex-deprived minds of single Christian men.

"The heart of a woman is a mysterious frontier," a pastor dressed like a P.E. coach says. There's no whistle around his neck, but he's sporting coach shorts, a baseball cap, and a clipboard. He paces the locker room as if we're all there for spring training. "In today's culture and world, how does a man intent on following Jesus not only understand a woman's heart but relate to her honorably, respectfully, and purely? What does this mean for you single men? And how can you prepare yourselves for the wife God has been preparing for you?"

I look around the smelly locker room packed with single guys and squirm.

"You start by keeping the vessel pure! Men, if you're entertaining lust, you're dancing on the edge of Satan's bonfire. James 1:15: *'Lust, when it is conceived, brings forth sin, and sin brings forth death.'* As men of integrity, you have to stay pure! Are you hearing me? Even St. Paul tells us in 1

Corinthians 9:27: *'Like an athlete I train my body to do what it should, not what it wants to do. Otherwise, I fear that I myself might be declared unfit.'* Who wants to be unfit?"

I notice the collective reaction of my fellow Christ-mates and not a one wants to be unfit.

"Sexual sin thrives in the dark," Coach Purity continues. "However ashamed you may feel about admitting your lust problem to a brother, the reality is this: You can't overcome this on your own. If you could, wouldn't you have done so by now? Take a hint from James: *'Confess your faults one to another, and pray for one another, that you might be healed.'* Never assume you've reached a point where you no longer need accountability. Never take on a flood alone. You need the guy on your right and the guy on your left when the water is rising. The adventure begins when you've locked arms and are facing the deep rising water together!"

I look to my left and see Tyler, to my right Jake and Wade, and in this moment, without saying a word, we realize the four of us are kindred spirits, brought together for a reason.

And already, I can feel the waters start to rise.

The following Saturday morning we are on the communal roof top deck of Jake and Wade's Venice Beach-adjacent apartment complex, the venue for our inaugural Promise Keepers Bible study. We've just returned from playing Rollerblade hockey at Venice Beach.

"This is cool," I say, admiring the view of the west side of LA. "You can see the ocean."

"On a good day," Jake says, checking the table for bird crap before setting down his Bible.

"If you use your imagination, the traffic on Venice sounds like the ocean," Wade adds.

Although Jake and Wade were strangers when we reunited at Promise Keepers, in the short time I've been around them, I feel an affirming camaraderie, as though I've known them forever.

"Are you a virgin?" Tyler asks me, nursing his shin where he got whacked with a stick.

"Am I a virgin?" I repeat the question, buying time, bushwhacked by his query.

I know my audience: all three went to Bible College. They don't cuss, don't drink, and are most likely virgins. I went to a secular university. My mouth is unclean. Alcohol has breached my lips, and when it comes to sex, it's complicated. I feel lucky to have been accepted into their fold, so I'm nervous about taking off my safety mask this early in the game.

Wade wipes the communal table (seagull toilet) as Jake kicks away a nasty sand bucket filled with cigarette butts. I can feel them all awaiting my answer, but my tongue is tangled.

"We're just starting out," Wade interjects. "He doesn't have to—"

"No, I'm not a virgin. And you?" I say, turning it on Tyler.

He nods his head confirming his virginity while covering his wound with a Band-Aid.

"What about y'all?" I ask Jake and Wade.

They nod. "My college girlfriend, we came close, but never, you know…" Jake adds.

"I didn't mean to put you on the spot," Tyler says to me. "I just thought, with all the talk last weekend about purity and accountability, it's good to bring the darkness into the light."

"It's cool," I say, pulling out the Promise Keepers Bible Study Guide we all pitched in to purchase at the conference: a teaching copy for the leader and individual workbooks for the rest. I pass out the workbooks like I'm their tutor. "Okay, so one lesson a week. We take turns leading, and there's homework, so no slacking. I'm not grading, but God is!" I say, lamely.

"What, we have homework?" Tyler asks, taking off his shirt and sunbathing/showing off.

"I love Jesus, yes I do, I love Jesus, how 'bout you?" Jake challenges, and we all laugh.

"Before we embark on this journey together, maybe we can pray," Wade suggests, and instinctually the four of us grasp hands, bow our heads, and start praying.

Since finding a church is crucial to my recovery, I join forces with Tyler on a mission to find one. I'd been attending Jack Hayford's mega-church in the valley, the pastor whose words at Texas Stadium inspired my change of direction, but in a congregation of thousands, I felt lost. For several weeks, Tyler and I had joined Jake and Wade at the African-American Baptist church they attend in West LA, where they are two of five white congregants. Wade is even on the fast track to become a deacon. The gospel choir is uplifting and the congregation friendly, but the preaching sounds like yelling, and it just doesn't feel like home. The church search continues.

After receiving a tip on a new church starting up, the next Sunday morning finds Tyler and me in my Cadillac, staked out in the parking lot of an elementary school in Santa Monica.

"Any church meeting in a school cafeteria is suspect," I say to Tyler.

"Should we flip a coin?" Tyler suggests as we debate whether to even go inside.

"Let's just check it out real fast. We'll duck in, get a vibe, and then cruise."

We leave our Bibles in the car and sneak into the cafeteria to find lunch tables replaced with rows of folding chairs all facing the cafeteria stage where a full band is rocking out contemporary Christian music. There are maybe eighty souls in the room, with many chairs left empty. It isn't traditional in any sense; most congregants are dressed in street clothes, many with hands in the air, eyes closed, and swaying back and forth to the spirited praise songs.

We quietly take seats in the back row for a quick exit if necessary. But when the bongo player emerges as the pastor and starts preaching, we go retrieve the Bibles from the car.

Over the next several weeks, it begins to feel like home, and with a congregation of less than a hundred people, it feels like a family—exactly what I need in the healing of my sexual brokenness.

The non-denominational Calvary Chapel was started by Pastor Chuck Smith in Southern California in 1965, who by reaching out to the hippies and the surfers, put the church on the frontlines of the Jesus People Movement of the late '60s and early '70s—a phenomenon making the cover of *Life* and *Time* in 1972. Its non-traditional, un-churchy approach to church caught fire, and by the '90s, more than 850 Calvary Chapels dotted the globe. Theologically, it shares the belief in the inerrancy of the Bible with fundamentalists, but also has Pentecostal leanings, embracing the Gifts of the Spirit, such as speaking in tongues or receiving prophesies from God.

I've never attended a non-denominational church, but I like seeing more tattoos than ties. And I appreciate how all the stuffy pretense, typical of organized religion, has been stripped away, leaving great music, inspiring messages, and down-to-earth people.

And Pastor Brody is not a typical pastor; mid-forties, sharply dressed, and goateed. He played football in college, surfs, *and* skateboards. The son of a Calvary Chapel pastor, he speaks freely about his rebellious, son-of-a-preacher days before following a calling to be a pastor. His wife Victoria is the hottest preacher's wife I've seen, their kids right out of a Ralph Lauren catalogue.

I make a connection with Pastor Brody, Victoria, and their three kids almost immediately. They are a down-to-earth Christian family, a rare find in fundamentalist folds. It's not long before I start taking the two boys, ages seven and four, after church on Sundays and drive them around the parking lot in circles in my Cadillac and then to McDonalds for Happy Meals. Since I'm pennywise, it becomes my way of giving back to the church. The two boys look up to me, even getting haircuts like mine after I get a shorter spiky-do. There's something about being invited to the pastor's house for dinner, their kids crying when I leave, and being included in their daily lives outside of church that I find comforting, as though they are my spiritual family.

In all the churches I've attended over the years (Methodist, Episcopalian, Baptist, Charismatic, Presbyterian), I've never had a personal connection with the pastor. But with the Brody's, I'm connected, not questioning for a minute that God has led me to them *for a reason*.

My new life plan is going great: I've found a great church and a solid men's Bible study. I'm meeting with Melvin the Mentor weekly and constantly listening to ex-gay tapes in my car.

I love Jesus, yes I do! I love Jesus, how 'bout you?

Three months into our Bible study, it is clear that the third promise of a Promise Keeper—the one about practicing sexual purity—is a challenge for all of us.

"Celibacy sucks," Jake says, as we huddle in my living room, finishing the pancake breakfast I prepared from scratch. The Mormon is out with his fiancée and her kids—soon to be *his* kids—making it easier for us to pray that God will free him from the delusion of that evil Mormon cult.

"What happened?" I ask Jake, opening my Bible and study guide.

"I had a tough week," Jake replies, looking down at the carpet.

"Minding your manners?" I ask, borrowing terminology from my days at Penn State where we used it as code for the big "M." Masturbation is a weed in our spiritual garden and Satan's backdoor to our soul. To keep one another accountable in this "common struggle," asking your bro if he has "minded his manners" is less awkward than asking if they've abstained from touching themselves. It's awkward, no matter how you ask it, but we are *fighting the good fight.*

"What happened?" I ask, the room silent as we gather around our fallen brother.

"Happened on Tuesday, and again on Friday. I even took a cold shower, but..." Jake trails off. Competitive by nature, he's sulking as though he's just lost a championship game.

"I stumbled, too," Tyler confesses. "I did fine all week but I couldn't sleep..."

"I think we should pray," Wade says. And so it goes.

Our hands-off approach to honoring God begins to feel like a contest. One by one, week after week, my weaker brothers arrive at Bible study shame faced, confessing to not minding their manners. But not me. I am in it to win it, obsessively guarding my eyes from erotic images and wearing blinders everywhere I go. And cold showers. Lots of cold showers.

At a men's retreat in Lake Arrowhead, Pastor Brody gives a Saturday morning talk to about fifty guys about the dangers of Internet pornography and sexual addiction. Apparently I'm not alone in my temptation to peer at lust-provoking images on the Internet—the only distinction being the gender of the erotic images. Since the best defense is a good offense, I join the Internet provider *Integrity Online* that filters out porn, often overzealous in its efforts to keep me pure. If, for example, I want to research the career of Dick Van Dyke, I'd be seriously "blocked" and reported to God. My email address, bchristopher@integrityonline. com, is a testament to my pious passion for purity. "I'm sorry, what was that email address again?" heathens sometimes ask, opening up the door to evangelize. "You see, each of us have a God-shaped vacuum…"

On my 121st day of masturbriety, I'm tested by the Devil while walking Wilshire Boulevard. For four months I've been so damn polite to my penis, the wind blows and it turns me on. Seriously. And then *out of nowhere*, I stumble upon torn pages of *Hustler* in the gutter, erotic male and female flesh fluttering in the breeze and rousing my hibernating hormones.

But the temptation isn't about me and the physical needs of my body; the conflict has a spiritual dimension: the temptation *is from Satan* working overtime to keep me broken.

Rebuking Lucifer and the lusty desires he's stirred, I walk on *in the name of Jesus*. My body is my temple and I must keep it clean, even if it means walking past gratuitous sidewalk porn. When I get home, I take an icy shower, the ancient Chinese secret to my celibacy success.

* * *

About six months into our Promise Keepers accountability group, I decide it's time to share the specific nature of my lust. After Bible study, as Tyler, Jake and Wade are leaving my place, I hand them each a screenplay I've written and ask for their feedback. It's titled, *Lost Among Men,* and details the struggle of a frat boy who answers a personal ad on the sly and has an experience with a dude, who later resurfaces as his fraternity brother and star basketball player.

It's a thinly veiled autobiography venting my inner-struggle—a way of getting it out without actually having to tell anyone. In the end one of the characters takes a gun to his head and pulls the trigger, so it's not a romantic comedy. As they leave with my truth in hand, I feel a sense of relief, followed by a sense of dread. I have no idea how they will respond. I feel vulnerable.

The first to call is Tyler. He calls late that night and wants to meet immediately and in person. We decide to meet in Venice Beach at a coffee shop on Washington Place open late, and when I arrive at midnight, he's already staked out a couple of sofa chairs upstairs. I notice immediately he's visibly shaken, so I prepare for the worst, anxiously sipping my coffee.

"So, how much of it is true?" he blurts out.

"Uh...well, there are some autobiographical elements," I confess.

"And the character of Shane is obviously you."

I nod, setting down my coffee mug because my hands are shaky.

He takes a deep breath, processing this new information. "Halfway into reading it, I was crying," he says, clearly shaken. "I don't know if it was the script or that I knew you wrote it."

I just listen, noticing I'm holding my breath, literally, and have to remind myself to breathe.

"Or maybe it's the fact that I understood it," he says, tears welling in his eyes.

And these words throw me completely off.

"I understand the conflict because I have the same struggle," he confesses.

All this time spent with him—praying and studying the Bible—and he's going through the same suffering. We talk for hours; he's never told anyone, so it's like opening up a musty closet and letting it air out. Afterwards, he walks with me to my Cadillac in the beach parking lot.

"You can't tell Jake and Wade," he says. "Promise me you won't tell them."

"I promise," I say, surprised at his sudden defensiveness.

"I don't want anyone to know. There's no point. It's a dead end path."

"Your secret is safe with me," I say, assuring him.

And then he looks at me with an almost flirty look—a look I've never seen before.

"I have a great book for you," I tell him. "It's written by the former president of Exodus."

"The ex-gay movement?" he asks, his body language changing and a tension stirring.

"Exactly. I have just about every book written, so I'll loan them to you," I say, hopefully.

"Thanks, bro. I don't know what I'd do without you," he says, leaning in for a hug.

I hug him back, but during the embrace there's a different energy behind it, and maybe because of the several months of celibacy, I feel a stirring inside that prompts a withdrawal.

"Well, I'm here for you, bro," I say, quickly opening my car door and getting inside. He watches me as I back away, and I have this strange feeling that Tyler is flirting with the chink in my armor. I've never been attracted to him. We're in Bible study together, fighting for our sexual purity as we prepare ourselves for our wives! On the drive home, I notice my inhibitions starting to unhinge, and I feel mortifyingly aroused and compelled to call him when I get home.

But I don't. He calls me.

"Hey," I say into the receiver. "I know, but I just—sure, come on over."

He's wired from all the caffeine and wants to come over for the ex-gay books. It's close to 3 a.m., and since the Mormon married last month, I have a new roommate, Martin, a brain surgeon doing his residency at UCLA. I never see him, but he's sleeping in the next room so when Tyler arrives ten minutes later, we slip into my room and I close the door.

"You should start with this one," I say, handing him *Desires in Conflict* by Joe Dallas.

"That sums it up for me right now," he says. "I have a sudden urge to kiss you."

"Which is why you need to read—"

And he does. He plants one on my mouth, and it's… weird. I'm stunned, unsure how we've gone from tearful confession to tearing off clothes; our hands just beginning to explore one another before we both abhorrently abort, my mind already hitting the delete button.

"I can't do this," I say, pulling away. "It's gross. We're in Bible Study together!"

Temptation can be deceiving, and in this instance, it's like salivating over a tempting slice of chocolate cake, only to take a bite and discover there's no sugar, just bitter chocolate.

"What were we thinking?" he says, putting on his shirt.

"I'm not even attracted to you."

"You're not?" he says, shocked because he assumes everyone is attracted to him.

On his way out the door, I follow him out to his truck, and we sit inside to debrief.

"We obviously can't tell anyone about this," he says.

"Obviously. You know, celibacy has this dangerous underbelly that no one talks about. Once you cut off all outlets, it can lead to insanity—like groping a Bible study bro."

"It's not like anything *happened* happened," he qualifies.

"Exactly."

"Can you imagine if Jake and Wade found out?" he ponders, shuddering at the thought.

"I'm all for telling the truth, and I hope you consider sharing yours when you're ready," I preach. "We need their help. But, in this case, I think some things are better left unsaid."

He's silent thinking about the ramifications.

"Let's pray," I say, bowing my head. "Father God, please forgive us for what just happened. Obviously we are broken creatures in need of healing. Please heal us, Lord. Amen."

"I forgot the ex-gay books," he says. "Do you mind grabbing them for me?"

The next day I receive calls from Jake and Wade. They've read the script and want to discuss, so I meet them at Rae's, a 1950s retro diner in Santa Monica. I sit on one side of the orange vinyl booth, and they sit on the other; that stupid song by the Dixie Cups, *"I'm going to the chapel, and I'm gonna get married,"* plays from the jukebox. My pancakes are cold and untouched.

"I'm seeing a Christian mentor, so it's something I'm working on. It's just...I thought you should know," I say, which is like telling someone you're an alcoholic but are in recovery.

"So what happened to Doug?" Jake asks.

I shake my head and shrug. "I don't know. I never looked back."

"Bro, you got to know that this doesn't change anything," Wade adds.

"If anything, it makes me feel closer to you," Jake says.

"Me too," Wade agrees.

And I feel it, a connection with both of them as the walls I've built come down.

"So how did Tyler respond?" Jake asks.

"Uh...well, he was supportive," I say, looking down at the table.

* * *

Exposing my truth proves to be a double-edged sword; for Jake and Wade, it deepens our bond, providing me with healthy, intimate relationships that, according to Joe Dallas, are key to outgrowing homosexuality. But for Tyler, airing my truth makes things worse. He's stubborn about his secret. Every Saturday morning at Bible study he plays the role of a struggling hetero, adding to his own and our group's dysfunction. And the fact we never again discuss those sixty seconds further strains our alliance. But Armageddon begins when Tyler moves in with Jake and Wade into a small house in West LA. I noticed a tension between Jake and Tyler during my audition at BIOLA, but living together just adds fuel to the fire. Or maybe Tyler has become intolerable. Following a promotion to senior film editor, he has new priorities that trump Bible study, often showing up having not done the homework. He shears the ponytail, bleaches his teeth, works out obsessively, and although he denies it, frequents a tanning salon. He even trades his truck for a flashy, black Trans Am, keeping the same license plate, "LA CWBY".

"I can't do this anymore," Jake confides to me and Wade in their backyard, almost one year to the day we began our journey together. "I thought I knew him, but I guess I don't."

"What should we do?" I ask them.

"Promise Keepers is in two weeks. Maybe it'll bring us back together," Wade offers.

A couple weeks later, I'm standing in the LA Coliseum for Promise Keepers '96 with Tyler, Jake, and Wade. And the only thing different this year is that *my dad* is standing next to us. At my invitation, he flew in from Texas to join me. Although he grew up in the Episcopal Church and attended a Baptist college and law school, in his adult life he's been more of a holiday churchgoer (maybe). So when he entered the stadium packed with men singing church hymns, he looked awed, maybe shocked. His mother was a devout Episcopalian who taught me to pray and inspired my creative side, and when she died my senior year in college, her dying wish was that my dad would go to church more. I thought Promise Keepers might ignite his faith.

Here's what I know about my dad: he plays tennis, not golf, water skis and snow skis, drinks Coors Light, smokes Marlboros, reads *Playboy* "for the articles," and for both my brother and me, was coach of every team we were ever on, from tee ball to soccer. He loves sports, *Star Trek*, and James Bond, and for discipline used his fraternity paddle (until my brother and I burned it in the fireplace). And when he used a belt, he was the dad that would say, "*This is going to hurt me more than it hurts you.*" And it did. And while not religious, he's always been the "cool dad" on the block, and as *my* dad, he couldn't have been more supportive and loving.

216

The theme of PK this year is *Breaking Down the Walls*, removing the "divisions within the body of Christ," with an emphasis on racial division. My dad is a good sport, but after two days of pastors preaching about sexual integrity, avoiding the demonic pitfall of porn and keeping promises to our brothers, our wives, our churches, and our God—we're ready for a beer. After the second full day, my dad and I break from the flock and head to Stratton's, my college bar that I actually discovered with him my first night in California when I transferred to UCLA.

We sit at the same table, look out the same window—but at a much different world.

"The guys in your Bible study seem like good friends," he says, lighting up a cigarette, blowing the smoke *away* from me, something I've trained him to do. I was the kid in the backseat always screaming to crack the window before I died. I was admittedly dramatic.

"I can't breathe," I say, mocking my childhood battle cry, making us both laugh.

He still has the same mustache he had in the 1970s. "How are you feeling?" he asks with disarming candor. As soon as my mother told my father that I had checked myself into a psychiatric ward for seventy-two hours, it's been a question that comes up on a frequent basis.

"Pretty good. The anti-depressant they put me on at the

New Life clinic wasn't doing the trick, so my doctor put me on Prozac, which, I don't know. I just feel...numb."

"Is this the doctor you've been meeting with since the clinic?"

"Melvin? No. He's not a doctor. He's not even a therapist, more of a spiritual mentor."

"What do you and this spiritual mentor talk about?"

"We just...you know, life stuff," I say, stumbling and reaching for my beer. "His approach is different than Dr. Kaufman's. Imagine the Promise Keepers version of therapy."

"You pray and sing, and then pray some more?"

"Exactly," I say, glancing upstairs at the booth where I first met Doug.

"So, have you been dating anyone?" he asks.

"Uh..." I stumble, taking a nervous gulp of beer.

With this one question the wall I've built is exposed. We've spent the weekend hearing about the importance of breaking down walls, but this proves to be one wall I can't bring down. I've never felt any pressure from him to get married and start building my white picket fence, although at my age, he was not only married, I was five years old. It's troubling that despite all the therapy and mentoring, I still can't be honest with the man responsible for my existence.

"No. Not right now," I say, adding another brick.

* * *

After a year of Saturday morning Bible studies, we collectively decide to disband our Promise Keepers accountability group, praying for each other as we go our separate ways.

Jake is getting serious with a girl he met at church, and Wade has been dating a girl he met at a Wycliffe Bible translation seminar, neither one able to scale the wall Tyler has built.

Despite a year of developing healthy, intimate, non-sexual relationships with godly and affirming men—the recipe for *change* according to my ex-gay guru Joe Dallas—I haven't outgrown my desire to have what Jake and Wade have with their girlfriends, just not with a girl.

And the floodwaters begin to rise.

I look to my left: no one. And then to my right: not a soul.

It's just me, fighting to keep my head above water, but being pulled down by a weighty loneliness. To quell my codependent craving for human intimacy, I decide to go swim laps at the UCLA pool. It's good exercise, and at the very least, it'll help me get my mind off me.

This is when I meet Nate.

And suddenly I'm a Promise Keeper on the verge of breaking one of my promises.

CHAPTER 8:

PLAYBOY BLUES

It's all in the eyes. Showering off before my swim at the UCLA pool, a glimpse of a strapping dude with a thorn-tattoo banding his left bicep has me switching to cold water, my body igniting with desires I'd hoped had been snuffed. I've made it six-months without a release. Nothing. Not even a ridiculous nocturnal emission, something I feverishly pray for every night. I'm seriously tense.

For a twenty-six-year-old male, spiritually castrating myself is a testament to my determination to conquer and alter my sexual nature. If I don't feed it, it will weaken, and it will *die*. But after months of starving, the gay gremlin is alive, pissed, and hungry.

The thorny dude leaves the showers. Instead of going out to the pool to do my laps, I return to my locker as if I've just completed a grueling swim, passing him as he towels off. And when his inquisitive eyes meet mine, it sparks the resurrection of my lifeless libido. It's a fleeting look but drenched with desire, causing my body to pulsate, mind to unravel, and soul to swell.

And it's *on*. As I unlock the combo to my locker, I think of Joe Dallas's words in *Desires in Conflict*: "*Sexual needs are natural to sexual beings. They are the result of the biological drive and the human need for romantic intimacy. There is nothing unhealthy or unusual about them.*"

Unless, you lack the biological drive and human need for romantic intimacy with the opposite sex, then you have no choice but to deny your needs. I've been doing that my entire life, but every human being has a breaking point. Including me, it appears. Shit. I throw on my jeans, T-shirt, and flip-flops, and as I flee the locker room, I glance back and as I fear (hope), the Italian is following. As I walk the slippery slope to my car, a slip from doing laps in a sea of depravity, I pray every step of the way. Once at the Cadi, I don't see him but feel his presence.

"Hey," says the thorny-tattooed Italian, his voice raspy and deep.

I turn to find him standing fully clothed, his thorns covered by a black T-shirt with the word *Triumph* across his chest. He's adjusting his NY baseball cap and eying me—dark hair dripping, charisma seducing, and green eyes penetrating. He looks like an Italian movie star, maybe in LA to promote a film or meet with bigwig Hollywood directors. He's probably 6'1", 180 pounds, with stubble on his face, and smooth, olive skin bronzed from the sun and deepened by his Mediterranean roots. And he's like Kryptonite, weakening my homo-aversion powers.

"Hey," I reply sheepishly, my face hot and tingly.

"I never do this, but I don't know, I got the sense that..." he says, sounding American.

My instinct is to play naïve: *I have no idea what you're talking about. I'm a Promise Keeper! See the bumper sticker!* Instead my eyes confirm what I've already conceded.

"I'm Nate," he says, extending his hand, the thorns peeking out from under his T-shirt.

I extend my hand, and when our hands touch, it sends a jolt to my pelvic girdle region.

"This is out of character," he confesses. "I have a girlfriend but there was something..." As he trails off, he's looking at me as though he sees the *me* hiding behind all the lies.

"You have a girlfriend?"

"Had. We recently went our ways," he says. "I'm not gay, I just...well, you know, sometimes someone like you comes along and..."

Here we are. I'm relieved he's not "gay." Since he has his own secret, my secret will be safe. I am torn, my stomach in knots, repressed libido springing to life and my mind trying to talk my body out of what will surely be repentance material. But my body has been held hostage by my militant mind for far too long, and on this day, is busting out of the chastity cuffs.

I open the back door of the Cadi as if he's a rock star and I'm his chauffeur. He takes the cue, crawling inside my love-shack Cadillac, and after I close the door behind him, I skittishly survey the parking lot to make sure the queer-smearing boogieman hasn't followed. I jump into the driver's seat, and under the cloak of window tint, I lock the doors and somersault into the backseat, ravaging him like someone whose libido has been incarcerated for a year. Just the simple touch is like fireworks; my unshackled hands can't get enough of him. He responds with equal passion, but before it gets too out of hand, he aborts, pulling away.

"Not like this. Not here," he says, peering out the window as a couple of college kids wander by. "Do you want to come over to my place?" he asks with irresistible charm.

"Where do you live?"

"Near the Hollywood Bowl."

As I follow Nate's vintage Land Rover east on Sunset toward the Hollywood Bowl, I play the *Desert Stream* ex-gay tapes, hoping it might inspire a turn of the wheel: *"Jesus is God's agent of freedom for the person whose divine image is marred by homosexuality,"* Andy preaches. *"He created us to reflect Himself, and where Satan and sin have defamed that image, He prepares the way for its repair. He also realizes how utterly help-less we are to restore that image ourselves. He knows our tendency to disobey Him."* I press eject, demanding to know why God hasn't freed or repaired me. Day after day, week after week, month after month of trying to starve the demon of homo-sexuality and here I am driving down Sunset Boulevard, mad with desire following a stranger I met at the pool! As we near the Hollywood Bowl on Highland Avenue, although it's Saturday afternoon at 4:30 p.m., the traffic is clogged, the air thick with jazz. I notice the marquis: *"Playboy Jazz Festival '96,"* an annual Bowl event. My thoughts go to Hef: *Does he miss me? Who's taken my place? Are there cameras in the grotto bathrooms?*

Sitting in traffic is like having a free seat at the concert; the bubbly blues spill out of the Hollywood Bowl and into the streets, stirring my soul and leaving me dizzy. Throngs of concertgoers packing coolers of wine and cheese weave in and out of the traffic on Highland, joining the steady flow into the Bowl. I notice Nate two cars ahead. It's not too late to change my direction. All I have to do is turn the wheel. But I'm being pulled by a magnetic force and its power is overwhelming. *Jesus, take the wheel!* I notice the date on the marquis: June 15th, 1996—one-year, one-month and ten-days since I was standing in the LA Coliseum with Tyler,

Jake and Wade at Promise Keepers for the first time. And a mere seven weeks since I was with them—and my dad—for the second time. A year of Bible study, accountability, and praying for my future wife, all for what? *To drown alone in a flood of dammed up desire?*

I think about my mom and how I'm not the son she thinks I am.

I think about Melvin the Mentor and how I'll explain my fall into sin.

It feels like I'm treading water in the deep end without a lifejacket and no sign of a divine lifeline. In the wake of heavenly silence, I sink deeper into the Playboy blues.

Nate turns off Highland Avenue before we reach the Bowl, checking his rearview mirror to see if I'm still there. I am. I follow him up the hill along a narrow lane winding through a hidden enclave of Mediterranean estates shrouded with lush foliage, red tile roofs, and unparalleled vistas overlooking the Hollywood Bowl and beyond. I become increasingly curious as to what he does for a living until we reach the top of the hill and begin descending down on the other side and the rent starts to drop. When we stop at an intersection of towering palm trees, the street sign Grace Avenue sends a shiver, making me wonder whether it's a sign or an omen. *If he lives on Grace Avenue, maybe God is sending a message that regardless of what happens at his address, it'll be covered by that Amazing Grace I've been singing about. Maybe*

God has sent Nate to me, so that I can—he turns on Whitley, down a steep hill and into the driveway of an apartment complex. I find street parking, and as I walk the palm-tree-lined incline back to Nate's place, I can hear the Playboy blues lingering in the balmy summer breeze.

Nate emerges from the underground parking garage, and I follow him into an antiquated Hollywood Hills apartment building whose glory days were back in the 1920s. We walk down a dimly lit and dorm-like hallway, passing door after door. When he unlocks his door and invites me in, I instinctually glance down the hallway to make sure there are no witnesses.

"Relax, no cameras in the hallways," he says.

I follow him inside, relaxing when the door shuts. Safely out of the public eye, my eyes scope Nate's private space: entry hallway with a walk-in closet, bathroom, small bedroom, and a kitchen with sliding doors that open to a balcony with incredible views of the ratty apartments next door. My eyes go from the original hardwood floors and vintage crown molding, to the king-sized bed that swallows the room, to the crucifix hanging above his headboard.

"Are you religious?" I ask, startled by the image of Jesus dying on a cross above the bed.

"Catholic," he says.

As a *Campus Crusade for Christ* Christian, I was taught Catholics aren't real Christians; they're too caught up with empty religious symbols and rituals, all of which is idolatry. I learned that Catholics could be extremely *religious* without having a *personal relationship* with God.

"You?" he asks.

"I'm Christian," I disclose, sparing him the drama.

"I'd give you a tour but this is kind of it," he jokes. "I'm always starving after swimming," he says, opening the fridge. "I know you skipped your laps, but are you hungry?" he slyly jabs.

"You noticed that?"

"I notice everything. I'm making a sandwich. You want one?"

"Sure," I say, noticing his place has old-Hollywood charm, sparking my curiosity as to who has lived here over the decades. The current resident sheds his black *Triumph* T-shirt, exposing his thorns—and mine. "How long have you lived here?" I ask, gulping my water.

"Here in Hollywood or here in this apartment?" he asks, the light from the fridge reflecting off his chiseled torso and eight-pack abs—the view that had me switching to cold in the showers.

"Both," I say, noticing that in his hot, sultry room, I have nothing to hose down the fire in my belly already burning like an inferno.

227

"I migrated from New York twelve years ago for college, and I've been here ever since. I'm coming up to one year in this place, which was supposed to be a temporary situation, but life happens," he says, whipping things out of the fridge, his kitchen morphing into an Italian deli.

"Did you go to UCLA?" I say, joining him in the kitchen.

"Pepperdine. My family summered in Malibu when I was a boy and I was sold. Going to a college where I could surf in between classes all year long appealed to me."

"Did you just say *summered*?"

"Yeah. Why?"

"It sounds kind of silver spoon-ish. Did you also *summer* in the Hamptons?"

He grins. "My family has a place there."

"What does your family do?"

"Mafia," he says, looking at me with a straight face. "It had its perks."

I chuckle, feeling surprisingly calm and relaxed.

"Commercial Real estate," he says. "My whole family. I'm the youngest of seven, the black sheep, more into surfing, writing, film, and art than the family business. My parents are these upper East Side New York socialites—I love them to death—but it's all about status, going to this black tie party and that charity event, like climbing a moving ladder.

That's why I escaped."

"And came to Hollywood, where it's nothing like that," I say, with sarcasm.

"Exactly," he laughs. "What about you?"

"I went to UCLA," I say. "And my family; we were highfalutin for Fort Worth, Texas. We went on vacations to the Gulf, but we never *summered*," I say, gaping at him standing shirtless at the open fridge, his sexy grin filling me with the urge to pounce.

"Do you want mustard, lettuce, tomato?"

I didn't expect I'd be driving to Hollywood for a pastrami and cheese, but I am starving.

"Do you have Grey Poupon?" I say, joking lamely.

"Why did I know that was coming?"

"Sure. Everything is fine."

Since you can learn a lot about a person from the place they call home, I turn my attention to his tidy dwelling: no dishes in the sink, no piles of dirty laundry, and no moldy pizza boxes. Even his bed is made. There is an antique bookcase housing a library of books on art, history, and philosophy, an eclectic mix of CD's, family photographs, and a pile of screenplays with the logo of a major Hollywood talent agency. On the dresser next to the TV is a framed picture of him and a pretty girl. "Is that your girlfriend?"

"Ex," he clarifies.

"She's pretty," I say.   She's blonde, actress-y looking, and stacked.

"Do you want a beer?" he asks from the kitchen.

"Sure," I reply, gazing at the picture of him and the girl. They look good together.   They really do.   I dig for more dirt.   "So, how long did you go out?"

"Three years," he says, entering the bedroom and hand-ing me a beer.

"Thanks," I say, taking the frosty Sierra Nevada lager.

He offers his bottle for a toast.   "To...what's your name again?" he jokes.

"John," I say, clinking my bottle against his, fizz bub-bling over and down the long neck of the bottle.   I don't want to drip on his hardwood, so I use my tongue, Nate watching wantonly.

"Is it hot in here?" he asks, opening a creaky window and inviting in a fresh breeze, as well as the soothing melodies of the blues.   He tends to the sandwiches and I start to relax. On the dresser next to the ex-girlfriend, I notice his college diploma in Art History from Pepperdine dated 1988—the year I graduated high school.   He's four years older than me.

"It's ready," he says, smiling at me snooping.   "This is just a snack.   If I really like you then you can stay for dinner."

"You're assuming I even can stay for dinner. You have no idea how popular and busy I am."

"I don't doubt that for a second," he says, moving in and kissing me gently on the lips, catching me off guard by how tender and romantic he is. "Have a seat," he says, pointing me to the kitchen café table for two and serving up sandwiches, the kind you find in a gourmet deli.

"Wow. This looks amazing," I say, impressed by his culinary cunningness.

He sits across from me, and for the first time in a long time, I don't feel so alone.

The night ends my bid for the *Guinness Book of World Records* for "sexual purity."

The next morning, my eyes open to find Jesus hanging from the cross above me. It's a startling image to wake to, followed by the even more alarming image of Nate sleeping soundly next to me. *It wasn't a dream.* As I lay motionless, my mind races to reconcile. The night felt almost spiritual, which could have been the reawakening of my dormant sexual drive, or the Enya CD he put on after the Playboy Jazz Festival faded into the night. Whatever the case, being with him felt normal and natural, which is worrisome—especially when I'm still in his bed.

I've never woken in another dude's bed. My encounters

had been limited, awkward, and bumbling, and after each I was convinced I'd never need to do *that* again. This is different. Beyond the physical, I feel a deeper connection to Nate I can't explain, sounding exactly like everyone else who's ever slept with a stranger. *"It's like we've known each other forever."* But with Nate, I feel connected, emancipated and *alive*. And *a lot* less tense.

The crucifix serves as a reminder that Christ paid the penalty for our sins, and as I take stock of the night, before I can ask the question, my inner truth brigade attacks: *"Of course, it's sin! Anything beyond sex with a wife is outside God's intent for human sexuality. You're in trouble."*

I need to repent, but decide I'll do it later. I'm curious to learn more about the intimate stranger lying beside me. I watch him sleep for a second, not in a creepy way, I just want to kiss him and touch him more. In my holy pursuit to straighten, I've fought to keep the animal in its cage until I could train it properly. With Doug, I had the animal on a choke collar. But with Nate the animal is running wild after being caged for six months without food or water.

Suddenly—there is a knock at the door, jolting Nate to consciousness and jump-starting my anxiety. With eyes wide-open, he looks at me, then the clock, before deflating in duress.

A louder, more impatient knock and a female voice: "Nate, wake up. It's me!"

I look to him for guidance, and he points to the picture of the girl, and to the box next to the door filled with CD's, ladies' shoes and toiletries. "Just a minute," he yells at the door.

We leap out of bed, both of us naked, and scavenge for our clothes. I consider the balcony as an emergency exit, but we're on the third floor. The only place to hide is under his bed, already taken with art supplies and canvases. Or his closet, which is where he's directing me. His eyes apologize as I take cover in his closet behind the mountain bike, easels, and Armani.

I hear him open the door. "You were supposed to call first," he says.

"I did. It went right to voice mail. I told you, Karen and I are going hiking up Runyon Canyon at—" her voice suddenly stops before gasping. "*Oh my god, you have someone here.*"

"No, I don't," he lies.

Her voice is softer. "You're hiding something. I see it on your face."

"Would you stop? Here's your stuff," he says, impatiently.

"I can't believe you're already…never mind. We're so over. It doesn't matter."

I hear him handing over the box and then a long silence. I notice Nate's closet is different than Hugh Hefner's closet.

When not wearing a Speedo, Nate must be an Armani model.

"Just tell me," she whimpers. "Is she the one you cheated with?"

"I didn't cheat on you. Would you stop it already?"

"It is, isn't it?" she asks again, not letting it go. The anger in her voice makes me feel that she might storm inside, exposing me and Nate. I hide deeper in his closet, trembling with the fear of exposure—a familiar fear that has kept me on the sidelines of my own life.

"We didn't break up because of another girl," he whispers angrily. "We broke up because we're not compatible."

"If there's no one inside, then why are you blocking the door?" she asks bitterly.

He answers with silence. I hear her crying. "Alison, please," he says, consolingly.

"Bye, Nate."

A moment later the front door closes, the closet door opens, and the lights turns on.

"I'm really sorry about that," he says, sincerely. "I forgot she was... Anyway, I'm sorry you had to witness that and for making you—"

"It's fine," I say, although I'm definitely on edge and not really fine.

I emerge from Nate's closet and into his firm embrace,

relishing a rare moment of intimacy with another human being who sees behind the mask.

"Do you want coffee?" Nate asks.

"One cup," I say, setting my limit. One cup and then I'll get out of there, repent, and forget this ever happened. That is the boundary I've set. One cup and then I'll leave.

By my second cup, Nate is looking less ruffled by the sunrise ex-girlfriend ambush. The girl has left, her box is gone, and it's just Nate and me: Sunday morning coffee at a table for two. He's leaning back with the *Los Angeles Times* pitched in front of him, wearing his *Triumph* T-shirt and NY ball cap. His eyes meander blissfully between me and the newspaper.

I notice the time: church is starting without me for the first time since I stumbled into that elementary school cafeteria well over a year ago. The congregation has since tripled, graduating from the elementary school cafeteria to the junior high auditorium. If I hadn't been snared by Satan's trap, I'd right now be greeting guests with Sunday morning worship bulletins. I haven't heard it from Pastor Brody, but higher up in the Calvary Chapel chain of command, founder Chuck Smith regards homosexuality as the "final affront against God." Sitting across from Nate, I am reminded, despite stirrings in my spirit, that romance with Nate is an *affront against God*.

"Ella Fitzgerald died," he says, looking up from the headlines.

"Who's that?" I say, sipping the dark French Roast, trying to shake the shackles.

"You don't know Ella Fitzgerald?"

I shake my head confirming my ignorance, my music awareness mostly Christian; when not listening to ex-gay tapes, the Christian band Jars of Clay plays on a loop in the Cadillac.

He reads from the paper, "*Jazz's First Lady of Song… The shy entertainer with flawless talent held the spotlight for decades until struck by ailments. She was seventy-eight.*"

"I don't think I've ever even heard her music," I say, recalling the time in college when I fasted from secular music. If it wasn't Amy Grant or Michael W. Smith, it was devil music.

"You have," he says, walking over to his CD collection, plucking one out and playing it. "This first one is called 'Summertime'—one of my favorite, with Louis Armstrong."

As I listen to the classic melody and the haunting saxophone, Nate is surveying the fridge. "Is there anything you don't like in your omelet?"

"You're making an omelet? All you've done is cook for me. You don't have to—"

"It's Sunday," he says, pulling things out of the fridge with the dexterity of a professional.

His kitchen is small, but I feel like I'm watching a cooking show. In the seventeen hours we've been acquainted, I figure Nate to be a pauper prince posing as a Hollywood screenwriter to disguise the fact he's an heir to a corporate throne. I'm not privy to his full story, and my imagination is rich, but I know he enjoys living simply, following his passions of cooking, writing, and painting. He makes a living as a screenwriter, with several projects in development, and just began an oil painting class. He isn't a practicing Catholic, surfs on Sundays, speaks Italian with his parents, and listens to KCRW public radio. He voted for Clinton, buys organic groceries, recycles—and when it comes to blokes, has had only a handful of encounters.

"So who taught you to cook?" I ask.

"My Sicilian grandmother. She taught me everything I know. She came over from Sicily every summer and stayed with us, tying me to her apron. It was my destiny she'd say, but really I was the youngest and her last best chance of carrying on the family traditions," he laughs.

"What about your mom?"

"Why cook when you can hire a chef? She can't even make spaghetti."

"You definitely have skills," I say as he chops, dices, and grinds.

"Wait until you've tasted my grandmother's lasagna recipe."

"Do I need to make a reservation now?"

"What are you doing tonight?"

I smile, unable to think of one thing I'd rather do than have a hot Italian seduce me with his grandma's lasagna recipe—a seriously gay thought.

"We can hit the Farmer's Market, and if you're up for it, hike to the top of Griffith—"

"Were you going to marry her?" I blurt, derailing his excited pitch of the day's itinerary.

He thoughtfully considers the question, before nodding. "Pancakes or French toast?"

"Pancakes."

"It's Father's Day, by the way," he says, changing the topic. "I'm not sure—"

"What? Are you—*shit!*" I can't believe I forgot. "It's also my dad's birthday!"

"Seriously?" he says, beating eggs into a frenzy with an eggbeater.

"I hate when it falls on the same day and I forget both."

As Nate scrambles my eggs, I listen to Ella and Louis

sing, struck by the fact that almost two months ago, my dad and I were praying together at the LA Coliseum.

"How often you see him?" he asks, chopping onions like a chef.

"You know, holidays, the summer," I say, choosing not to disclose that my dad was out last month for Promise Keepers, or that I'm an aspiring ex-gay on Prozac living a stale new life.

Sometimes, the truth is easier to take in installments.

"I'll finish breakfast. Go call your dad. You can use my phone."

"You sure?"

"Of course," he says, shooing me away with a spatula.

I move to his bedroom—and after a few moments of psyching myself up, preparing my story should my dad ask what I'm doing—I dial my dad's number, relieved when he answers.

"*Happy Birthday to you, happy birthday to you*—is that enough torture? You don't want me to finish. I get my singing talent from you," I say, laughing while perusing Nate's bedroom; the disheveled sheets and Jesus dying on a cross above his bed prove unsettling.

"With your birthday out of the way, *Happy Father's Day*! I should be there. It's the double whammy. But I just saw you less than two months ago which should last me until Christmas," I joke. Our rapport is easy, until he asks awkward girlfriend questions or why I'm not at church. "No, I'm feeling fine, I just took a day off. Did *you* go to church? What? *You did?*"

There's another knock on Nate's door. *Are you serious?* I muffle the phone and retreat to the open window, in case I need to escape. Nate enters, gesturing an apology.

Another knock.

"So what are you doing today?" I say to my dad into the phone.

Nate looks through the peephole and deflates, giving me the 'just a minute' gesture. I watch him crack the door and slip into the hallway. I instinctually start making the bed with one hand, holding the phone with the other, doing my best to straighten up the room just in case.

"What's the lake level?" I ask, my anxiety rising when I hear *her* voice again. I can't make out words, but it's heated. "It's up to the sea wall? Wow." And then from the stereo, Ella sings a poorly timed tune, "Makin' Whoopee":

Another bride, another June,

Another sunny honeymoon,

Another season, another reason,

For makin' whoopee!

"What are ya'll doin' for dinner?" I ask, covering up the headset to muffle Ella and her stupid Whoopee song. And Nate's jilted lover hollering at him in the hallway.

And then I hear the ex-girlfriend yell: "If you're not hiding anything then let me in!"

"What?" I say to my dad who heard the screaming. "Oh, just neighbors. So—"

And the smoke alarm goes off in the kitchen—bringing Nate bolting in, the door flinging wide open leaving me face-to-face with Alison, the girl from the picture—just without the smile.

"Hey dad!" I scream into the phone. "No, it's just the smoke alarm. I'll call you back!"

Ella's crooning competes with the squealing alarm:

Another year or maybe less,

What's this I hear?

Well, you can't confess,

She feels neglected, and he's suspected,

Of makin' whoopee!

I walk toward the door, and Alison's entire body language melts to complete relief.

"Oh my god," she yells over the alarm. "I'm so embarrassed. You're not—I'm Alison!"

"I'm Bryan," I yell over the piercing alarm, awkwardly shaking her hand.

Nate opens the kitchen sliding door, fanning the smoke with a newspaper until the alarm stops, leaving a piercing silence, except for Ella:

She sits alone 'most every night,

He doesn't phone her, he doesn't write,

He says he's busy, but she says, 'Is he?'

He's makin' whoopee!

"Oh my god, it's Ella," Alison says, wistfully. "She died yesterday. Can you believe it?"

I shake my head, commiserating with her grief. "I know. Awful."

"Anyway, I'm Nate's girlfriend, now ex," she says, leaning in and whispering. "All morning I thought, I don't know, he was with the girl he left me for. I'm not sure there's another girl, but he was acting so guilty. I feel kinda crazy, like Glenn Close, *Fatal Attraction* crazy."

Nate enters, looking at Alison and then to me. "Where there's smoke—"

"There's fire," Alison completes.

"Not always. Sometimes it's just smoke," he says with a tinge of bitterness.

"Was it the pancakes?" I ask.

"Oh my god, are you making your famous gingerbread pancakes with walnuts?" she shrieks.

"No. Multi-grain with blueberries," he says, tipped with venom.

"I'm sorry, Nate," she says, laughing, while looking at me. "I created this whole other—"

"It's okay," he says, moving to the door, waving it back and forth to create ventilation and a not so subtle hint that it's time for Alison to move her body to the other side of the door.

"How come I've never met you?" she asks me. "I thought I knew all of Nate's friends."

I shrug, deferring to Nate. "Not all," he says, impatient with the nosy ex-girlfriend routine.

"Well, I should call my dad back. It's Father's Day," I say, because it's so awkward and I have to say something to fill the verbal void. "Very nice to meet you," I say to Alison.

I leave them at the front door, taking the phone into the smoky kitchen, my fear of exposure preventing me from going outside on the balcony. Instead I put my nose to the screen, trying to breathe the outside air without going outside. I'll call my dad back later. I'm too shaken up.

I overhear them talking at the door, inspiring me to click my heels. *There's no place like—*

"He's cute. Has Karen met him?" Alison whispers to Nate. "She would totally—"

"Bye, Alison."

"I talked to your dad this morning," she says. "To wish him Happy Father's Day."

"Why are you making this harder than it needs to be?"

"He thinks you're making a mistake. In his eyes, I'll always be family," she snaps.

"Take care, Alison."

"I don't even get a pancake?" she asks, jokingly serious.

"They're burned. Goodbye, Alison."

And the door closes. I sit down at the table for two, my head spinning while Ella croons:

You'd better keep her

I know it's cheaper

Than makin' whoopee!

Nate joins me in the kitchen, collapsing across from me at the table, his face falling into his hands, shaking his head. And when he looks up at me, we both start laughing hysterically.

CHAPTER 9:

JAVA FOR JESUS

On Monday morning when I wake to Nate's alarm chirping at 5:00 a.m., my eyes open to find Jesus hanging on the cross above me. His face looks peaceful, so I can't tell if he's mad at me or not. Nate groggily rolls into me, groping for me in the darkness. "You awake?"

"Yeah," I whisper. I'm awake. Wide awake. I woke at 3:11 a.m. with a debilitating sense of dread at the prospect of returning to my failed new life. "Go back to sleep," I tell him.

"Help yourself. There's granola in the—"

"I'm good," I say, grabbing my clothes and sprinting to the bathroom.

The race is on; it's Monday and I open the church coffee shop, a part-time summer gig.

While showering in Nate's shower, I realize that his place feels like a safe haven where I can just *be*. And I don't want to leave. The rest of Father's Day was like a movie montage: edgy, hip music playing while Nate and I playfully shopped at the Farmer's Market, hiked to Griffith Observatory for the sunset, and then had a storied Hollywood night with Nate making his grandma's lasagna from scratch. I dread putting my mask back on and returning to my evangelical world where Nate and I could never exist.

As I roll out of Whitley Heights in my grandma's Cadi, Nate's Hollywood bachelor pad in my rearview mirror, I have a sinking feeling as the most passionate, romantic, sensual mistake of my life is now but a memory. As I drive, it's a troubling transition from homo-liaisons with an Italian stud in Hollywood to serving java for Jesus in Santa Monica.

With the clock ticking, I have thirty-seven minutes to drive to Santa Monica, pick up pastries and open the doors at 6:00 a.m. or risk the wrath of the decaffeinated yoga students who expect their herbal tea within the first ten seconds of opening the doors. One morning when I didn't open until 6:12 a.m., one lady told me I'd upset the entire rhythm of her day. And when I served her Chamomile tea, I was tempted to slip her a *Smooth Moves* tea bag—*how 'bout that for rhythm, lady*! But it's a church-owned operation, and Jesus signs the checks.

I helped build Higher Grounds from the ground up, mostly painting, and believed in Pastor Brody's vision of serving the local community of Santa Monica by creating the *Cheers* of coffee houses, a place for locals to call their own. And it's working. Most patrons don't know it's a church-owned operation; with the exception of the giant Michelangelo etching of God's hand touching Adam's artfully rendered on the acid-stained concrete floor—or the halo that on humid days can be seen floating above my head—there's nothing churchy about it. No religious tracts to peruse with your cappuccino or preaching with your pastries, just a hip neighborhood coffee house with a vintage interior and a nice, chill vibe. Although the coffee beans aren't handpicked by the Holy Spirit and delivered like manna from heaven, they are of the highest quality, and in taste tests, four out of five evangelical Christians prefer our coffee to the other brands.

I'm ten minutes late; there's a line of impatient yoga students standing outside the shop waiting. I'm off-rhythm, and nothing is moving smoothly. On the outside, I maintain a buttoned up exterior, but on the inside I am torn, trying to reconcile the irreconcilable. I'm on autopilot until Victoria, Pastor Brody's wife, comes into the shop with her three-year-old hanging on her hip and the two boys in tow, both playfully ambushing me behind the counter.

"Where were you yesterday?" the now eight-year-old asks.

"Yesterday?" I stall, as both boys look at me wide-eyed. They look forward to our Sunday adventures. So do I. In my daily prayers for a wife and kids, I pray my sons will be just like these two kids. "I was sick," I finally say, hating that my truth requires me to lie to them.

"You feeweng bettah?" the little one mumbles.

"I am feeling better," I lie as Victoria approaches, smiling a genuine down to earth smile.

"They missed you," she says. "You have no idea how much they look up to you."

"Only because he's taller," the older one jokes, both climbing on me like I'm a tree.

"Can you watch them for two minutes? We have women's study and I—"

"Of course. I'll put them to work," I say, as she joins a woman from the church to prepare for the night's Bible study. During business hours, Higher Grounds is a legitimate business serving secular needs. But *after hours*, it's a venue for spiritual activities such as Bible studies, church meetings, and Friday and Saturday night acoustic Jesus Jam concerts.

"What do y'all want to make?" I ask the pastor's boys, my shift almost over.

"A mocha with extra chocolate and—" the older one starts.

"Wots of chocowate and cherrwees and *boogers on top,*" the younger one says, laughing.

"How about an ice-blended booger mocha with hot snot on top?" I suggest.

They both laugh. As an older brother, I understand sibling psychology. But according to the church leadership, it's more than that: working with kids is one of my "spiritual gifts." I can't speak in tongues, but since the kids follow me around like the Pied Piper, I was recruited for children's ministry, a fancy term for babysitting, during a leadership weekend at a private house in Newport Beach a few months ago. It was three days and seven kids. While the adults plotted the future of the church, I led the kids on nature hikes, judged coloring contests, and read to them from Amy Grant's *Heart to Heart Bible Stories* before naps and bedtime. All weekend I listened to the parents tell me what a great father I'd be—a comment that cut both ways.

With my two helpers I finish my shift, but before I get out the door, Victoria approaches. "I know someone who has a crush on you," she singsongs, sounding more like a girl on a playground than a thirty-eight-year-old hip pastor's wife and earth mother of three.

"Who?" I say as she opens a can of worms I'd rather keep closed.

"She might not be your type, I don't know, but she's such an amazing girl. She's just shy, convinced you don't even know who she is. It's so cute; she gets so nervous when you're around. Anyway, I'm not trying to play cupid, but you're both so great, I just thought I'd…"

My face must reflect my horror, because she stops pitching.

"I'm just a little bird. Sunday night we're having a barbeque, and she'll be there," she says, grinning, as though she's planted a seed and one day will be toasting us at our wedding and telling the story of how she brought us together. "I really do think you two would hit it off."

Of all the days to be struck by a cupid arrow from the pastor's wife, I break a leg acting smitten by the idea of being set up, already rehearsing an excuse for missing the barbeque.

After clocking out on the Westside, I race to the Valley for my 4:30 with Melvin, who greets my whoopee-making news as warmly as a sponsor learning an alcoholic under his care went to a bar.

And stayed there all weekend.

"It didn't feel wrong. It's the first time I'd ever——"

"That's the nature of *sin*! It twists things, makes us think what is wrong is right and even pleasing to God. You can rationalize it, but Satan is attacking your weakness, and it's my job as your mentor to speak truth in love and steer you away from what is obviously Satan's trap!"

Melvin has been my mentor for a year and a half, and since my third session, we've been breaking breadsticks at a family-owned pizza joint in Van Nuys, which according to him is less clinical. Every week we sit at the same red corner booth. I order iced tea and he orders a Coke, sometimes a slice of pizza. I pay the tab and tip, and leave a $30 check for Melvin.

Mentoring is different than psychotherapy, my dynamic with Melvin less therapist-patient and more grandfather-grandson. On the days he takes the train from Orange County, I drop him at the station after our session. During my years with Dr. Kaufman, I never saw him outside of his office. We never shared a pizza, discussed train schedules, or prayed. Melvin is genuinely good-hearted but clueless about treating my issue. And I'm sick of talking about myself, frustrated that after a year-and-a-half of meeting with a men's mentor in Van Nuys, there are still no signs of "healing." Our sessions have become the movie *Groundhog Day*: I enter and vent my deplorable bent, he listens and affirms traditional values—and then we pray. Repeat.

But having met Nate, the cycle is broken and I'm in the danger zone.

"There's a connection, an intimacy, like none I've ever experienced with another human."

"What about that other one?" he asks, a question jaded with judgment.

"Doug? And did you seriously just say the '*other one*'?"

"I meant Doug," he says. "We just haven't talked about him in a while, and I—"

"I know you think he was a mistake. But for the record, we were physically intimate a few times in the beginning. That's it.   We developed a bond, an emotional connection, and—"

"You checked into the New Life clinic," he says, shaking his head, eating a slice of cheese.

"*What*? Why are you shaking your head?"

"You still reframe this past relationship, and this one with Nate, in a way that undermines the severity of the issue. These emotional connections you have, it's not how God designed us to relate to our own gender. Just because you feel affection for someone *doesn't make it right*."

"And marrying a woman who I don't feel any affection for is somehow better?"

He doesn't have an answer, so he sips his Coke as I push away the cold breadsticks.

"According to the Bible, celibacy is an honorable way of life and a gift from God," he says, reminding me of my one-and-only option, as if celibacy is supposed to provide solace.

"I know. But I don't have that gift! So then what? What am I supposed to do?" I say, scanning the empty Italian eatery, making me crave another piece of Nate's lasagna.

"I believe our Father will open your heart to receive a woman and—"

"You keep saying that, but look at me! I'm *twenty-six*! Do you have any idea what it's like to be celibate at twenty-six? You don't, because by my age, you were married with four kids."

"In the Garden, God declared that it wasn't good for man to be alone, so he created Eve for companionship," he says, going back to the basics, which is like cartwheels and Kindergarten.

"Yeah, I get that. I'm not new. I'm obviously still not digging on Eve, and breaking breadsticks with you once a week hasn't made Eve any more desirable!"

"What you experienced with Nate is contrary to the way God created you and—"

"How do *you* know? How do you know how God created *me*?" I say, steam releasing.

"Because I have God's Word," he says, his loaded Bible levitating above the tablecloth.

When Melvin prays, he can ramble, but when he hangs up with God, he always ends with the words "In Jesus's name." "Lord, I lift up my brother, Bryan. Guard his heart from the lies of the enemy, oh Lord. Prepare him for his wife, Lord. Mold him into the man you created him to be.

We ask that you'll give him strength and heal his heart *in Jesus's name.* Amen."

"Amen," I say, looking up to find his eyes looking at me welling with compassion.

In the eight years I've been orbiting the evangelical Christian universe, the tag, *"In Jesus's name"* is on the end of every prayer request, regardless of how trivial, and much like hitting the send button. Jesus is the courier, delivering your request to the foot of the Almighty. Sure, there are other couriers, but Jesus is the only one who can positively get it there overnight. The message from Christian radio and "family values" mailings: "Lord, protect us from the *gay agenda,* convict the *homosexual activists* of their sin, and help us defend godly values and our way of life *in Jesus's name.*" I'm becoming increasingly aware of how the things said and done *in Jesus's name* are slicing away at my soul. Gay equals sin. Period. Full stop. Case closed.

"You need to reach out to your pastor and the men in your church to help you fight this," Melvin mentors. "You can't do this alone. You need someone to call when you're weak."

"You need a ride to the train station?" I ask, digging into my empty wallet.

"If you don't mind."

* * *

After dropping him at the station, it's close to 6:00 p.m., and I have a voice mail on my pager from Nate. He's in Malibu surfing and asks if I'd like to meet him for dinner somewhere on the Westside. I decide I won't call him back, but after an hour of stewing in traffic, when I see the Sunset Boulevard exit, I take it and start looking for a payphone. He's in Brentwood at a friend's place, so we agree to meet at A Votre Sante, a healthy, upscale bistro on San Vicente Boulevard.

When I arrive, Nate is sitting at a candle-lit, white-table-clothed table-for-two next to the window, far more exposed than I would've liked. He looks like a movie star, wearing jeans and a sporty black button-down with sleeves rolled up and hair slicked back. When I approach, thankfully there is no slaphappy grab-ass Italian greeting, just a disarmingly sexy smile that puts me at ease. Until I remember we're in public. When I sit down, I instinctually glance around, hoping we look like two straight guys having a romantic dinner and not two fags on a date.

"Would you rather have the booth in the back?" he says, noticing my paranoia.

"Your ex-girlfriend's not a waitress here or anything?"

"She's off tonight," he says, before leaning forward and whispering. "I'm glad you met me. You're all I've thought about all day."

Of course that comment sparks the fire, the ensuing silence turning steamy in an instant.

"So what's good here?" I ask, turning my attention to the menu.

"What are you in the mood for?"

My face flushes at the flashbacks of our weekend. The eye contact smolders, until the evangelical voices inside my head, a chorus of condemnation, begin shouting apocalyptically: *Dinner with Nate is a slap in the face of God, a perversion of humanity, and will never be accepted, tolerated, or embraced by the Body of Christ! God loves you, but He hates your sin!*

"Are you in the mood for a Cabernet or a Merlot?" he asks, studying the wine list.

The apostolic arguments are playing on a loop, and I can't shut them off. All day I've been wallowing in the crevice between my two worlds, the schism inside only growing larger.

"They also have some good Italian Pinots."

We're sitting next to the window among a row of boutique shops, so people keep strolling by window-shopping. And when they look at us, I feel like we're on display. I feel exposed, my down-low, up-front and center for the world to see and judge, as though the more lurid details of the last forty-eight hours are playing on a video screen above my head. I feel vulnerable, like bully bait; any second a gay-bashin' redneck is going to pass the window, call us out, and smear us for our blatant faggotry. The fears snowball into an insidious form of gay panic: *Are those people staring? Do they think...?* I begin to anticipate what I'll say if my pastor passes by, or Melvin, or someone from church. I'll be forced to lie, like I did to the pastor's kids earlier, and I'm already becoming tangled in the web I'm weaving.

"You said you were coming from the valley?" he asks, making conversation.

"I had an appointment," I say, deciding to remain mute on Melvin the Mentor. "How was surfing?" I ask, hyper aware of the older well-to-do couple within earshot at the table next to us.

"Good," he says, browsing the menu. "Would you split a salad?"

"Can't we get our own salads?" I say, noticing the elderly woman look at us, and although she doesn't say anything, I use her blank stare as a canvas on to which I project all my queer fears.

"We can. I just thought—*oh, I get it*," he says, reading me. "Too g-a-y," he spells out.

I force a smile. He grins, continuing to browse the menu as I browse for bullies.

"So are you?" I finally say.

"So am I what?"

"Don't make me spell it out."

"I told you. I'm more...in the middle," he says, looking back at the menu. "Do you know what you want?"

I do. And that's the problem.

Over the summer, I have a foot in both worlds, spending the night with Nate on Saturdays and racing to church Sunday mornings to take Pastor Brody's kids for Happy Meals. I am living two lives and never the twain shall meet. There are times when I have to choose.

On July 4th, instead of being with Nate, I'm with Pastor Brody and family, heading to the Harvest Crusade, a Billy Graham-inspired big tent revival at Anaheim Stadium. Pastor Brody is driving, Victoria in the passenger seat, and I'm in the back seat with the two boys and the girl in a car seat. We've just been to In & Out, a popular West Coast burger chain and are examining the Bible verses printed discreetly on the bottom of our drink cups.

"John 3:16," the eight-year-old says, reading the bottom of his drink cup.

"Mine too," I add. "Do you know John 3:16?" I say, creating a "teaching moment."

"Duh. I'm like a pastor's kid. *'For God so loved the world, he gave his one and only Son, so whoever believes in him will not perish, but have eternal life,"* he says, then blows a bubble.

"Nice," I say, giving him a high five.

"Is Stacwee your gwirlfriend?" the five-year-old asks me, taking me by surprise.

"What? No, Stacy is not my girlfriend."

"Then who's your gwirlfriend?" he asks. The *Who's your Girlfriend?* game is my least favorite.

"I know who his girlfriend is," the older one says. "Jenny!"

"Ha, ha! You wuv her! You wuv Jenny!"

"No, I don't love Jenny. And no, she is not my girlfriend."

"Then who's your gwirlfwiend?" the younger one presses.

"I don't have a girlfriend?" I say, sheepishly ashamed.

"Why not?"

"I don't know..." I say, my spirit shriveling.

"She'll come along when you're ready," Victoria assures me, then looking over at Pastor Brody. "We didn't meet until I was twenty-seven. How old are you?"

"Twenty-six."

"See, you're young. You've got plenty of time to meet Ms. Right," Victoria assures me.

Once inside a packed and spirited Anaheim stadium, Harvest Crusade feels like Promise Keepers, just with the noticeable addition of women and children. I am standing in the masses, shoulder-to-shoulder with Pastor Brody and family, singing along with Crystal Lewis as she sings from the outfield the song, "Come as You Are." All the while knowing that I can't.

Later that night, the Fourth of July is almost over, but the fireworks are just beginning. Nate is house-sitting off Melrose Avenue and asks me to come over. Having just spent the weekend lying to my pastor and family, I can't wait to take the mask off. On the drive over, I feel the transformation from Dr. Jekyll to Mr. Hyde; when he opens the door of the Spanish Bungalow on June Street, the way my heart leaps at the sight of him standing in his swim trunks is such a blatant violation in the world I've been immersed, it's jolting.

"How'd it go?" he asks, knowing I've spent the weekend harvesting for souls.

"Fine. Do they have a pool?" I ask, referring to his swim trunks.

"And a hot tub," he says, inviting me in, and once inside, giving me a tender kiss.

"You didn't tell me. I would have brought my swimsuit."

"You don't need a swimsuit," he says, words that complete my transformation to Mr. Hyde. "Do you want a glass of wine?"

"Sure," I say, checking out the place, a tastefully

furnished bungalow.

"Who lives here?"

"Friends of friends. It's a cool place, huh?"

"Real cool," I say, moving to the hallway lined with framed photographs. It takes less than ten seconds to notice that most feature the same two middle-aged men, just standing in front of different landmarks across the globe, from the Eiffel tower to the Great Wall of China.

"Exactly, who are the owners?"

"Bob and Terry," he says, from the kitchen.

"And Terry is a man?"

"That is correct," he says, joining me and handing me a glass of wine. "And so is Bob." He points to a picture. "That's Bob and that's Terry. Great couple."

"Couple? This is a *gay* couple's house?"

"Is that a problem?"

"No, I just..." I start. "Do they know about you?"

"No. I actually know them through Alison."

"And there aren't any cameras or any chance they'll show up?"

"No cameras, and they're in Europe. So, no."

I gulp my wine, my imagination substituting Nate and me onto the wall of pictures. It's a sobering reminder that unless I stop this train, one day we may have our own wall in our own house, which means one thing: I failed God, failed my family, and failed myself. Not to mention the fact that photos of Nate and me would never make it to my mom's hallway of pictures. As I peer into their life together, I judge them, and in so doing, judge myself. They've given in to *sin*.

I start to revert back to Dr. Jekyll, knowing that Mr. Hyde will eventually destroy me.

By the end of the summer, the stress of living a double life has taken its toll, and I've reached the breaking point. My bond with Nate has deepened to a degree that I know I can't extricate myself alone, so one night I reach out and call the deacon from my church to confess.

Deacon Dale grew up surfing with Pastor Brody in Huntington Beach before both finding God and starting up a church. Dale is in his late thirties, has a wife and a toddler, and lives a few blocks from me. As soon as I spill the beans to Dale, he thinks we should call Pastor Brody.

"You want me to tell...I can't tell Pastor Brody! Besides, it's almost 9:30 p.m.!"

"He'll be up. You have to tell him. He should know, Bryan."

In the car with Deacon Dale en route to Santa Monica to meet Pastor Brody, I'm starting to get panicky. His family has taken me in, and I fear my truth will change things.

I don't want to lose them.

When we walk into the Coffee Bean on Main Street in Santa Monica, Pastor Brody is sitting by the window dressed in flip-flops and board shorts, looking more like a surfer and less like a preacher. He holds a Bible in one burly hand, extending the other warmly, which I take timidly.

"You're hands are sweaty," he says.

"Yeah, well, I'm kind of nervous."

"You have nothing to be nervous about. You're among friends."

After buying them coffee drinks, we find a table, away from others. Pastor Brody places his Bible on the table, stirs sugar into his latte, and looks to both of us, trying to get a sense of why we're all there. I know Dale wants to tell him, give him some warning, but defers to me.

"So what's going on?" Pastor Brody asks.

And I begin hemming and hawing for well over an hour, avoiding the real issue, as they listen patiently. "And then when I was seven..." I ramble, my Iced blended Mocha already melted until Dale finally intervenes. "Why don't you just tell him what you told me?"

Easy for him to say. "Well, I've been struggling with..." I choke. "Well, with lust."

Expecting something far worse, Pastor Brody breathes a sigh of relief. "You're not alone. Every man struggles with lust."

I look to Deacon Dale for guidance, and his eyes push me to take the plunge. "My struggle is a little different," I expand, cautiously.

"How's your struggle different?" he asks, seemingly puzzled.

"The object of my lust is...well, not women."

"Oh," he says, looking to Deacon Dale, who raises his eyebrows, and then back at me, as if he hasn't wrapped his head around my words. "What is the object of your lust?"

"Other guys," I confess, looking down at the table ashamed.

He wants to help me. I can see it in his face, but he seems stumped. I don't feel judgment, just a sense of being thrown. He quickly recovers, treating it like any other lust issue: Flee temptation. He grabs a Coffee Bean napkin and a pen lodged in his Bible and begins outlining my deliverance plan, starting by asking me to list things that cause temptation.

This is when I tell him about Nate.

I watch as he scribbles Nate's name on the napkin, making it clear I must cut all ties. They are both supportive of my desire *to change*, but one comment from Pastor Brody as we wrap up forces me to clarify my struggle. He assures me he won't tell Victoria or the kids, and that it won't change the way he feels about me hanging out with his kids, but he might "have reservations should there be a sleep over or something of that nature."

"What? Wait a minute!" I recoil. "I'm not talking pedophilia. I'm not attracted to kids. Let's at least get that straight," I make clear. "I'm attracted to dudes *my age*. Big difference!"

He seems to comprehend the distinction, but it leaves me wondering how well he understands my struggle. With the beans spilled, we start prayer-walking down Main Street. From outward appearances we're having a conversation; our eyes are open, and we're in motion, but the words coming out of Pastor Brody's mouth aren't directed at us, but to the Almighty, who we hope is tuning in on this cool, breezy Santa Monica night. As Pastor Brody and Deacon Dale pray for me, I clutch the Coffee Bean napkin outlining my deliverance.

The easiest step: meeting with Pastor Brody weekly for pastoral counseling.

The most challenging step: saying goodbye to Nate.

The day after my caffeinated confession, I call Nate and make plans for the final goodbye.

Nate is dog sitting in Malibu, and since I've started waiting tables in Malibu, I agree to meet him at the beach for a dog walk before my shift. It will be the last time I ever see him.

At least that's the plan.

I pull into the crowded parking lot off the PCH to witness the amusing spectacle of Nate trying his best to corral two wild Great Danes the size of ponies from the back of his Land Rover. He's yelling at the crafty canines that appear to have had some trauma associated with leashes and are playing hard to leash. Nate is not enjoying this portion of the program, and when he sees me, I notice that he's definitely on edge, maybe even suspecting my intentions.

I approach cautiously, wearing my waiter uniform of white shorts and white *Gladstone's* T-shirt, and attempt to facilitate the disembarking of the two hyper hounds without getting dirty. Before we get out of the parking lot, the dogs take elephant-sized craps, prompting an angry lot attendant to appear. I quickly fish two plastic bags from the trashcan as Nate struggles to pull the dogs back to assist me, but the Great Danes already have the beach in sight.

"Go ahead! I'll meet you at the beach," I say, picking up the dog crap.

* * *

He reluctantly concedes as the beasts yank him like a rag doll.

I toss the bags of crap and approach the narrow path leading to the sandy shores of Malibu beach. Nate is about twenty yards ahead, and as I step onto the path, I stop in my tracks. Seagulls circle. My face is prickly, my palms clammy, and I'm frozen—trapped inside a body attempting to reboot. I watch Nate reach the sand, but as he turns to look for me, the dogs sprint for the surf, taking Nate with them. I want to follow, more than anything, but know if I do I'm not strong enough to look him in the eyes and have the conversation I've rehearsed.

I just can't do it.

I stand there and watch Nate and the dogs fade into the horizon, allowing the image to burn on my brain so I can remember him. I know I have to change my direction, and with my heart ripping, I turn and walk away, leaving him waiting for me at the water's edge in Malibu.

It's another twenty minutes before I receive a page on my pager, prompting me to pull off at a pay phone at a gas station in Santa Monica. He's upset that I left without saying anything, and I regret my action immediately. He's aware of my spiritual conflict and concedes to not wanting to be a roadblock in my spiritual path, but is saddened by my decision. To experience such a deep level of intimacy is rare, so closing the door feels like I'm severing a part of myself.

Standing at a pay phone on Lincoln and Interstate 10, I'm wiped out by a tumultuous tide of emotions. I call in sick for work, spending the night instead walking the beach and praying—and fearing I'll never feel intimacy and companionship with a woman, like I did with Nate.

Two days later, I'm behind the counter at Higher Grounds, feeling low, when a man in his late thirties enters, comments on the interior, and begins browsing the menu. I rarely mention the church connection, but because of his inquiry as to the owner, I tell him briefly about the church.

He becomes hesitant. "What kind of church?"

"It's a non-denominational church affiliated with Calvary Chapel in Costa Mesa. It's cool. I've been attending for over a year now. We meet at the junior high down the street," I say, attempting to assure him, although the church-coffee connection concerns him.

Then he asks a question that not only highlights my own personal drama, but forces me to make a spontaneous judgment on God's love: "Where does your church stand with gay people?"

"Uh, well..." I stumble, his inquiry triggering an

earthquake in my psyche.

Since severing all ties with Nate, I've been drowning in a sea of doubt and unanswered prayers. Silenced by my own shame, my hesitation has him anticipating rejection. "Where does the church stand with gay people?" I repeat the question. What *would* Jesus say? I don't have the answer, so I simply regurgitate what I've been taught. "Well, they'd treat homosexuality just like any other area of sin," I say, being as sensitive as I can be with my piercing judgment.

He recoils at this, even backs away from the counter.

"They believe in the grace of God and would treat gay people with love and compassion. They would love the sinner, just not the sin," I say, hating the way I sound saying it.

"Well, I can't support a church that believes *who I am* and *how God created me* is a sin," he says bluntly. "I'll have to get my coffee elsewhere. Have a good day."

He turns and walks out, leaving me silent and stunned.

Part of me wants to run after him and offer a free cup of coffee as a consolation for my condemnation. Instead I deflate behind the counter—tears welling, soul splitting, spirit drowning. Since I can't control the impending emotional tsunami, I distract myself by making a fresh pot of coffee, which makes me think of Nate, and suddenly the silent storm envelops me. I pull out my deliverance napkin and stare at Pastor Brody's inscription of Nate's name.

And then with shaky hands, I grab a pen and put a checkmark next to his name.

CHAPTER 10:

FLIRTING WITH FEMALES

Although companionship with Nate felt divine, it's clear from my meetings with Pastor Brody and Melvin—and listening daily to Focus on the Family with James Dobson—that being with Nate is a sin, so I begin again my search for a human being with lady parts that I can love.

I vow to find my wife, the one who will save me from ever having to tell my mother.

I've been here before. Some define doing the same thing over and over again and expecting different results as insanity. Others call it faith. It's the spiritual X-factor that keeps my flame from flickering out. My stubborn *faith* in a God that can, *and will*, fix what the church, society, and my family all agree is egregiously broken. Besides, the world is full of miraculous accounts: if a cancer patient given six months can baffle doctors by mysteriously becoming cancer-free, or a paralyzed patient inexplicably walks again, why can't a patient suffering from same-sex attractions one day wake up craving the succulent center of the *Playboy* centerfold?

As insane as it may seem, *I still believe.*

I dismiss my summer of iniquity as a stumbling block, but not a defeat. I'm back in the saddle, continuing on in my holy crusade to rewire my desires. I have a new tactic: any time I catch myself entertaining thoughts of Nate, I'll abort the thought—and *pray for my future wife.*

I've been doing a lot of praying for my wife, and it's working: not a week has passed since I left Nate standing at the water's edge and Jenny McCarthy is sitting in my section at Gladstone's 4 Fish! She's back, and this time she's taking me with her. My fellow waiters swarm, each offering their first-born to trade tables so they can serve Jenny McCarthy her steamed clams. But I resist their bribes. We have unfinished business. "No," I tell them. "She's mine."

As I walk toward Jenny's booth, the sun is setting on the Pacific Ocean and the waves are gently lapping the beach— the perfect backdrop for our reunion. I just hope she doesn't make a scene. I've seen her on that MTV show and she's not exactly subtle. I also prepare for the distinct possibility that she might not even remember me. It's been three years since I've worn a butler uniform. As I get closer, I begin to strut a little, waiters jealously watching on as I boldly approach God's Siren. And *I'm feeling good*—until I get closer and it becomes apparent the man with her is more than a friend.

I do my best to dial down my creep level, opting to act as though I wasn't the one serving tea the night she met Hugh Hefner at the Playboy Mansion.

"Hey, how y'all doing?" I say, trying to act cool. She's wearing cut-off jeans, a tank top, and not a stitch of makeup, looking more like a pretty mortal than a *Playboy* goddess.

When she looks up, her slow-mo smile puts me at ease, as if she too knows her mission: God is using her to save me and bring about His divine will. Out of the thousands of restaurants in Los Angeles, she is at Gladstone's, during my shift, and *in my section.* It's obviously fate.

"Hi," she says, her excitement clearly stifled by the dude hovering like a dark cloud.

"Can I bring y'all something to drink?" I say, but really: *Jenny, I'm more desperate now than before. You have powers. I know you do. I've seen them at work. Touch me with your finger, or wiggle your ears, or do that I Dream of Jeannie-arm thing—just do something!*

"Waters with lemon," she says, but I hear: *"I'm totally glad I've found you. I've been sent here in a Touched-by-an-Angel way. Consider yourself saved!"*— "Do you have specials?"

"Today we have blackened swordfish served on a bed of jasmine rice with a lemon butter caper sauce."

"We'll start with a bucket of steamed clams with extra napkins?"

"Of course. They can get messy," I say, my eyes flirting as hard as they can flirt.

"And yummy! I could eat like five buckets on my own. Oink, oink," she says.

As the sun sets, it's clear she's with the dude and I'm playing the fool. And how juvenile to think that every little coincidence has some sort of cosmic meaning. It's all chance. Jenny isn't in my section for any other reason than she likes steamed clams and Malibu sunsets. And although she gave a big tip, her number wasn't on the receipt (although I know it's 867-5309).

"She's even prettier in person," a female voice says, bringing me out of my daydream.

It's Jill, the hottest waitress on staff, watching me watch Jenny leave without me.

"And aggressive," I reply. "She wouldn't leave until I'd given her my phone number."

"I don't blame her," she says, balancing a tray of steamed mussels.

Jill is a sun-kissed, beach-babe, jazz singer from Florida, in Los Angeles to pursue her lounge-singing *Fabulous Baker Boys* career. She looks like a young Carly Simon, with thick, brown hair, striking Caribbean blue eyes, and a body that has some of the male staff and customers wishing she were one of the daily specials. She's the Coppertone Girl, all grown up.

"They're going to start pairing us up tomorrow," she says. The outdoor decks are about a mile away from the kitchen, so management is pairing waiters to work as a team: one takes the customer orders while the other makes the trek, back and forth, with the food. "Do you want to be partners?" she says, making the plain white company uniform, shorts and a T-shirt, look sexy.

"Sure," I say, surprised that out of all the eligible waiters, she's picked me.

And it proves to be a perfect match. On the shifts when we are paired, we find a natural groove and work becomes fun for both of us. We're a good team: she deals with the people and I do all the heavy lifting. Eventually, we ask management to schedule all our shifts together.

On the day she expresses interest in attending *my church*, I know she is "the one."

Since I'm casting the role of my wife, Jill is a logical choice: foxy, funny, and totally down with J.C. Over the years I've developed more than adequate flirting skills with females, and soon our coworkers are catching us flirting. It's not long before it even begins to feel like we are a couple, many of the staff assuming we are. While I never fantasize about her naked, I do imagine walking down the aisle with her into the land of heterosexual bliss.

Although our Bible study has disbanded, Tyler and I have remained friends and still attend the same church, so during this exploratory flirting phase with Jill, I often talk about her, sharing with him how much I like her and how all the ex-gay reprogramming is actually working.

One night Tyler and Jack, a friend of his visiting from Ohio, show up at Gladstone's while Jill and I are working, and after our shift, Jill and I join them in the main dining room for dinner. Tyler craves being the center of attention and this dinner is no exception. Strangely, he becomes so zoned into Jill, asking all sorts of flirty questions, it's as though his friend Jack and I have disappeared. After dinner, we carry the awkwardness into the parking lot where Tyler is still hamming it up, being a version of him that is becoming an aversion to me.

Jill is polite and seems to tolerate Tyler's aggressive attention.

A couple of weeks later, I feel it's time to make a move with Jill and ask her out on a real date outside of the restaurant. We've had a few post-work pseudo-dates, ordering half-priced seafood entrees and dining together in the empty banquet room, but they aren't real dates. About the time I'm ready to turn up the heat, Jill asks me to lunch. My initial thought: she's grown impatient with all the flirting, and if I'm not going to make the first move, she will.

She suggests a café in Westwood, and when she shows up, it takes me off guard to see her without her apron and deck uniform. Her hair is down, her crystal-blue eyes sparkle, and faded jeans hug her Buns of Steel (proof the videos do work). I give her a long hug, something we do a lot of, and after ordering, we agree it's nice to have someone serve us. Just as I'm about to go into my semi-prepared *"I'd like us to begin our journey toward the altar"* speech, she begins.

"I've asked you to lunch to talk," she says, squeezing a lime wedge into her Diet Coke.

I anxiously stir more *Sweet 'n Low* in my iced tea; she sounds serious.

"I've noticed that...well, you like to flirt. I don't know, but I sense that maybe you have feelings for me. Or maybe you're just a flirt, and it means nothing," she says, treading carefully.

I smile (fake), but don't like the direction she's taking this conversation.

"I feel like it's only fair to tell you," she starts, looking away while searching for the right words. She seems unsure how to proceed, flicking a lock of hair out of her eyes.

I can hear my heart beating faster and my breathing becomes shallow.

"Tyler and I are seeing each other. We didn't know the best way to tell you, so we both agreed that I'd talk to you first," she confesses, taking a nervous sip of Diet Coke.

"Tyler? My friend Tyler?" I ask, unable to fathom the possibility.

When she nods, my brain goes into a catatonic state of shock.

"I didn't want to hurt your feelings, but felt you should know I think of you as a *great* friend. But that's all," she says, unintentionally driving the stake deeper into my heart.

I'm still stuck on the Tyler part.

By the time I make it back to my place, there's a message from Tyler. They had it choreographed, my conversation with Jill a cowardly ploy to make it easier on Tyler. I call back the traitor at work and he answers with a chipper tone of voice that makes my skin crawl.

"How could you? You *knew* how I felt about her!"

"Hey, bro. We should talk," he says, deflecting my accusation.

He asks if I want to meet in person, which inspires a vision of me strangling him. I agree to meet him at his fancy editing suite in Hollywood. When I arrive, I tell the receptionist I'm there to see Judas—I mean, Tyler. She buzzes his office, and he surfaces wearing jeans, his standard black T-shirt (two-sizes too small), and his stupid cowboy boots. He struts like he owns the place, extending his hand, which

I look at as though it's a serpent, turn and walk outside.

We get into his black Trans-Am with LA CWBY plates, and the LA cowboy drives to a trendy outdoor cafe on Melrose, the kind of place actors go to be noticed (or editors who are wannabe actors). I don't like the idea of meeting in public because I'll be forced to edit what comes out of my mouth, and I've already rehearsed a few choice words.

We're sitting at a dainty café table on Melrose Avenue, and of course I catch him sneaking a peek of his biceps, which seem to please him. He does a cursory look of the place for famous faces, a name he can drop later (and to see if anyone has noticed his biceps).

The steam coming out of my ears focuses him and I begin by clarifying his backstabbing antics. "So, you called the restaurant the next day and got her number?"

"I had to pretend to be her brother but they gave it to me," he says, seemingly gloating.

"You knew how I felt about her," I say, making a statement, not posing a question.

"But you two weren't *dating*," he says, twisting the knife in my back. "I felt a connection to her. It was obviously mutual." I can't believe he's actually justifying his betrayal.

"And so for the last two weeks you've been sneaking around seeing her?"

He nods, leaning back in his chair; perhaps to create

some distance beyond the length of my arm should my fist accidentally fly across the table and knock the smirk off his smug face.

"How much have you been seeing her?"

"Does it matter?"

"It matters to me. How much have you been seeing her?"

"Enough to know that we may have a future," he says, unveiling his agenda.

Silence. I know I shouldn't hate him, but I do.

My mom and grandmother arrive the next day for a visit. My grandmother wants to treat my "friends" to dinner, and I have to question whether Tyler and Jill are still on that list. Both offer not to attend if it's too awkward, but I take the high road, asking them to join us. In my fantasy, this would be the night my mom meets her future daughter-in-law; my attempt to quell any fears she might harbor since finding ex-gay books in my closet. Jill and Tyler show up separately and keep their budding romance in the closet. But I've already mentioned Jill, so I have to correct my mom and grandmother every time they refer to her as my girlfriend.

Work isn't the same after that, and neither is church. I ask our manager to stop scheduling our shifts together, and when we are together, I pull the plug on the flirting, making work a real drag. At church, it never fails. I pull into the parking lot every Sunday just in time to witness LA CWBY strutting around his Trans-Am in his designer shit kickers and opening the door for Jill to step out in her Sunday's best. Our church meets in a junior high auditorium, but you'd think they're walking the red carpet. I always stall, watching safely from the Cadi as they flaunt into church, each with a Bible in one hand and holding hands with the other. I do my best to avoid them at every corner, but after the church Christmas party at a hotel ballroom in Santa Monica, the parking garage elevator opens to Tyler and Jill holding hands, forcing a duel.

"Going down?" Tyler asks, in a chirpy tone, cloaking the volatile subtext.

It's the holidays in Los Angeles, but there's a chill in the air. Tyler is dressed in a tailored black suit with a snowflake tie and Jill is stylishly dressed in a groovy red cocktail dress.

"P2 please," I say, trying to play it cool, although on the inside it's tearing me up.

Elevators are always awkward, but these are the longest five levels ever. As we go down, I'm tempted to ask Tyler to return the ex-gay books I'd loaned him, but decide to bite my tongue. They stare at the numbers as I stare at my scuffed, worn-out shoes, a bargain at Ross several years ago. I notice Tyler's shoes are polished, expensive, and probably the latest in men's fashion, *GQ* being the magazine that inspires his style and who knows what else.

"What are your plans for the holidays?" Jill asks, breaking the subzero silence.

I turn and face them, rising above. "I'm going home to Texas to see the family."

"Sounds fun. Tell your mom and grandmother hello. They are so sweet."

"I will." I force a smile. "What are your plans?" I ask Jill, not Tyler.

"Well," she gushes, looking over at Tyler. "I'm going to Ohio to meet Tyler's family."

I force myself to actually look at Tyler, an arrogant grin accentuating his fake-baked face, and my right fist clinches. My eyes penetrate through his charade; he quickly loses his haughty façade when he sees that I have a weapon, the truth, and in an instant I can destroy him.

He's unable to hold the eye contact and turns to Jill with an uneasy smile.

The door opens just in time, and I step out, but not before turning and saying, "Merry Christmas!" in a way that probably comes out less than merry.

They reply in uppity unison, the doors shutting, leaving me alone in a cold parking lot more than two years since beginning my so-called new life. The parking garage is empty, only a few other cars. I find the Cadi, afflicted with more than a few battle wounds since returning to LA. There are fender benders in the front (my fault) and the back (not my fault), and both side mirrors hang by wires (misjudgment of the width of my garage). Even with duct tape, they flop.

I open the door and slump in the driver's seat, the luxurious burgundy leather still intact and pleasurable. As I loosen my tie, I think about Jill. I'm not in love with Jill. I'm in love with *the idea* of loving Jill. Love requires intimacy, and there's too much I'm still hiding.

With Jill, I've been playing a role, one that failed miserably.

As I put the key in the ignition, I think about Nate and raw emotions begin to seep through the cracks in my antidepressant defense shield. With Nate, I'm the most authentic version of me, a realization that continues to shame me. It's been four months, and the image of him being dragged by two Great Danes into the Malibu sunset still haunts me.

In weaker moments, I imagine running toward him, instead of away from him.

I start the Cadillac, which turns over a few times before igniting; the *Check Engine* light illuminates, as it has for the last six months. There's a whirling sound of a belt that's loose or broken, and I'm praying it doesn't rain because the windshield wiper on the driver's side is broken. Two of the four hubcaps are missing, and the paint of the gold trim is starting to peel.

Los Angeles is a tough place for cars.

CHAPTER 11:

COMING OUT CELIBATE

There's a season for everything. When you're a seasonal deck waiter, a change of seasons means looking for a new day job, which explains why I'm with Jill and we are sitting in the audience for a taping of the TV show, *Love Line*, where Dr. Drew and comedian Adam Carolla field questions about sex, love, and S.T.D.s. Before it was a TV show, it was a late-night radio show that I listened to on the sly as a senior in college, its frank candor about sex refreshing and amusing. I've never seen the TV version, but it's forty bucks, and at this stage in my so-called career, every penny counts.

Since returning from the holidays, I've made an effort to accept their "relationship," forgiving Tyler for his betrayal, although I will never forget, and Jill for not picking me.

Since Jill is also out of season, she has recruited me for this job.

We've been instructed to bring a change of wardrobe, since we're filming two shows, and to expect an eight-hour shift with a one-hour lunch break in between tapings. During the first taping, it hits me just how desperate I've become: I'm earning $5/hour sitting in an audience and applauding when the stupid *Applause!* sign lights up as a doctor and a joker answer questions from callers and the audience. When the producer encourages audience members to approach with questions to ask on air, I know we've become sad Hollywood clichés when Jill and I seriously consider asking a question. At the very least we'll be on TV, which is *exposure*. Exposure could lead to bigger and better things. We could be discovered! *We got our big break on Love Line!*

During the lunch break, Jill and I drive to Melrose Avenue and grab lunch at the California Chicken Café, and although she's still dating Tyler, we explore questions we can ask together. Since we're both evangelical Christians, and that side is rarely presented, we see this as a golden opportunity to champion celibacy through the airwaves by playing the role of "engaged couple" wanting to wait until our wedding night to have sex. We consider asking Dr. Drew if there is a medication we can take to lower our sex drives to help ward off sexual desire until we're ready.

While Jill and I plot our bid to become the poster couple for abstinence, I notice a guy from my acting class, Vince, eating alone at the far end of the communal table. I don't know him well, only that he had a small role as an assassin in a David Fincher film. With his tattoos and wife beater shirt, he's not the kind of guy you want to mess with or that you might find in my circle of evangelical church friends. Since our class has just begun, I tell him my name again and introduce Jill, confessing we're on break from taping an episode of *Love Line*, making forty bucks for the day. He tells me he works at a film production company in Hollywood and that they're looking for another runner. He gives me his number, and we race back to the studio.

Jill and I approach the distracted female producer, hand in hand, acting engaged.

"You're celibate?" she asks, registering her disbelief.

"We want to wait until we're married," Jill says, smiling at me adoringly.

"We want it to be special," I explain, looking at her and gushing.

The producer studies us as though we've just landed from another planet.

"And we're struggling because intimacy is a slippery slope," I confess.

"Our bodies are saying 'yes,' but our minds have to say 'no' because we want to honor God with our commitment," Jill adds, batting her eyes.

"We want to ask Dr. Drew if there's a drug we can take to *lessen* our sexual drive to help us wait until our wedding night," I pitch. "You can't imagine how hard it is to keep my hands off *this*," I say, referring to Jill, who blushes, playfully jabbing me on the shoulder.

The producer looks horrified, but writes down our names and seat numbers, qualifying that maybe they'll get to us, maybe not. During the taping, studio cameras are whizzing by while Jill and I hold hands, acting all lovey-dovey, which in light of our history is surreal.

As we're sitting in the audience acting like we're in love, even though we're physically intimate, it fails to spark a fire, only confirming my fears. I've spent a lot of time imagining what might have happened had Jill picked me: Would I be able to sustain a relationship with her despite not being fond of her anatomy? And what kind of relationship would that be?

We don't get called on, which is a relief, and as soon as the show is over, we stop playing the role of the engaged couple and are back to being friends. We get our forty bucks, and I make a vow to pursue acting with a vengeance so I never have to sit in an audience again for "love."

"You're not having sex?" Vince asks, completely shocked by my chastity.

We're sitting at an outdoor cafe on Third Street Promenade in Santa Monica. Shortly after bumping into him while on break from *Love Line*, I followed up with the production company where he works and have been criss-crossing Hollywood as a courier. It's the ideal day job, giving me freedom to audition and a step up from being paid to be a stupid face in the crowd.

Vince and I are doing a scene together for acting class: the *Odd Couple* by Neil Simon. He's Oscar and I'm Felix—roles that mimic our roles in real life as well. Sitting across from him now at a café, I'm the ultra-conservative Republican at the table, making sure my dinner fork lines up with my salad fork, and he's the foul-mouthed tattooed bad boy visually molesting every woman that walks by our table. He's on the prowl. If you take his wife beater, tattoos, and piercings—mix in his Portuguese blood and hard-knock ghetto-Jersey roots—he's a thug with a heart of gold. In Tinseltown, that keeps him typecast as the "bad guy." From our rehearsals, I've learned he loves movies and idolizes Marlon Brando, shocked beyond belief that I've never seen *On the Waterfront* (*"I coulda been a contender!"*), is a single dad to an adorable five-year-old girl, and when he's on stage he's always the most interesting actor to watch.

I use the large cross tattoo on his forearm to explain why I'm not having sex. "I'm a Christian, and I want to honor my future wife by saving myself for her," I say with conviction.

He laughs as if I just told him the funniest joke he's ever heard, except I'm not laughing.

"I'm waiting until I'm married," I explain, a bit too proud of my prudence.

"Get out of here! Are you serious?" he asks, eying me like I'm a nut job.

I stand my virginal ground, but he's distracted by a couple of ladies sauntering by dressed to attract. He looks at them in a way that makes clear his intentions; he's not only undressing them with his eyes, he's doing other things as well, which makes me take a nervous gulp of wine.

"What's wrong with sex?" he asks, looking from them to me with a dirty grin.

"Nothing when in the context of marriage," I explain, sounding like a righteous prude.

"I've been married. It's overrated." The ex-wife is a thorn in his side. "The only good thing that came out of my marriage is my daughter," he says. His daughter is his pride and joy. "So you weren't tapping that girl I saw you with that day?"

"Jill? No. We're just friends," I dismiss. "Long story."

"She didn't look so virginal," he says.

"I wouldn't know."

And I wouldn't.

A few weeks later, I'm sitting in the back of a 1983 Bentley limo, adjusting the antennae on the tiny TV, but it's fuzzy, the signals most likely being disrupted by the massive florescent XXX-sign towering above me. Parked in the lot of a seedy-strip club near LAX, the limo tint is dark enough to protect me from the sinful rays and allows me to observe my surroundings undetected. I feel like I'm Jane Goodall observing gorillas. *Who are these human females who dance and the males who pay them? I believe it must be some type of mating ritual.*

To supplement my part-time pittance as a package peddler at a production company, and the peanuts I'm making as a born-again barista at the church coffee shop, I've been driving a limo for a middle-aged bachelor Bel Air real estate broker looking for love in all the wrong strip clubs. Gordon, a former UCLA linebacker, is pushing forty and single, so his outings on the town usually involve picking up his bachelor brat pack and hitting LA's hotspots, where he uses his wealthy charm to slip past ropes in Hollywood and impress the ladies with his vintage limo and "personal driver," my role a vital part of his charade. While Gordon and his entourage get lap dances that cost more than I earn in a month, I'm holed up in the back of a Bentley immersed in ex-gay materials and praying under XXX signs. Gordon occasionally invites me in, but I always decline, making it clear donating to G-strings conflicts with my faith. Once again, I'm able to cloak my female intolerance with my evangelical Christian identity.

On this night, with LAXXX safely in the rearview mirror, I drop them at an exclusive strip club in West LA and then park in the quiet residential neighborhood. I've barely cracked the Bible when a tap on the window from a naughty Dorothy from Oz startles me. She's wearing the slut version of the blue-and-white checkered dress, the same Judy Garland pigtails, but her ruby red slippers have stilettos. I crack the tinted glass of the limo, but only partially.

"Are you Bryan?" she asks with a flirty twang.

"Uh...yeah," I reply, annoyed that Gordon and friends would send me a stripper.

"Jordan sent me to check on you," she says, as if paid in advance to have a quickie with me.

"Gordon," I clarify.

"Right," she smiles, playing the wide-eyed character but with a sex-kitten edge.

"Did they pay you to come out here?" I ask, removing the Bible from my lap.

She smiles. If they paid money, I'm at least obligated to have a conversation, so I step out.

"Nice ride," she comments on the Bentley limo. "Is it easy to drive?"

"Like driving a long station wagon."

There's a chill in the air; she's shivering in her stilettos, so I offer my navy blazer.

"Now ain't it interesting I have to leave the Gentleman's Club to find a gentleman," she says, sliding it on, her buoyant breasts busting out of my blazer, creating a provocative visual.

She opens a tiny purse, pulls out a pack of cigarettes, and offers one. "Smoke?"

"No thanks."

She lights up, takes a long drag, and courteously exhales away from me. "Are you really celibate?" she asks unexpectedly, dropping the Dorothy character.

"Uh...why?"

"Gordon said you were holding out until you're married. Which I think is *great!*"

I look down, embarrassed and thrown by her inquisition.

"It really is sweet. The girl you marry is gonna be one lucky gal," she says, eying the door to the club where a beefy bouncer sits on a stool watching her like a prison guard.

"Where are you from?" I ask, making obligatory small talk.

"Kansas," she says. "And I ain't jokin'. I've been clickin' my heels for like the last five years." She reaches down and liberates her feet from the ruby reds, taking a long drag. "When I packed up ten years ago and headed west, I thought... I don't know... there'd be a pot of gold at the end of the rainbow. I didn't expect I'd end up here. Who does, right?"

"Yeah, well me neither," I say, referencing the limo.

"Are you an actor?"

"Working on it."

"I thought so. You have that whole Tom Cruise thing going on," she says. "I'm an actress—at least in the day-time. Do you have an agent?" she asks.

"William Morris is sending me out for pilot season, but I haven't booked anything. A few callbacks, but I'm still driving limos."

"At least you have an agent. I've been through three managers and two agents, all with an agenda other than promoting my career," she says bitterly, the fire now just a flicker.

"Has working here changed the way you view men?" I blurt out, surprising even myself, as though I'm trying out my psychology degree. "You don't have to answer that. I don't know—"

"I didn't like men before, and I still don't like them. I have nothing against men as a species; it's just as a lesbian, I have no desire to be intimate with one. It's way gross."

"You're a lesbian?" She doesn't exactly fit the stereotype.

"You'd be surprised at how many strippers are lesbians. I know you're probably judging me right now. Gordon said you walk the straight and narrow, and I saw the Bible in the limo."

"I'm not judging you," I say, although I'm thrown. I suspected the Tin Man, but Dorothy?

"I took my girlfriend home to Kansas for the holidays. My parents are ultra-conservative and still recovering. They call themselves Christians, but put them in the same room as a black person, or my girlfriend, and see how Christ-like they act. When we were home, they recruited my high school boyfriend to win me back. It was humiliating. They invited him over for Christmas dinner. I have my girlfriend on one side at the dinner table and my ex-boyfriend on the other, with my parents across the table expecting a tug of war, praying that Tommy would win me back over from the dark side," she says, working hard not to become emotional.

"What do your parents think about...?" I ask, referring to the Gentleman's Club.

"I haven't told them. I'm not ashamed of my relationship with my girlfriend, but I'm not exactly proud that I do lap dances for a living," she says, taking one last drag before snubbing out the cigarette on the curb. "So, I better get back inside. They have me on a tight leash."

As she straps back on her stilettos, I find myself wishing she didn't have to go.

"And thanks for this," she says, handing me back my blazer. "You're such a doll."

"It was nice to meet you," I offer.

"You're gonna do well. I just know it," she says, surprising me with a friendly kiss on the cheek. "Pray for me, will ya?" she asks with a sweet vulnerability that eclipses her sexy exterior.

"I will. Just stay away from tornadoes," I joke lamely, but I'm touched by her request.

She smiles sublimely, and as she struts away in her spiky ruby reds, I notice something different: I see a human being, whereas five minutes prior, I simply saw a stripper.

And then, clicking my own heels, I say a prayer for Dorothy.

A couple months after signing with a new talent manager, I'm in his office stapling my 8x10 glossy to my resume. The TV is tuned to Oprah on the landmark day Ellen Degeneres and Anne Heche are on her couch. There's been so much hype about this Oprah episode, I have the sense that all of Hollywood has shut down to witness the event. Ellen's made a splash in recent weeks by coming out on the cover of *Time* with her truth plastered in print: "Yep, I'm gay."

Manager Don, his assistant Ivan, and I are glued to the screen, taking me back to 7th grade and the Phil Donahue episode with the two gay guys, who I learned from my mother were a "waste." I'm not sure how Don, being a "spirit-filled Christian" will respond, but I find myself already bracing for disparagement. The concept of an *openly* gay actor is a new frontier that Ellen is courageously forging, and according to Don, it's the end of her career. Not only is there the phobia of being pigeonholed, and there aren't exactly an abundance of gay roles, according to my manager, audiences won't accept a gay actor playing a straight role—a fear that kept movie stars Rock Hudson, Montgomery Clift, and Tab Hunter in the closet during their careers.

Since I'm the one stapling a resume to my 8x10, I wonder how my own career prospects would be affected if people knew the role I'm playing isn't on stage but in my everyday life.

Focus on the Family warns that *freedom from homosexuality* is not easy because, *"Satan is not pleased when someone sees through the deception of homosexuality and discovers the way out."* Their claim that thousands have left homosexuality and married has been fueling my fire—although the follow up claim that, *"others remain celibate, yet lead joyful lives devoted to God's service,"* is worrisome because I'm not sure how long I will last on the celibacy train.

There's a significant distinction between a homosexual celibate and a full-fledged heterosexual, and I'm holding out for the latter. I want to experience *real change*, something some of the ex-gay voices claim when they refer to an *enlightenment* that takes place during their journey "out of homosexuality" where they begin to crave "the other"—a miraculous moment where the desire for the opposite sex becomes a budding need. Now in the final act of my twenties, I still have no desire for "the other," I'm still waiting for this great enlightenment.

The challenge with celibacy is it requires denying that I'm even a sexual being, the only way I've been able to tolerate myself. It's with a healthy dose of denial that I've been able to weather the storm of my shame, *almost* forgetting the truth lurking deep within.

Yep, I'm *celibate*!

CHAPTER 12:

HOLLYWOOD CRUSADE

It's been almost three years since I began my new life, and I still have the *Pursuing Sexual Wholeness: How Jesus Heals the Homosexual* tapes in heavy rotation in my car.

The tapes almost blow my cover the night Kate and her evangelical Christian mom visiting from Colorado invite me over for a *Melrose Place* slumber party. Kate has landed a recurring role, and I've been summoned to join them at Kate's new boyfriend's place in The Colony, the exclusive celebrity enclave in Malibu where getting past the gate requires your name on the list.

Kate's scientist boyfriend is out-of-town, so my name is on the list.

When we worked at Baskin Robbins as teenagers, Kate started running with the wild crowd, and it was rumored her puritanical mother made her swear on the Bible after a night out that she didn't do drugs or engage in sexually promiscuous behavior. The image of her mom in my head was monstrous, but when I met her, I found her kind and warm, and we developed an immediate connection based on our fundamentalist roots. I quickly took to calling her "Mom" as well. We both championed traditional values and wished Kate would go to church more.

Watching the episode through the lens of fundamentalist Christianity, I'm terribly offended by the blatant sexual-immorality and wish one of the characters would find God. I mean, if only Heather Locklear's Amanda would see the light and usher in a revival on Melrose Place! Kate's character has some steamy sex scenes; watching them with her mom makes us all laugh uneasily.

After suffering through the episode, Kate suggests we eat at Nobu, a star-studded sushi spot on the PCH in Malibu. I always stash the twenty-cassette reparative tapes in the trunk when others are on board, but on this night I hadn't planned on driving, so when I start the car, a tape starts playing and Andy is praying, "...a father hunger that only Lord Jesus—"

I frantically press eject just as Kate finds the rest of the cassettes in the backseat.

"Pursuing Sexual Wholeness: How Jesus Heals the Homosexual," she reads the title, peering at me in the rear view mirror with one eyebrow raised.

I feel exposed, but launch a quick defense. "Oh, how

funny! It's a part of a Bible study at the church I was telling you about. We're learning how to minister to people struggling with... well, you know, homosexual tendencies," I say, shrouding myself with another lie.

"Homosexual tendencies?" she asks, incredulously. "You mean gay people?"

"Well, people who are looking to..." I stumble, trying to be politically correct.

"Change?" her mom finishes, reinforcing our conservative Christian views.

"Change? You seriously think gay people can change?" Kate asks.

I turn to her mom and then back to Kate—the verdict isn't quite in, but I'm still optimistic. "With God, all things are possible," I say, deflecting with a cliché.

"Some of my best friends are gay. My brother is gay," Kate says, as if to remind her mom. "It's not something that needs to be healed." I notice her mom squirming. Ron is her stepson, and I sense his gayness might still be difficult to reconcile with her fundamentalist values.

"Ron has had a lot of stuff happen to him in his life," her mom says.

Kate rolls her eyes. They've been through this tired nature versus nurture argument before.

"How does Jesus heal the homosexual?" Kate asks, point blank.

"Through worship, prayer, and having same-sex intimacy needs met through healthy non-sexual intimate relationships," I say, giving the textbook conversion therapy answer.

I watch Kate's reaction in the rearview mirror. She thinks I'm joking and laughs out loud, until she realizes she's the only one laughing. "You can't be serious. *Same-sex intimacy needs?*"

§ § §

"*Same-sex intimacy needs?*" Adam, a coworker at the production company, replies to my explanation of his gayness.

"Well, certain needs—needs we all have for male-intimacy—were somehow *sexualized*, which is why you use illegitimate means to fill legitimate needs," I say, spewing ex-gay theory.

Adam's a Yale graduate and he's not buying it.

"Look at the plumbing. It just doesn't work!" I cry out in defense of traditional order. "The complementary nature of the male and female genitalia, at the heart of reproduction, is evidence of Creative Intent. It's pretty obvious where God intended you to stick it!"

"I'm sorry, but have you seen a vagina? It's like an open wound that won't heal. I'm not sticking it anywhere near that thing!"

Adam's whole world is rainbows and White parties. He lives in a gay neighborhood, eats in gay restaurants, takes his gay laundry to the gay cleaners, shops at a gay supermarket, and works out in a gay gym. He's gay 24/7 and my closest friend at the company, besides Vince.

"God created Adam and Eve, not Adam and Steve!" I say, countering with a cliché.

Adam just rolls his eyes. "Oh, now *that's* a new one. Never heard that one before."

At the Hollywood production company, my temp job is beginning to feel more permanent, as pilot season didn't lead to my own TV series. Most of the jobs I auditioned for went to stars or actors with actual credits, leaving me just another unknown waiting to be discovered.

I'm not alone. The city is swarming with desperate people trying to make it, and I'm finding chasing after my big break is leaving me broke. So I continue to work at Propaganda Films, a cutting edge film/TV production company located in an architectural warehouse in the heart of Hollywood. It's not a white-collar environment with cubicles and fluorescent lighting, but a funky, MTV, Hollywood hipster atmosphere. I can arrive at work with holes in my crotch and a ratty T-shirt and no one bats an eye. We have a blue-haired, tattooed, and pierced lesbian mail girl. There's a lot going on, and everyone is famous and important. On any given day, there are several commercials, music videos, and feature films, all in various stages of production. To maintain freedom to pursue my acting career, I'm content staying on the bottom rung of the ladder and doing the work that requires the least responsibility, such as running packages, delivering mail, answering phones, or sharing Jesus with gay people.

I've never in my life been around so many gay people.

You can't walk through the lobby without tripping over a gay person. Several assistants to the producers and directors are gay; even the owner of the company has two gay male assistants, Adam being one of them. When I first started, I "came out" as a born-again Christian to clarify my orientation to any inquiring minds, making a point to build friendships with all the gay folks first, before I let my conservative views known. I'm careful not to judge, just love.

I'm an ex-gay *in the closet*, which is a challenging evangelical position.

I begin to pray for my gay and lesbian coworkers, convinced God is calling me to lead my own Hollywood crusade. Perhaps I'm at the production company for a reason: this is my *mission field*. I will minister to others who are like me—men and women in desperate need of a Savior who loves them too much to let them live in sin. I will send a message of hope for those struggling with homosexual temptations. You don't have to be gay! You can be free from the bondage of sin! God desires us to be *sexually whole*!

"I feel whole. And what makes you think that I'm broken sexually?" Adam inquires, amused by the debate. He's been "out" since birth. "What's wrong with being gay?"

"I have nothing against gay people, but the Bible is clear that homosexuality is a *sin*," I reply with words that have been programmed into my psyche and regurgitated.

"And who wrote the Bible?" he challenges. Adam has a minor in Religion from Yale.

"Well, it was inspired by God, but written by man," I say, knowing where he's going.

"The men you call inspired were Middle Eastern men with a Middle Eastern worldview and walked the planet *two to three thousand years ago*! The sixty-six books that made the cut—the ones *selected by man* and *packaged by man* into what we call the Bible—were written in Greek and Hebrew over a span of 1,000 years, from 1,000 B.C.E. to 135 C.E. You can have faith it's Holy, and call it the Word with a capital W, but the fact is, it wasn't delivered from on High in its current form or sprouted from some burning bush. It's the work of humans. Even if you believe the original authors were inspired, that doesn't mean the text hasn't been tainted, or the original message lost in translation. Think about it. Before there was a printing press, the text had to be translated, interpreted, and copied by hand. It's a great leap of faith to assume the human hands that wrote the original words, the human hands that translated their words, and the human hands that copied their words, made no errors. Your faith in a divinely inspired Bible is just that: faith. And when we look at these ancient texts, faith doesn't translate into facts."

"Even without the Bible, homosexuality goes against nature. It's just not *natural!*"

"Natural? Maybe not for you, but for me, being with a female is definitely *not* natural," he says, making a sour face. "It's repulsive, much like being with a man might repulse you."

No comment.

"Are the gay penguins at Central Park Zoo unnatural or a part of God's diverse creation?"

"Gay *penguins?*"

"Roy and Silo are totally gay and have been together for years. Even when offered lady penguin tail, they refuse. At one time, they seemed so desperate to incubate an egg, their keeper gave them a fertile egg needing care, and a chick, Tango, was born. They raised Tango, keeping her warm, feeding her food from their beaks until she could go into the world on her own. In the animal kingdom, Roy and Silo aren't unusual. Scientists have documented more than four hundred and fifty animal species that engage in homosexual behavior, everything from courtship, to sex, to parenting. Should we not look to *nature* when defining *natural?*"

"But that doesn't mean it's natural for *humans,*" I say, reflexively negating the nature argument, but secretly intrigued by the concept of Roy and Silo. "It's a question of *morality!*"

"Do you think homosexuality is a choice?" he asks, putting me on the line.

"Uh...probably not," I say, masking my own insight.

"If homosexuality is not a choice, but a result of natural forces, how can it be *immoral*, especially when love is involved?" He poses a question I can't readily answer. "What does Jesus say about homosexuality?" he asks. "Ain't nothing in the red letters about gays, but plenty of red ink devoted to divorce and adultery. And to think we're blamed for the destruction of family values. Anyway, Jesus loves me so fuck off!" he cracks, and we both laugh.

Debating with Adam is like a good game of tennis. We work hard to win the match, but when the debate is over, we shake hands at the net.

The conflict climaxes on the pages of several newspapers, including the *LA Times* and *USA Today*, when *Exodus International* runs a full-page ad featuring a group of smiling men and women with the caption: *"I questioned homosexuality. Change is Possible. Discover how."*

Adam and the other gays in the office were *outraged* by the ad. I quickly begin defending the men and women pictured by preaching tolerance. "They have the right to—"

"Offer hope? As if being gay is a disease to be cured?" Adam challenges.

What Adam and the other gays and lesbians at work don't know is that I am involved with the very organization that placed the ad. I've questioned homosexuality as well.

I'm just still working out the details of the *"change is possible"* part.

"What about the guys who started Exodus?" Adam baits. "They fell in love and spent the rest of their lives trying to undo the lies they told," he says, leaving me silent because it is true.

Adam and I go to lunch regularly and he is my first official gay friend.

For his 30th birthday, his family flies out from Connecticut, and he invites Vince and me to the party at a restaurant in Hollywood. Most of his friends in attendance are gay, many of whom I know from the office. But it's surprising to see how his rather traditional East coast family, brothers and sisters, as well as his parents, seemingly accept him unconditionally.

He is out and still accepted and loved by his family. His friendship is enlightening.

Regardless, I hold tenaciously to the belief that *change is possible*. I'm careful not to preach, simply standing up for traditional family values when appropriate, like the time I share my concern about lesbians raising children with one of the office lesbians. Janice has been with her partner for seven years; they even had a ceremony shortly after joining the office. She showed me the rings. On their honeymoon at an exclusive couples only spa resort in Mexico, when questioned by fellow guests, they felt more comfortable just telling people they were sisters. Her honeymoon story saddened me. They clearly love one another but are forced to exercise caution when expressing that love publicly. When the discussion turns to motherhood, she challenges me to explain how their gender makes them unfit to be mothers.

"I just think a child needs a mother and a father," I lament, echoing my indoctrination.

"What if the drug dealing father took off and the unemployed mother is a crack head?"

* * *

As a born-again Christian working on working in Hollywood, I'm not only proselytizing the gays and lesbians at work, but have enlisted myself in the larger crusade to win Hollywood for Jesus—a mission crystallized by my involvement with the Hollywood Presbyterian Church.

The awe-inspiring gothic sanctuary on Gower Street has soaring cathedral ceilings, stained glass windows, and dark wood pews, and on Friday nights, it's *the* place to be for the mostly twenty-something, mostly-single, mostly-unemployed Hollywood evangelical crowd. The weekly networking events are intelligently designed to bring together like-minded people in the industry with the common mission to create entertainment that promotes family values and faith. Even I find myself saying things like, *"If the Lord blesses me with success in my career, I won't be swept away by the world. I'll use my gifts for the Kingdom!"*

When possible the church spotlights those in the industry who champion Christian values *and* actually make a living. The night that glorifies Kirk Cameron, from the '80s TV show *Growing Pains,* and his wife, draws the masses as we pack the church to hear how God is working in their lives. I'm inspired to learn Kirk and his wife read the Bible in the limo on their way to work. But when their new sitcom is subsequently cancelled, I begin to doubt God's involvement, at least to the degree they so zealously claimed. There are few examples of successful Christian entertainment, and movies produced by Billy Graham don't exactly bolster my faith that God cares about filmmaking. If the Almighty is interested in using Hollywood to reach people, then why aren't Billy Graham movies winning Academy awards?

I spend countless Friday nights praying God will save Hollywood from the grip of Satan.

One of my evangelical missions is Howard, who becomes a friend after I reach the Master Class. Howard knew he was gay as a kid growing up in Rhode Island where he found refuge in the theatre. He's active in his Jewish Synagogue (welcoming of gay people), but surprisingly has never been to any of the gay clubs on Santa Monica Boulevard in West Hollywood.

"It's adolescent," he says. "My theory: most didn't experience adolescence like their straight peers because they were closeted. It wasn't safe to be who they were. So, they get to be in their twenties, come out, and go through a second adolescence. I have no need to go there."

For the Oscars every year, he comments on the performances for the *Los Angeles Times*, and one year gives his opinion on CNN, which my mom sees in Texas. She calls to ask if he's my acting coach, commenting that he sounds smart before asking if he's gay.

"He's gay and Jewish and one of my favorite people," I say. And he is. Howard is gay and Jewish, and I'm ex-gay and Christian, but he doesn't know about the ex-gay" part.

I play the role of "straight guy" hoping that I'm convincing.

We've had many conversations about Jesus, as I'm curious to get his perspective as a Jewish person. For his birthday, I give him a fully loaded King James Bible with Jesus's words in red and his name engraved in gold letters on the genuine leather cover.

For my birthday, he gives me the full compilation of the works of Shakespeare.

Since I've never been to New York City, he makes a pact that if I haven't been to the Big Apple by the time I'm thirty years old, he'll take me as a birthday gift.

I'm in the twilight of my twenties and on a Hollywood crusade, convinced God is using me to minister to the gays and lesbians around me. I have faith that Jesus will come through for me, and them, and soon we'll all be on Oprah talking about how change is possible.

There is freedom from homosexuality through Jesus Christ!

I'm not exactly lusting after females, but I haven't been lusting, period. The anti-depressants are squelching my libido, a blessing in my obsessive pursuit to repress all sexual urges. I still practice preventative measures such as cold showers, Internet filters, and wearing blinders when walking the planet, but my denial is so advanced, the high dose of anti-depressants so numbing, my immersion in ex-gay theology so deep, I'm at a place where it feels as though I've spiritually neutered myself, seducing me into thinking that maybe celibacy is an option. Although I continue to pray for a wife—and the desires that should only be natural when I have one.

And then one day I'm in the lobby of the production company getting coffee, and as I'm stirring half and half in my French roast, I look up, and who do I see rushing through the front door, sharply dressed in one of those Armani suits I'd spied in his closet a couple of years prior?

It's one of those moments that freeze in time.

I haven't seen Nate since I left him standing on the shores of Malibu, so seeing him standing in the lobby where I work is surreal. What makes it more unsettling: I'm wearing *his* black *Triumph* T-shirt, the one he was wearing the day we met at the UCLA pool. Of all the days to pull this shirt out of my closet! I'm not even sure how it came to be in my possession, whether he gave it to me or I borrowed it, but over the last couple years it's become one of my favorite shirts, mainly because it fits so well.

As I languish in the lobby wearing his *Triumph* T-shirt, my coffee cup trembling, I am flooded with feelings—broken feelings I'd hoped would be healed by now.

He's looking at me with the same look of dismay, both of us stunned, not knowing how to act or what to say. I become conscious of all my coworkers in the vicinity and attempt to play it cool since Nate is a threat to my rebooted new life and born-again identity.

"Hey," I say, trying to act casual, but inside I'm unraveling.

"Hey," he replies, noticing the T-shirt, a strange accent to an already weird moment.

"What are—" I start, but Penny, a Jewish girl with whom I've had several conversations about Jesus, interrupts me.

"There you are! Oh my god, we're so late!" she says, running toward him, and to my horror, they share a quick kiss before she notices me. "Oh, do you two know each other?"

We both look at each other, and then to her, and my mind is blank.

"Yeah," Nate says, "from the UCLA pool where I used to swim."

"It's been a long time," I say, forcing a fake smile, my mind going numb. It feels like I'm in a dream and at any minute I'll wake up thinking how bizarre it was.

"I didn't know you swim?" Penny says to Nate.

"Used to. Not anymore," he says, his eyes locked on me.

"Yeah. Me neither," I reply, our eyes communicating the rest.

"Well, we are so late it's crazy," she says. "We're trying to make a six o'clock screening in Culver City. You better let me drive!"

"Good to see you again, Bryan," Nate says, taking Penny's hand.

"Good to see you, too," I reply.

He leads her out of the building, and as he lets her exit the door first, he takes another look back at me, and we share a lingering glance that sweeps me away like a Kansas tornado.

There's no place like home, there's no place—

"What's up, bro?" Vince startles me.

He's pouring himself coffee, eying me as I try to recover. "Nothing. You?"

"You got drama brewing," he says, reading me better than I realize. "I ain't dumb, biatch."

"I'm just...you know, it's been one of those days," I cover.

"Cruise over after work. You know what tonight is?"

"What's tonight?"

"*Temptation Island* and you know how much I love hating that red headed bitch!"

* * *

That night I'm with Vince and his three feisty pit bulls in the *Hollywood Forever* cemetery on Santa Monica Boulevard, the final resting place for several Hollywood legends such as Rudolph Valentino, Jayne Mansfield, and Cecil B. Demille. Two of the bullish canines are hiking legs on headstones, while the other remains on leash, punishment for eating another neighborhood feline.

We're in the part of Hollywood where chicks with dicks turn tricks, drug dealers deal drugs, and Vince rents a small, detached studio in the backyard of a nice, Hispanic family, an oasis in the jungle. His daughter, now in 3rd grade, fell asleep watching *The Little Mermaid*, as she does most nights, her voice better than Ariel's. Now we're letting his pack of bulls do their business. I've become close with Vince and his daughter, even babysitting on Thursdays when Vince bartends at a trendy club in Hollywood. He pays me with Guinness.

He lets Buster off leash, now that we're in the heart of the cemetery and away from the living. This is where Vince comes to think, his solace in the city. As his dogs chase rats across fallen stars, I'm bewitched, bothered, and yes, bewildered that Nate walked into the office and back into my life. His hair was shorter, making his five o'clock shadow look later. I'd never seen him in one of those Armani suits I spied in his closet, and he looked ready for a runway in Milan. Seeing his face was like

315

a whiff of smelling salts, waking me from my celibate slumber.

"Bro, you want to talk about it?" Vince says, pulling a tennis ball out of his baggy jeans and throwing it long. He knows me well enough to know I'm clearly acting out of character.

"I'm cool. I'm just...my job satisfaction level is low," I say, covering with a dirty white lie.

"Tell me about it," says the single father fighting his way through the Hollywood jungle.

The next day I'm taking a break outside of the production company, trying not to breathe the downwind smoke coming from the punk mail girl and her actress girlfriend, when I notice Nate trying to park his Land Rover into a tight space. I start to flee, but he signals me to wait as he makes another attempt, requiring me to jump in and direct him. He gets out of the truck, dressed casually; there's a puppy in the back, a lab mix—the canine element taking me back to the fateful day with the two wild Great Danes.

"What's his name?" I ask.

"This is Roscoe," he says, with affection.

"Hey, Roscoe," I say, talking to the dog because it's easier. "He's cute. How long have you had him?"

"About a year. He's a rescue," he says. "You're a lucky dog, aren't you, buddy?"

I reach out and pet the dog; our hands accidentally touch making us both laugh. I was nervous about seeing him, but for some reason, it's all just disarmingly familiar and normal.

"I was hoping I'd run into you. I would have called, but you were pretty clear," he says.

"Yeah, I'm sorry about that."

It seems like a million years ago. So much has happened since then. Obviously.

"So, you and Penny, huh?" I ask.

"Yeah," he says, smiling awkwardly. "She's great."

"She is. She's one of my favorite people here," I say. And she is.

"How 'bout you?"

"How 'bout me what?" I deflect.

"You seeing anyone?"

I smile and look away, unsure how to answer. The truth is I haven't been with another human being since him. "No," I reply, keeping it short and turning my attention back to the pup. "You're a good boy, aren't you?" I say, speaking stupid dog talk.

I can feel Nate looking at me. When I look at him, our eyes connect, and for a moment, it's just the two of us. The eye contact ignites something in my body, taking me back to the first time we met. "I should get back inside," I say, respecting the new boundaries that seem to disappear when we're together. He's dating Penny, for crying out loud!

"Take care, Bryan," he says, as I turn and flee like escaping a house on fire.

The next week Vince and I are driving down Santa Monica Boulevard through West Hollywood and I use our geography as an opportunity to take off my mask. I've since learned that not only have Nate and Penny been dating, they're *serious*. I haven't seen him again, but it's just a matter of time. The only people I can talk to about it are Pastor Brody, Melvin the Mentor, and my new Promise Keepers accountability partner Ethan (he and his wife are the directors of Campus Crusade at UCLA; we meet every Saturday morning for Bible study and prayer).

Pastor Brody, Melvin, and Ethan all believe I'm going through serious spiritual warfare: Satan is using Nate as a pawn for my soul. This is a sentiment reinforced by Andy Comiskey in the Living Waters tapes: *"Satan delights in homosexual perversion because it not only exists outside of marriage, but it also defiles God's very image reflected as male and female.... Another related source of demonization is the homosexual relationship itself.... that attachment and communion are indeed inspired, but the source is demonic."* Andy repeatedly refers to homosexuality as "spiritual disfigurement," and when I'm around my support network—the men I've recruited to help me heal—I'm keenly aware of just how disfigured I am. During this tenuous time, they pray I'll be able to outfox Satan's sly deception and remain a godly man.

It'd be nice to have a friend with whom I can really talk, and looking over at Vince—all muscles, tattoos, and machismo—he doesn't exactly fit the profile on paper. But I think out of all the people in my orbit, he's probably my closest friend, maybe my best friend.

He's behind the wheel of his vintage 1955 Ford F-100 pickup, tattooed arm hanging out the window. He's the guy you don't want to piss off in traffic. And then there's me, cowering in the old-timey cab, terrified how he'll react to what I'm about to tell him.

"I have something to tell you, and I hope it doesn't affect our friendship because...well, you're one of the best friends I've ever had," I say, petrified as words of truth begin to form.

"You're my number one homeboy. Don't know what I'd do without you, bro. For real."

Sometimes he refers to me as his "other bitch," which admittedly sounds gay, but it's a term of endearment. His real "bitch-of-the-month" is a sultry actress from acting class (who strips a few days a month at a high-dollar New York City strip club to subsidize her Hollywood acting career). They're rehearsing a scene for acting class and "rehearse" two to three times a day.

He looks over at me, definitely the Oscar to my Felix, and so I let the cat out of the bag.

"I'm not gay, but I struggle with same-sex attractions," I confess, without confessing.

"Shut the fuck up," he dismisses, as if I'm joking. I wish I were.

Our geography has us in the heart of West Hollywood as it pulsates with gay life. At a stoplight, I watch young gay humans, all shapes and styles, congregate outside the clubs. I glance inside *Rage*, beating with club music, and notice a burly drag queen working the door and catch glimpses of male exotic dancers gyrating on blocks, dollar bills tucked inside G-strings.

I can't help but consider Howard's theory of adolescence.

"Are you serious?" Vince asks again.

My face signals I'm telling the truth. "It's something I'm working on changing. My pastor knows and I've been in therapy working...well, you know, trying to not be."

"Have you ever been with a dude?"

And so I start with Doug, working my way up to Nate and his tornadic cameo last week.

"Holy shit, man," he says, completely thrown off guard as we drive out of West Hollywood and into Beverly Hills.

He's still taking it all in, blindsided it seems. "I had no idea."

I hold my breath. The big fear in telling someone is that they will withdraw.

"Well, you gotta know, bro, this don't affect our friendship," he surprisingly affirms. "There ain't nothing wrong with being gay. It's just how some people are. I don't judge them. I know you're all caught up in religion and think the Bible is more than a book written by man, but I don't buy into all that. I believe in God, and I believe he made you the way you are. You're my homeboy, and I support you no matter what," he says. "You big homo," he jabs, giving me a playful punch on the shoulder, and we share a good laugh.

I start to breathe, stunned that in his eyes, I'm not disfigured. Just brainwashed.

"What are you gonna do about Penny's boyfriend?" he asks with genuine concern.

"I don't know."

And I don't.

Over the next few months, conversations with Penny are just awkward; she's always dropping Nate's name: *Nate and I did this. Nate and I did that. Nate and I went here. Nate and I went there.* They're obviously serious, which should've prepared me for the day she waltzes in with a ring on her finger, beaming with pride. I feign excitement, but inside,

I'm not so excited.

About a week after I learn of their engagement, Nate comes into the production company, catching me off guard because I know Penny is in Santa Monica for a pre-production meeting.

"Penny's not here."

"I know. I'm not here for her. Can you take a break?"

I follow him outside.

"How much time do you have?" he asks.

"Maybe half an hour."

We get into his truck, and he drives to the adjacent residential neighborhood and parks. I look over, unsure as to why I'm here, but knowing I wouldn't want to be anywhere else, a realization that troubles me. He's wearing his NY baseball cap, jeans and a T-shirt.

"So, I guess you heard the news," he says.

"I did. Congratulations!" I offer, trying to sound enthusiastic, but it's obvious I'm acting.

"I love her," he says, thinking out loud. "But I still think about you."

These words take my heart out of hiatus. Looking at him I feel alive...and scared. "I haven't been able to rid you from my thoughts either," I confess.

He looks at me with hungry eyes, and I know I should

open the door and run as fast as I can. But I don't, or rather I can't. I'm stuck in a moment I don't ever want to end. He puts his hand on my shoulder, breathing life into my dormant body. I pull away, "You're getting married!"

"I know. And I don't mean this sexually, but I wanted to... I just wanted..." he stops.

I have one hand on the door, but the energy between us, or chemistry, or whatever the hell that is—that connection between two people that has the power to trump even the best intentions—has taken over, rendering my mind useless and giving my heart more slack.

"Do you ever wonder...you know, you and me..." he asks, endearingly vulnerable.

I nod. This seems to satisfy him. The eye contact is too intense, so I look away. When I look back, his eyes are trained on me and all the suffocated yearnings receive a healthy breath, proving to be more powerful than both our wills. I feel like I'm outside of myself, watching in horror as I lean across the center console and take him in my arms, clinging to him like a human who hasn't had a crumb of physical intimacy for years. He hugs me back, and in the comforting space of his embrace, my mind imagines what a future with him might look like.

I force myself to detach, which feels like refusing food when I'm starving. I gaze into his green eyes, and unconsciously, almost instinctively, our lips connect. It's not a lusty kiss, but a tender, sad, goodbye kiss. I pull away savoring the moment, knowing it will be the last.

"I should get back," I say.

When he pulls up near the office, we sit in silence. I look over at him, and his eyes are teary. Mine are too. I force myself to open the door and step out, closing the door behind me.

It isn't a melodramatic, lingering goodbye like in the movies where I chase the car and we wave for blocks with a heart-tugging soundtrack. I just stand there in a cyclone of silence, going numb inside as Penny's future husband drives away, taking a piece of me with him.

CHAPTER 13:

HIDING FROM MYSELF

My new life has lost that new-life smell. When I hopped on the ex-gay bandwagon four years ago, I joined the mailing list of a handful of Christian organizations: Focus on the Family, Family Resource Council, Christian Coalition, American Family Association, Pat Roberson's *The 700 Club*, and the Traditional Values Coalition. I wasn't on Jerry Falwell's list, but when he lashed homosexuals with his venomous tongue, I'd feel it. I had hoped that by immersing myself in the newsletters of the Religious Right, I might draw inspiration for my crusade. But when I hear Pat Robertson tell his audience of millions: "*[Homosexuals] want to come into churches and disrupt church services and throw blood all around and try to give people AIDS and spit in the face of ministers.*" And his warning: "*...the acceptance of homosexuality is the last step in the decline of Gentile civilization,*" I'm finding the newsletters not so much inspiring, but terrifying and wounding in a fundamentally destructive way. By demonizing homosexuals, Pat Robertson fuels the hatred of them *in Jesus's name*. And by saying: *"[Gays seek] to destroy all Christians,"* he casts gays as the enemies of God, sparking a showdown between my fundamentalist faith and the fundamentals of my reality.

From my pro-family indoctrination, I've learned that not only is traditional marriage under attack by homosexual activists and activist judges, but the increasing tolerance of homosexuality in the media and politics, if not battled on every front, will lead to the end of the world as we know it. The rabidly anti-gay propaganda I've been receiving weekly in my mailbox for years has an apocalyptic sense of urgency, serving as a call-to-arms and a battle cry for action: from boycotting companies that advertise in gay publications or support gay rights, to writing letters to TV networks that blasphemously feature gay characters.

Every time I open up a letter from Tony Perkin's Family Research Council or Don Wildmon's American Family Association, it reinforces the now deep-rooted perception that it's an *us*-versus-*them* world. And although I'm one of *us*, I'm really more like *them*.

I'm a soldier in the Religious Right army, one secret away from becoming the enemy.

My involvement is not unlike a black person obsessed with removing all traces of color so as to be accepted into the KKK. When I look in the mirror, despite my charade, I see the enemy.

On a psychological level, this proves destabilizing, and as my psyche splinters, so does my identity, the crisis culminating the day I decide to change my name. I've grown weary of Bryan Christopher; he's self-loathing, and I've had enough of him. To reinvigorate my *new life,* maybe I need a *new name.* No plan to change my birth certificate, just adopting a stage name—a lady-loving, leading-man name to set me apart from the Hollywood abyss of the undiscovered and provide me with a procreating, pro-family, alter ego that won't be forced to sit in the back of God's bus. It's not that I expect that by changing my name I will somehow miraculously change my nature, but I'm just so sick of myself, I have to change *something.*

For my new, family-friendly *movie star name*, I decide to stay in the family, at least be true to my roots. After studying all the names that adorn my family tree, my great-grandfather on my dad's side, affectionately known as "Pops," had the most unique name: Tarleton Broadus.

Later that week I'm in Howard's office, and I've just reintroduced myself as Tarlton Brodus, eliciting a puzzled, concerned look on Howard's face. He sits back in his chair, legs crossed, hands clasped, head tilted forward, trying to read me. "What are you doing?"

"I just thought maybe I should try a new name."

I see it in his face. He feels bad for me, listening with the patience of a psychoanalyst.

"I need something to set myself apart. That audition for Ken Olin's pilot—an Olympic gymnast whose dreams were dashed finds redemption in coaching. I know they're looking for Cinderella, but that shoe fit perfectly! And then I made the mistake of walking into the casting room and do you know how high the stack of headshots were for just for that one role?"

I gesture waist high. Howard is my Miyagi, but I'm sick of waxing on, waxing off.

"But you got a callback. Not many make the first cut. You met Ken," he reminds me.

"Yeah, but I didn't book it." I say, hearing students shuffling on their way to the studio.

"In all my years of coaching, I've never met anyone like you," he reassures. "Early on I expressed faith in your ability, and you've made tremendous progress. Some of the work you've put up on my stage is as good as the best actors out there working. I know it may seem all the powers are conspiring against you, but changing your name will not solve your core issue."

"What's my core issue?"

"You fear success," Howard says. "Success would force

you out of your comfort zone, and that's scary. For some reason, you're hesitant to really put yourself out there."

Howard doesn't know the reason, but I do. Putting myself out there increases the odds someone will see through my charade and call me out. You can't fool all the people all the time.

"I believe in you. But until you believe in you, you're facing an uphill battle making believers outside of this studio. This has nothing to do with a name. It's never about a name anyway. It's what you bring to the name. You have a great name. Stick with *you*."

Stick with me? That's the issue. I'm trying to escape me. Obviously. I look down at my stylishly tattered jeans, holes in the knees, and think how ridiculous they are—and *not* me.

"Have you given any more thought to the role?" he says, gathering his teaching notebook.

He's directing a production of *Bobby Gould in Hell* by David Mamet. Jim Belushi is set to play the Devil and Howard has offered me the coveted role of the Devil's apprentice.

"I don't really think I'm right for it. I mean, do you?" I ask, squirming.

"You'd be working with Jim Belushi! This is a great opportunity, and yes, I think you'd be perfect in the role, otherwise I wouldn't have offered it to you."

"I just...the subject matter. I'm not comfortable playing the assistant to the Devil."

"It's a comedy. It's David Mamet!"

"I'm going to have to pass, Howard."

"Do you know how many actors would kill for this role?"

"I appreciate you casting me. I really do. But I don't think I'm right for the part, and I just can't compromise my values for an acting role, regardless of how it may help my career."

He leans back in his chair, exasperated. He wants to help me, but I'm getting in the way.

"To thine own self be true," he says, conceding with the words of Shakespeare.

I'm in a Hollywood casting office, waiting to audition for a Wrigley's gum commercial—a job I plan on booking so I can quit my ridiculous day jobs and focus on acting full-time.

This is what they call a cattle call. Wrigley's is auditioning anyone with a pulse. I'm in the holding pen, surrounded by a herd of actors, all different breeds, waiting for the gate to be released to the next stable, where a Wrigley's "How to" video is playing on a loop, a three-minute tutorial designed to illustrate the proper way to "load and chew" Wrigley's gum.

As I wait, I study the other actors, realizing I'm about as unique as a snowflake.

A short, punk girl, armed with the sign-in sheet and a camera, eyes the room of actors like we're filthy rodents, barking out names: "Tarlton Brodus!" She has purple hair, piercings in her ears and nose (and God knows where else), and bad energy. I try to ignore her until my turn.

"Uh...*hello!*" the casting gnome yells. "Not saying it again: *Tarlton Brodus!*"

In my mind, I wish the guy would answer so she'll—*and then it hits me*: "That's me!" I say, raising my hand like I'm in a classroom, all eyes in the room burning into me.

She whips around, her face saying: *You stupid, pathetic actor. How dare you make me wait!* "Are you like deaf," she yaps. "I've been calling you for like days! Follow me."

I follow her into a hallway like a scolded schoolboy. She points to the wall. I stand with my back to it, she aims a camera—and without counting to three or giving me time to say "cheese" —she snaps, the camera spitting out a Polaroid.

"Wait in there," she snaps, throwing me the Polaroid and returning for her next victim.

I detest Polaroids, but they're standard protocol in commercial auditions. They want to see what an actor really looks like, not how good the photographer is. Even a bush pig can have a nice headshot. I return to the casting room with the budding Polaroid, my face just peeking through, but with each second, I become more horrified. *Is that really what I look like?* My fatal flaw has long eroded my self-image, but the distortion in recent years has become so severe, I actually go out of the way to avoid mirrors, my reflection in store windows, and Polaroids.

My success as an actor, my victory as a Christian man looking for a wife, my ability to fit into society and be treated as equal are all dependent on how well I can mask the gay part—and in this picture, *I look like a faggot!* I break out of the holding pen, seeking refuge in a bathroom stall. Analyzing the abominable Polaroid, I sink deeper into the quicksand of shame: If they see this picture, they won't hire me. Wrigley's is looking for FCC-friendly and unobjectionable heterosexuals to chew their gum, not obscene, indecent, and profane homosexuals. The kids could be watching! The second a homosexual is spotted chewing gum in a Wrigley's commercial on television, the American Family Association will strike back against the liberal media for promoting the "homosexual agenda" by filing a complaint with the FCC and firing off a mass email to its family values flock, calling for a boycott of Wrigley's.

If my true colors shine through, not only will it limit my career potential, but I risk becoming a target for those who find it justifiable to discriminate against, bully, and even *murder faggots*—my fragile frame of mind perhaps in response to the recent news of a university kid who was pistol-whipped and tied to a fence in a remote, rural area of Wyoming and left to die *because he was gay*. Adam and all the gay guys at work were deeply affected by the murder of Matthew Shepard, attending several candlelight vigils. At the trial, the defendants used the "gay panic" defense, claiming they were driven to *temporary insanity* by alleged sexual advances by Shepard (although their girlfriends testified they went to a gay bar to hunt their target).

There's no question: gay people are not safe. Not at this time, not in this world. They are still victims of hatred and discrimination, and *sometimes* they are the victims of their own hatred and discrimination. This internalized version of homophobia is insidious and dark, and at this moment, manifesting in a certain casting bathroom in Hollywood.

Staring at the Polaroid, anger raging inside, all the "pro-family" vitriol I've been marinating in begins to spew, directed at the deviant in the photo. I try ripping him to shreds, but he won't tear, so I crumble him up and throw him in the trash. I march right up to Punky Brewster with the camera, in no mood for her 'tude. "I lost my Polaroid. I need you to retake it."

She eyes me up and down, clearly not the first time an actor has "lost" their Polaroid.

With my new Polaroid still black and unformed, I pledge

not to look, but as I enter the casting, I inadvertently catch a glimpse and the sight of the guy in the Polaroid shames me.

His name is Tarlton Brodus, but he still looks like me.

Back at home, the evangelical voices in my head are shrill in their condemnation, reminding me of my detestable disposition, leading to yet another standoff with the man in the mirror.

To make a dire moment even more cringe-worthy, I'm listening to Michael Jackson's, "Man in the Mirror."

I'm gonna make a change,

For once in my life,

It's gonna feel real good,

Gonna make a difference,

Gonna make it right.

Is God speaking to me through Michael Jackson, or am I teetering on the edge of insanity? It's bad.

And then it starts, my own form of "gay panic" — as if the murderers of Matthew Shepard have joined forces with the bullies of my youth — and they are chasing me inside my head and I'm running scared. *Die, faggot, die!* As I loathe the man in the mirror, I realize changing his name doesn't solve the problem, so I let Tarlton Brodus die, leaving me stuck with myself.

I'm starting with the man in the mirror

I'm asking him to change his ways

"Why can't you change, you fairy?" I gay bash the queer in the mirror, my adrenaline pumping and fist tightening. I've been here before: *Why does it keep coming to this?*

I want to destroy him. *Faggots deserve to die!*

I hate the way he moves, the way he talks, the way he walks. *They're not real men.*

I hate his face, his nose, and his hair. *Pretty boy!*

I hate his very existence! *Queers deserve to be smeared!*

My bulimic approach to sexuality is only making me sicker.

I want to destroy the man in the mirror, and this is the closest I've ever been.

And no message could have been any clearer,

If you wanna make the world a better place,

Take a look at yourself,

And then make a change.

Desperate to change something, I mindlessly grab a pair of clippers and begin shaving my head, each aggressive swipe of the clippers across my scalp feels like mowing a lawn, my spirit cracking as I watch large clumps of hair hit the floor. When I'm finished, I'm shaken by my impromptu act of self-sabotage, dropping the clippers and staring at my freshly shaved head.

As I confront the bully I've been hiding from, the one tormenting and chasing me around the hallways of my mind since that menacing summer before 7ᵗʰ grade, I discover his face looks like mine. It *is* mine. I've become the enemy, the disparaging voice echoing the shaming anti-gay, "pro-family" rhetoric of the church. I've become the judger, the hater, and the murderer.

(*Na Na Na, Na Na Na, Na Na, Na Nah*)

To escape the brutality of my own hatred, I must hide from myself.

CHAPTER 14:

PLAYING IT STRAIGHT

The morning after shaving my head, Kate calls from Vancouver. She's working on a new TV show, just read the script for the next episode, and there are two roles for which I might be right. I tell her I shaved my head, but it doesn't deter her from faxing the script and arranging the audition. I have less than twenty-four hours and prepare for both: the "bad guy" and the "nerdy sidekick."

She warns that a couple of her friends have auditioned for roles but did not get the part, so it's not a sure thing. About halfway to Culver City for the audition, I have an epiphany.

I know this will be my last audition.

Despite whatever talent I may or may not have, I just don't have the passion for acting to deal with the constant search for the next acting gig. The fact this door is opening from the inside gives credence to the idea it's *who* you know. I approach the audition as if it's my last, an attitude that

337

works to my advantage. At the casting, I feel good about my reading, and before I make it out the door, the producer tells me to start packing my bags for Vancouver.

When I get home, Kate calls, ecstatic and genuinely proud of me. She tells me she's flying into LA that weekend to plug the new show on Jay Leno, and since they're putting her up in a hip hotel on Sunset Boulevard, she insists that I join her and some friends for dinner.

When I enter the trendy lobby, it is hopping with Hollywood hipsters, and I immediately feel less than hip. The swanky restaurant is a white-on-white, modern extravaganza, illuminated by hundreds of tiny candles, creating a warm, romantic glow. The patio, with its giant clay pots of ficus trees and panoramic view of the city lights, feels magical. I spot Kate at a large, round table with four females, none of whom I know. I approach the table, prompting her to do a double take before standing and giving me a warm hug, playfully rubbing my shaved head.

"It looks good," she says, looking like a glamorous Hollywood star.

I take a seat, and she introduces me to the group: One of the girls is a young, wide-eyed Canadian production assistant for the TV show who accompanied Kate from Vancouver. I'm seated next to a lesbian couple, Monica and Kirsten, and after talking with them, learn they hardly know Kate but are friends with Zoë, a new-agey, slightly annoying girl on the other side of me who I learn is also a lesbian with an obvious crush on Kate.

"She has such good energy," Zoë says, referring to Kate. "She's a total Sagittarius," she says, smiling adoringly at Kate sitting across the table. "What's your sign?" she asks, reading my energy, which feels like I'm being spiritually raped.

"Taurus," I lie, in a lame attempt to test her abilities.

"Exactly! That's totally what I figured."

"Well, actually, I'm a Capricorn," I confess, putting her sixth sense under scrutiny.

She studies me again, as if reexamining my energy. "You don't believe in astrology?"

"I don't believe you can spend five minutes with a person and claim you know them because of the month they were born. Surely you don't believe all Capricorns are alike, just as I'm sure you'd concede not all lesbians are alike. Stereotypes may be useful in simplifying a complex world, but ultimately they're dehumanizing," I say, smiling lamely as if I'm on the high school debate team. The table is silent, all ears tuned to my spirited response. "But it is a full moon and my horoscope did predict I might act out of character tonight," I qualify, like an idiot.

It's an unusual dinner, taking a bizarre turn when the lesbian couple begins trying to set me up with a friend of theirs. "Do you have a girlfriend?" Monica asks.

"Uh...no. Not right now," I say, playing it straight, avoiding eye contact.

Monica turns to Kirsten, "Can't you see him and Sarah hitting it off?"

"Totally," Kirsten replies.

"You would *totally* dig our friend. She's also from Texas and very funny," Monica pitches.

"And hot!" Kirsten says, a little too emphatic.

"Kirsten had a total crush on her before I came along," Monica says.

"I did not!" Kirsten defends, her face becoming flushed.

"You did so! It was cute. We've all had crushes on straight girls," Monica says, throwing a piercing look at Zoë.

"Anyway, we should give you her number," Monica says.

"Sounds good," I reply, playing along, relieved I'm passing straight with the lesbians, calming fears that my truth is showing. Playing it straight is clearly a defense mechanism, an instinctual act of self-preservation, and a preemptive measure of protection against persecution.

But in the presence of a seemingly well-adjusted lesbian couple, it feels like cowardice.

* * *

After dinner, Kate and I head up to her posh hotel room to watch the Jay Leno segment taped earlier that afternoon. After raiding the minibar and watching the interview, we decide to crash the infamous Sky Bar, the so-called hottest bar in Hollywood. After we pass trendy hipsters lounging poolside on plush mattresses on the roof of the hotel, we ascend stairs to a tiki bar, entering the celebrity Twilight Zone. Kate runs into an actor friend from *Melrose Place*, introducing me as a high school friend and bragging that I just booked a role on her TV show.

As they head off to the corner to catch up, I begin pushing my way through the mob toward the bar. As I find myself flying solo at the Sky bar, I begin to withdraw inside.

"This place is funny, huh?" a deep voice bellows, bringing me out of my shell.

I turn to find a guy that, at first glance, looks like a rugby player. He's short, stocky, and sipping a beer like a jock. "It's like everyone is trying so hard to be noticed."

The stranger is striking up a conversation and any minute I expect talk about hot chicks and which one I have my eye on. He seems the frat boy type—until he makes an off-handed, joking reference to the size of his member. "Ten inches," he says, almost complaining, much like a woman with triple D's might complain of back pain or finding shirts that fit.

"Excuse me?" I say. I must have missed something. It is loud in here. Is he talking about—

"It's more of a burden than a blessing," he says. "Sometimes it just gets in the way."

His delivery is almost clinical, and I'm simply speechless.

I glance over at Kate, still deep in conversation, and then back to the endowed stranger. The desires I've repressed begin bubbling dangerously close to the surface. I wouldn't have pegged him as gay, so the detour in the conversation is bizarre.

"You don't believe me?" he taunts.

"I believe you," I say, knowing I should flee.

He takes a gulp of his beer, eying me to gauge my reaction.

"Ten?" I say, jokingly.

I take a nervous gulp of my beer, scanning the place. It's packed. I look back at the stranger, and he has a mischievous grin on his face. His eyes point south, leading my eyes downward to find he has discreetly exposed himself, confirming his claim and exposing the part of me I've been fixing, healing, and loathing. The part of me I can't stand to acknowledge rushes to the forefront as the unzipped rugby player slyly takes my sweaty right hand and discreetly introduces it to his hefty appendage, as if to prove it's no prosthesis.

I recoil. "Dude, I'm straight," I say, my hand confirming it's definitely real.

He smiles at me knowingly. "Dude. Me too."

And it hits me: even while groping a rugby player in public, I'm *still* playing it straight.

"You want to get out of here?" he asks with a sexy grin.

"I do. But just so you know, I'm not ... you know."

"Dude, I know. Me neither."

Ten minutes later, I'm in the back seat of the Cadillac on Sunset Boulevard with "John."

"You were the hottest guy in there, you know," he says, putting his hand on my knee.

"*Please.* I'm sure you've been strutting round all night with your willy hanging out. It started getting late, you started getting desperate, and then I came along and took the bait."

He laughs as I warily watch clubbers stumbling by through the tinted windows.

"So what's your deal?" I ask. "Are you gay?"

"I'm not 'out,' but I'm definitely... Well, it's complicated."

"No one knows about you?"

"My close friends, but in my line of work, it's better to be discreet."

"What do you do?"

He pulls his hand off my knee, peering out of the tinted window at a group of girls passing by dressed for a night on the town. "Well, you have to promise to keep this in your Cadi."

"Dude, I'm not exactly 'out' either."

"I'm an actor," he says.

"Everyone's a friggin' actor in this town."

"I've been on a soap for the last ten years. No one knows, except my close friends. My agent and manager know, but I have to be careful. If the network were to find out, I don't know. I play a character that is quite the womanizer on the show, and my fans are mostly women in the Midwest. My reps think it might be better to, you know, play the role."

I look away, his reality sobering.

Suddenly, we become aware of the girls, this time walking the other way. Upon closer inspection, they are most likely tourists on a "girl's weekend" in LA, stalking celebrities to have stories to tell their coworkers on Monday morning. As they saunter by, one stops, and to our horror, walks right up to the window of the Cadillac, sending us both diving into the floorboard.

With us cowering only inches away, she uses the tinted glass as a mirror.

"I thought LA wasn't supposed to be humid! *Oh my gaw!*" she says, furiously teasing her hair into a 1980s poof. "No wonder that asshole didn't let us in. Look at me!"

Two girls pull cigarettes out of tiny purses and light up, while a hefty gal, wearing clothes that don't exactly flatter her full figure, yells into a cell. *"Bitch, I thought you said our name was on the list!"* The girl doing a makeover is so close I can see her wrinkles, looking more like a divorced mother in her forties than the skimpy twenty-something she's trying to pull off.

"I'm so over this," she says. "I'm getting Botox. I don't care what you bitches say."

"You can't polish a turd!" quips one of the women as she sucks on a cigarette.

As the woman puts on lipstick, puckering into the glass, my heart is racing so fast I fear it might overheat. If this woman were to see beyond her face, how might she respond when she notices a TV soap star and me having a panic attack in the floorboard?

"I need to get laid!" she says, before stumbling away and joining the other girls.

We come up off the floorboard as though we just dodged a bullet, both of us watching warily as they proceed down the boulevard looking for their own true Hollywood story.

And it hits me: *Maybe God sent the girls to provide me a way out of a fall into sin?*

"I live just right up the hill there. Follow me to my place?"

"I go to an evangelical church, and I'm in an ex-gay program," I say, the ultimate buzz kill.

"Wow," he says, looking at me with a kinship we didn't have two seconds prior. "I thought my situation was rough. I come out and I may lose my fans and my career. You come out—"

"And I lose my soul," I finish.

"That must be... Wow," he says, searching for words with a compassion that disarms me.

"You work on a soap opera. You don't need my drama."

For a moment I think he's just going to open the door and flee, but instead he looks at me.

"At work, I have to give this illusion that the role I play on TV is who I am in real life. I'll never be able to reconcile the two. In a way, we have a lot in common."

"Except you get paid to play a straight guy."

"Exactly. I'd still love for you to come over tonight—and not for sex. We don't have to do anything. Just open a bottle of wine and talk. See what else we have in common."

He really is hard to resist, and for a second, I feel like I'm on a soap opera.

"I promise I won't even flirt with you," he says, flirtatiously.

I look out the window, the proposition tempting.

"Come on. What do you say?" he asks, playfully punching me on the shoulder.

"Okay. I'll come over, but just for one drink—and no sex."

"Deal. Give me two seconds; I'm four cars back."

He puts one hand on the door and then reaches over and rubs my shaved head in a playful way. He ducks out, and I watch him walk away. Just in case there are paparazzi hiding behind the bushes, instead of getting out of the car to get in the driver's seat, I climb over the seat.

I look in the rearview mirror and am horrified to see the girls who had walked by earlier huddled around him. And he appears to be reluctantly signing autographs! I slink down in my seat and watch him hop in his car. *What am I doing?* I say a prayer as he pulls up in a sporty BMW. And I begin following him in my battered Cadi, heading east on Sunset Boulevard.

But when he turns left on La Cienega, I keep going straight.

* * *

Kate's mom picks me up at the Vancouver airport with Kate's two dogs in tow. We immediately take the dogs on a walk along the river with downtown Vancouver as the backdrop—an absolutely stunning city. After getting settled, we go to the set on location in downtown Vancouver. When we arrive, the film crews are set up outside a market, Kate inside filming a scene with an Asian man playing the owner. I enjoy watching her in action, doing several takes and joking with the crew in between. After the scene wraps, she emerges, giving me a hug, and I immediately notice she has more padding up top, and when I pull away I can't help but joke.

"Well, you're all growed up," I play, making reference to her rather ample breasts that weren't there the week prior in LA.

She looks down at her boobs as if they're aliens. "Oh, you have no idea the crisis this morning. Wardrobe couldn't find my bag of boobs and—"

"Bag of boobs?"

"Oh, yeah. I'm not getting a boob job, and god forbid we have a flat-chested leading lady! It's in my contract," she says. "Anyway, shooting got held up while every PA frantically searched for my boobs. Finally I told everyone, 'Look, I'm sorry for the inconvenience my flat chest is causing, and

I'll buy everyone a drink after we wrap.'"

"It's not your fault," Kate's mom says, taking some responsibility, referring to her chest.

I can't help but notice the circus of activity surrounding us: the crew breaking down the set, producers barking orders into walkie-talkies, and production assistants chasing their tails.

"I can't believe you're actually here," Kate says, leading me away from the chaos and introducing me to members of the cast as well as the director of the episode I'll be working on.

Over the next two weeks, we shoot in and around Vancouver, one weekend taking a road trip into the Canadian countryside, shooting white-water rafting scenes. I have my own trailer, the size of a closet, alongside four of my co-stars. Kate has her own wagon where I spend my downtime—one of the perks of being friends with the star of the show. Every day is an adventure, and it's satisfying to finally be paid for acting, but I know this will be it for me.

On the one day we both have off, Kate takes me hiking through the forests on the outskirts of Vancouver: mountains, trees, rivers, and clean air. She received a package from Zoë the day before filled with homemade soaps and spa products, opening up a conversation about lesbians. Kate played a role as a lesbian in an independent film a few years prior, and her candid openness about sexuality gives me the courage to open up a little. I trust her. We've been friends for over twelve years, and when it comes to gay people, I know she won't judge.

"I had an experience," I say.

"Really?" she asks, leading me down a fern-lined trail, the sun peeking through the forest canopy above. I inhale the crisp air and feel faint.

"In college," I confess, quickly backpedaling as fast as I can.

"When in college?" she asks, as there was a short time I had a toothbrush at her place.

"After you and I...you know."

"I have that effect on men. I'm sure there's more than a few guys I've dated that end up at Rage," she jokes, referencing the gay bar in West Hollywood.

"It was just once and confirmed I'm definitely straight," I say, aborting the truth.

By playing it straight, I place another brick on the wall.

§ § §

On New Year's Eve, 1999, I arrive at the Burbank airport with Vince waiting for me at the gate. I'd planned on partying like it's 1999 in D.C. with high school buddies, but after a few days of playing the role of someone other than me I made an excuse and left early.

Strangely, Vince has made plans for us to attend the New Year's Eve Gospel service at the First A.M.E. church, a largely African-American church in Los Angeles. It's not the type of event I'd expect Vince to attend, but it's his suggestion. He's actually dressed up; a long-sleeved black shirt covers the tattoos, and his hair is slicked back and his goatee trimmed. With Vince behind the wheel of his vintage Ford, I roll down the window, my blood beginning to thaw after being frozen over the holidays. I look over at Vince, and I thank God for him.

With him, there's no playing (or lying). I can just *be*.

I'd spent the last two days with Luke, my best friend in high school, who ranked higher on my heart than my girlfriend, and Henry, my Promise Keepers bro from Texas. Luke works in the West Wing of the Clinton White House, but lives in a loft in Virginia. Since his roommate was out of town, Henry and I shared the room. Luke made it clear the roommate wasn't a friend, perhaps to create distance from the large Confederate flag mounted on the roommate's ceiling.

"I spent last night staring up at a Confederate flag in Virginia."

"What? I thought you were with your high school homies?"

"It wasn't Luke's flag. It was his roommate's. I never met the guy."

"Well, we'll just have to pray for that racist son of a bitch tonight," Vince says, smiling.

"I can't believe it's your idea to attend a church service on New Year's Eve. What's gotten in to you?" I ask, suspiciously. "Are you dying?"

"No, I'm not dying! I figure what better way to start out the New Year, right? If we're not high on the Holy Spirit by midnight, we'll go get wasted afterwards."

What makes the evening more colorful is that Vince's manager, Stanley, a balding, plump gay man in his late forties, who discovered Vince in a showcase several years prior, joins us.

Vince pledged to never tell a soul my truth, so I play it straight with the manager.

When we arrive at the church, I quickly discover we don't exactly blend, and I pray the congregation looks beyond the color of our skin and to the content of our character. From the sharply dressed black men handing out pamphlets at the door, I learn A.M.E. stands for African Methodist Episcopal, and the church was founded by Bridget "Biddy" Mason, a former slave freed in the 1850s. Now almost 150 years later, it has a membership of well over 15,000.

An elderly woman dressed in a frilly hat ushers us in just

as they start steering others to the auditorium set up with a satellite TV. The magnificent chapel has the energy of a pep rally, giving me the impression that Jesus is not only coming back tonight, but he'll be stopping here first. The spirited hymns, powerful enough to make even an atheist nervous, are led by a full gospel choir reminding me of the movie *Sister Act*, after Whoopi Goldberg gives the nuns permission to really let loose. The elder leads us to a pew near the middle of the chapel, and we walk past the familiar faces of Arsenio Hall, Quincy Jones, and Magic Johnson.

As I sing in unison with a church full of African-Americans, I am jarred by the juxtaposition of having spent the night before in a stranger's bed in Virginia staring up at a Confederate flag. As I raise my hands in the air, reaching out to the same God as those around me, I'm stunned there was a time when leaders in the church interpreted the Bible literally—mainly a passage in Genesis 9:20-26—to preach the justification of segregation and slavery from the pulpit.

I look at Stanley, who recently lost his partner of fifteen years to AIDS, and he's wiping tears, prompting me to put my arm around him in comfort. As I stand with my arm around a grieving gay man in a church full of black people singing the hymn, "Just as I Am," questions percolate that challenge my theology and worldview: *Is Stanley beyond the Lord's embrace simply because the person he loved and committed to for fifteen years was of the same gender? Is the church making the same mistake excluding gay believers as it once did black believers? Will history show that one day the church will view its unrepentant discrimination against gays and lesbians like most, but not all, now view the Confederate flag?*

As I mouth the words to "Just as I Am," knowing these words still don't apply to me, I notice an impeccably dressed black man flanked by a large black woman and two young boys dressed identically with bow ties. Everyone is singing in unison, but I'm pulled out of the moment when I observe the man scrutinizing Stanley. I'm not sure if I'm projecting my own fears, but I notice him shake his head, almost in disgust, and then his eyes go to me. I turn away, self-conscious of my arm draped around Stanley. *Did he just judge us or am I being paranoid?*

At the time Jesus is believed to have walked the earth, the Pharisees were a powerful political and religious Jewish group that upheld an interpretation of Judaism that insisted on the strict observance of Jewish law. They were determined to catch Jesus breaking a law so they could imprison him. They once tested him by encircling a woman caught in adultery—and with stones in hand—asked Jesus what should be done. The law clearly stated that she should be stoned to death. Jesus responded famously by saying, "He who is without sin among you, let him be the first to throw a stone."

There is so much stone throwing in the church that when I notice the man's wife, now eyeing Stanley and me with one eyebrow raised and no longer singing, I sheepishly withdraw my arm. This instinctual act of self-preservation, again, feels cowardly. But if I'm exposed as heterosexually challenged, there are many—even in this very church—who might feel justified throwing stones my direction. At one time the stones flying from the church were directed at black people. And now they're being thrown with reckless abandon at gay people.

To avoid the stones, I *must* play it straight.

PART III

CHAPTER 15:

THURSDAYS WITH SEQUOIA

It came out of nowhere. I was turning into Goodyear Tires, where I just spent $367.50 on two new tires, only to leave and discover they weren't aligned properly. I was returning to have them realigned when a BMW ran the light, broadsiding me and realigning more than just my tires.

With my brain still jostling from the impact, I look over into the passenger seat and notice it's been replaced with the front end of a Beemer, the reality just beginning to register. Stranded on the Sunset Strip, I'm trembling inside the once luxurious, now mangled, leather womb of the Cadillac. I notice traffic crawling around us, heads rubbernecking, a few even aggressively honking as they pass, as though we've done this on purpose to further complicate their day.

Physically, I seem intact and instinctively crawl out to check on the driver of the other car, a spoiled rich kid brushing off the powder from his deployed airbag. He's fine and already on the phone with his dad and his attorney. We are in front of a Rite Aid, so I run inside and buy a disposable camera and take pictures much like a coroner documenting a dead body.

It's totaled. The wrecker arrives, hooks it up, and instead of having it towed to the salvage yard, I have the driver tow it to my garage. As the once shiny chariot that delivered me to my Christ-centered Second Act in Hollywood is being entombed in my garage, I notice what's left of the Promise Keepers "Seize the Moment" bumper sticker that's been slowly peeling away since our zealous return. The duct tape holding the mirrors has long given way, the gold trim has chipped away, and all the dings and fender benders (that I thought added character) are now just cruel reminders of how unforgiving a place the City of Angels can be. And not just for cars. Pulling down the garage door feels like shoveling dirt on a casket of a loved one, leaving me with a sad, sinking feeling knowing that the Cadi will never drive again.

Since I only have liability insurance, I will have to take the snotty teen driver to small claims court to recoup my loss. In the interim, I'm forced kicking and screaming into the world of public transportation. I've seen buses in the city, but don't know one person who has actually set foot inside one. During the first week, I discover the closest bus stop to my permanent temp job at the production company is smack dab in the seedy seat of the Hollywood red light district. When I approach the bus stop for the first time after work, I notice guys with tight muscle T-shirts and loose jeans hanging below their asses strutting the boulevard and eying me as if I am competition. I, of course, put my shirt back on and take a seat at the bus stop, eying the horizon to communicate that I'm actually here for the bus. About the third time a car stops and I'm asked "my rate," I decide I will walk the extra two blocks to the less cruise-y stop at La Brea.

At the corner of Santa Monica Boulevard and La Brea —the second closest bus stop to a job that leaves few extra dollars in my wallet—I am singled out by an angry, drunk, transvestite hooker with a craving for something that requires the dollar burning in my wallet.

"Hi hansthome. I'm Sequoia. Can you spare a dollah?" he slurs at me, eyes bloodshot.

He's the ugliest woman I've ever seen.

There are transvestites out there who can fool just about everyone except their mothers, but Sequoia is not one of them. Not even close. The permanent 5 o'clock shadow peeking through the layers of gaudy makeup, the raspy voice saturated with testosterone—not to mention an Adam's apple even a turtleneck can't hide—all serve to betray his/ her flamboyant charade, leaving little doubt amongst his/ her clients what they will get when they unwrap the package.

There are no *Crying Game* moments for Sequoia. He's a real life Hollywood transvestite hooker in need of "a dollar for some food. Not drugs. I don't do drugs—I mean I do, and I know they're bad, and I'm trying to quit, but this is for a cheeseburger at McDonalds. I'm hungry. They have that, um...ninety-nine cent Big n' Tasty. And I ain't talking about me!"

My mind races through the database of programmed responses that have succeeded in excusing me from the slippery slope of goodwill in the past and none seem appropriate.

"What you looking at?" he accuses an elder Jewish lady weighed down by two shopping bags, his tongue dripping with venom, his vile nature undoubtedly fueled by the copious amounts of alcohol and drugs coursing through his veins. The result is a belligerent monster I am convinced is demon possessed. The lady looks away, adjusting her bags, searching the horizon for a sign of the #4 bus, her exodus on wheels from this god-forsaken corner of the city. This isn't her part of town. It's not my part of town either. This is Sequoia's turf, and we all feel it.

"You just want a dollar?" I ask, digging into my wallet and forfeiting the dollar, just as the old woman throws a glance my way, communicating nonverbally I am a sucker.

It's just a dollar. Besides, it's charity. What would Jesus do?

"You're a doll," he/she mumbles, quickly turning his attention to the next wave of cars cruising through the intersection, geographical victims to his flamboyant solicitation. As much as "she" is used to walking this boulevard, the disadvantage of having a size 11 man's foot stuffed into stiletto heels creates a balancing act that keeps all of us innocent bystanders on our toes. Add a cheap bottle of whiskey and drugs to the mix and it's a recipe for disaster.

I feel bad for him/her and question the destiny of my dollar and whether my small act of charity is helping or hurting: is the money for a cheeseburger or more drugs?

The question presents itself again a week later when our paths cross for the second time, but this time is different. This time he is sober, and his charade seems less amusing and more desperate. His solicitation of passing cars has a sense of urgency, and when he asks me for a dollar, I sense he is truly hungry. Before I'd seen a demon monster, now I see a human being.

"Are you hungry?" I ask.

"Starving," he replies, with conviction.

"Carl's Jr. or McDonald's?" I offer, surprising even myself.

He's hungry. And since I'm blindly chasing after the footsteps of Jesus, asking the neighborhood man tramp to lunch just seems like the Christ thing to do.

From the reaction of the kids behind the counter, Sequoia is no stranger to the golden arches. As I order, I can't help but notice the judging stares his existence elicits from other customers. With the gaudy makeup, stiletto heels and short-short skirt, he doesn't exactly blend. As I wait for the food, he scouts for a table outside, away from the obnoxious stares, but with a clear view of the street should one of his regulars be on the prowl. It shocks me he has regulars.

As I approach with our tray of McFood, he's applying another layer of makeup to his chiseled American Indian features. There's nothing feminine about his bone structure. His limp, greasy hair is shoulder length and pulled into a ponytail, his flat halter-top revealing he's still saving up for the breast implants. The Y in his genetic code seems to be the major obstacle in his desperate attempt to sync his exterior with how he feels inside. Is he a woman trapped inside a man's body or just insane? I'm curious, so I listen as he talks incessantly about his tragic life with a natural flamboyance that is both entertaining and devastating.

"You know, I say screw him. It's always the same bull-shit," he says, wiping off the lipstick not on his lips with a McNapkin. He peers into the pocket mirror, examining his chapped ruby reds. "But I love him. I do. I know he treats me like shit, but what can you do?"

And that's how it all begins—the most unlikely of friendships forged over a couple of Happy Meals in Hollywood.

I've been taking the bus for a month now, and since I live and work off Santa Monica Boulevard, the bus ride is a daily safari tour through the jungle of LA: Westwood, Century City, Beverly Hills, West Hollywood, and final stop, the slimy underbelly of Hollywood.

From my corner at the Mormon Temple, it takes thirty-four minutes from the time I board until I pull the cord—an hour of my day when I don't have to fight traffic and can just relax, read, and reflect on how my Hollywood story isn't turning out the way I scripted. The reality is that I'm watching the city from the back seat of a metro bus, further loosening my grip on the seductive idea that out of the millions who flock to Hollywood to make it, I might somehow be different—a belief that fueled my twenties as I clung to the desperate hope that success was right around the corner. For many, Hollywood promises fame and fortune—a magical place where dreams come true—spawning a pulsating, dehumanizing desperation that leads everyone in the whole city to look at every situation and every person as someone who might advance their career. It's annoying. Hollywood is the one place where people die of hope.

From the back of the bus, I also have time to reflect on all the ways my new life has gone stale. After three years of driving to the valley weekly to meet with Melvin—week after week, month after month, year after year—where I laid bare my soul for mentoring, while Melvin mainly listened, reinforced traditional values, and prayed the Almighty would heal me and bring me a good Christian woman, I haven't changed one iota. This reality, along with the inconvenience of taking a bus to Van Nuys, prompts a pulling of the plug on the so-called mentoring. Melvin the Mentor will have to find another ride to the train station.

Given the prayer hours logged, I can't help but wonder if God is even listening. I haven't lost all hope, but my faith is being tested. As I witness the poverty and need of the residents of the City of Angeles, I just wonder where He is. It's time for His close up.

And not just in my life.

It's hard to remain an optimist from the back seat of an LA bus.

Regardless, it's time to change tactics, and I vow to find a *real* ex-gay therapist.

Already on the other side of promptness, I resolve myself to the back of the bus and grab a book from my duffel bag. I'm reading the *Left Behind* series, a fictionalized account of the End Times, loosely based on the book of Revelations in the Bible. It's a bestseller among evangelical Christians because it extols a fundamentalist worldview and begins with the Rapture, the apocalyptic event when true believers will be snatched up in an instant into heaven while non-believers remain stuck on earth as punishment for their lack of faith. There's the rise of the Anti-Christ and Jesus's Second Coming, and as I board the bus today, I find myself hoping that Jesus returns before I get off at the corner of La Brea because I don't know how much longer I can live in Hollywood when my dreams have already started to fade to black. Or how much longer I can walk the straight and narrow without seeing at least a glimpse of the Promised Land.

As I watch the world pass me by from the back seat of an LA bus, filling my head with fantasy-inspired visions of the end of the world, I am still haunted by a fundamental question, the answer to which is no longer clear: *Will the "ex-" part of "ex-gay" ever be permanent?*

I also find myself, again, rethinking the *"Everything is for a reason"* philosophy that people love to say when bad things happen. Am I in Hollywood for a reason—a reason I once believed actually had divine origins—or am I simply another Hollywood statistic?

It's a legitimate question, given that I am on the #4 bus on my way to a dead end job and the highlight of my day will be having lunch at McDonalds with a prostitute named Sequoia.

When I pull the cord, I walk to the production company, wondering if today will be my last day. A few months ago, the production company was bought out by a bunch of idiot investors clueless about the entertainment industry. Since then, it's been like working on the Titanic. For months I've been punching the clock at Satellite Films, an autonomous division within the larger company that represents a highly successful stable of directors—producing their films, commercials, and music videos. There are twelve people on staff, so it's like a family, and they've been requesting me to do menial office work. I feel like a foster child, and they're still deciding whether to keep me or throw me back in the temp pool. Since the company was sold, Satellite had been operating without a captain until our senior staff hired an advertising executive from Weiden Kennedy in Amsterdam. When Charles showed up the first day, I thought he looked young, only mid-thirties, to be running our division. With a perfectly shaved head, he looked more like a rock musician than hotshot executive producer. His casual confidence put everyone immediately at ease, and under his guidance, the ship has been righted.

As I race toward our corner of the sinking ship, I rehearse my tardiness apology for Charles. When I swing open the door, Charles falls out and into me, juggling a pile of contracts in one hand and a Starbucks coffee in the other. He was using his foot to open the door, so when I opened it, he lost his footing and fell right into me, my arms bracing his fall.

"I'm sorry, I didn't—" I start, but stop when I realize I've got both hands on his shoulders.

"Good morning, Bryan," he says, regaining his balance, his eyes trained on the sloshing hot coffee in his hand. "And look at that, didn't even spill a drop."

"Good morning," I say, withdrawing my hands and chuckling nervously.

"I was wondering how I was going to get that door open," he says, with a warm smile.

"Sorry, I'm late," I say, holding the door for him. "I really tried—"

"It's cool," he says, my tardiness minor to the major company issues he's confronting. "I'm late for another silly staff meeting, so you can just put all my calls through to Janice."

"You got it," I say, relieved.

He takes a few steps and turns. "When you get in tomorrow, could you buzz me? There's something I want to talk to you about," he says, before rounding the corner and out of sight.

I'm going to be fired.

That afternoon, I'm at the bus stop reading about Armageddon when Sequoia surprises me.

"Hey, doll. I was hoping I'd see you today," he says, plopping down next to me.

I put down my *Left Behind* book, strangely happy to see him. "Are you hungry?"

"Starving. But, oh my gawd, you're not gonna believe the shit that when down last night."

We've met several times so far, usually on Thursdays, when my shift ends at 2 p.m. This is his slow time, so we've developed a Happy Meal routine: I listen while he talks incessantly, exposing all the ugly details of his tragic life. Of course he didn't set out to be a prostitute. Who does? His father kicked him to the curb when he was sixteen: a boy dressing as a girl was blasphemous. That was fifteen years ago, and he's been walking the streets ever since.

And it shows.

I don't know what I'm hoping to accomplish breaking bread with a man harlot in Hollywood. Maybe being around him makes my situation seem less desperate. I may be a frustrated ex-gay without a car taking a bus to a dead end job, but at least I'm not giving $10 blowjobs on a seedy corner in Hollywood.

Things could be worse.

Or maybe listening to another human spill their soul makes me feel like I'm making a difference, my psychology degree not in vain.

Whatever the case, if there's a silver lining to my car wreck, it's Thursdays with Sequoia.

"You're my guardian angel, you know that?" he says, nibbling his fries.

"I'm hardly an angel."

I haven't told Sequoia I'm a disillusioned "ex-gay" and not once have we discussed his "gender inferiority." My recycled theories on gender identity or the origins of homosexuality seem irrelevant to his plight. He needs food, shelter, and love from someone not paying him.

"I don't know what I'd do without you."

"Starve," I crack.

"You got that right," he says, genuinely grateful.

He eats his fries one at a time, like a lady, betrayed only by meaty man hands with nubby black nails. "So why do you help me?"

"Well, I believe if Jesus were to return, this is where He'd be, having lunch with you."

"That's so sweet," he says.

He unwraps the cheeseburger, delicately cuts it in half and takes small bites, enjoying every morsel as if it's the last meal he'll ever have. He eats slower than a turtle, and I wonder if it's a way of delaying the reality that is his life outside the safe haven of the golden arches.

"Do you want your toy?" he asks.

I hand him the toy that comes with my Happy Meal, as I do every week. He collects them.

After he finishes his meal, he always breaks out a pocket mirror from a sequined purse (missing more than a few sequins) and begins a miracle makeover: freshening lipstick, covering the 3 o'clock shadow with another layer, and applying eye liner with the dexterity of a pro. His makeup ritual is performed with the diligence of a soldier preparing for battle, and I fear not armor enough to protect him from the cruel world that awaits. Although he seems immune to the vile words thrown freely from people driving by, sticks and stones do break bones.

When we talk, I mostly see him as female, despite the deep voice and Adam's apple, but when *she* excuses herself to go powder her nose in the men's room (usually sending any men inside fleeing in horror), I realize she is very much a chick with a dick, which is unsettling.

After our McSessions, as we walk back to the bus stop, I'm forced to recognize the fleeting impact of a Happy Meal as Sequoia slips back into character, seducing each car that passes, waiting for a taker. This part is the hardest to watch because it's so desperate. If I had the money, I'd pay his rate just so he wouldn't have to sell himself on the open market.

I know him well enough to know it's destroying him.

The next morning, I'm in Charles's office—by far the most stylish office in the building, accented with vintage mid-century pieces. I squirm in an Eames chair as he straightens a stack of papers and lines them up with the edge of his desk. I chuckle because I do the same thing. Although Charles is in charge, I get the sense he hates firing people, especially when it's about budget cuts and not job performance. Although he is the ideal boss to have when being fired, being next on the block still makes me sweat. He focuses on me, his blue eyes popping against his blue sweater.

"So, I've been discussing you with Human Resources and the gang here," he starts, and I'm already preparing my exit speech to everyone: *I'll be okay, really. Selling my body on the open market is not as bad as it seems, and I've already made some great connections. I'll be fine!*

"I understand you've been here a few years and have been offered positions to move up the ladder but have declined. This is a day job while you pursue an acting career?"

"That's right."

"I'm just curious if that's where you still find yourself today. The reason I bring this up is I think your skills are being wasted, and given the opportunity, you could play a larger, more significant role in this company. But if that's not what you want, then I need to know."

"What are you getting at?"

"Well, you're very well-liked by the gang here, and if you want to continue doing the job with the least responsibility so you can pursue other things, then I, or we, support that. But, if you're ready to step up and take on a new challenge, I think you'd make a great director's rep."

"Really?" A director's rep is a big step up the ladder.

"You're friendly, people like you, and I think you'd be great. If you need time to—"

"I'll take it. I'll definitely...thank you," I say, still thunderstruck by his endorsement.

Charles stands and extends his hand, which brings me to my feet.

I take his hand in mine, grateful and still a bit shocked.

"For this to work, I'll need a corner office with views and at least two assistants," I joke.

"Why don't we start with business cards," he says, smiling.

"Okay, fine," I say, turning and walking toward the door.

"You're going to do great. I know it."

And when he says this, I actually believe him.

That afternoon, I skip to the bus stop, looking for Sequoia to share the news. I just got a raise, taking on a real job representing some of the top directors in the business. I don't see Sequoia, but just as I'm about to board the bus,

I spot him walking toward the alley behind Carl's Jr.

"Sequoia!" I yell, as he disappears behind the building.

I let the bus leave me behind and follow after Sequoia.

As I round the corner, I find him sitting on a crate crying, and when he looks up at me, I reflexively take a step back: his face is so swollen, so black and blue it looks deformed, as if someone took a crowbar to it. His lip is bleeding and a bloody napkin trembles in his hand.

"Oh my god, what happened?" I say, leaning down to help him.

"Hey doll, I'm fine. It's just a busted lip, that's all. Really, I'm fine."

"You're not fine! Who did this to you? What happened?" I demand. If the bullies are close, I'll call Vince to chase them down and make them pay!

"Don't worry about it, really. I'm fine."

"Who did this to you?" I press.

"I don't know. Last night I was up near Sunset and there was this car full of guys and they jumped out and..." he says, shuddering at the memory. "They laughed the whole time."

"Have you been to a doctor?"

"I'll be fine. Although I am a little hungry."

As we sit at our usual table outside near the playground, we finish our Happy Meal, but it's not all that happy. It's the first time he hasn't filled the silence with manic chatter.

"And you didn't get a license plate?"

"What, you think the police are going to help me? That's not how it works, doll."

"But they beat the crap out of you!"

"The risk you take doing what I do," he says, matter-of-factly, giving me chills.

He takes out his pocket mirror, his trembling hands struggle to apply another layer of makeup to cover his bruised and swollen eyes, and I worry he'll poke his eye with the eyeliner. The heaviness of his heart is devastating to watch, and I pray silently: *"Dear God,"* I pray, as he examines his bruised eyes, wincing while applying the makeup. *"I pray you will help Sequoia—"*

"I've been worse," he says, his bloodshot eyes glancing up from his pocket mirror.

"This has happened before?" I ask, shocked at the cruelty of people.

He looks at me as if I don't know the half of it.

And I don't.

The next week I'm at the corner and it's Thursday, but there is no sign of Sequoia.

We've met at this time for the last several months, so his absence has me concerned. It's not that I expect the neighborhood tranny streetwalker to be prompt and responsible, but our meeting the week prior concerned me. On that day, as I boarded the bus and walked to the back, I noticed him wave at me, and as I waved back, I was overtaken with emotion. The sight of him standing on the corner—broken and bruised—was a haunting visual that will never leave me.

Perhaps because it would be the last time I'd ever see him.

Many Thursdays follow, but Sequoia is nowhere to be found.

God only knows.

After my initial encounter, I really did think he was demonic, and I looked the other way. I ignored him mainly because I didn't know how to deal with someone like him. As a transgender person, his true colors had more pink tones than blue, but pink is a color in the natural spectrum. God made pink, and for whatever reason, Sequoia came into the world the way he is, his true colors not his fault. What do you do when the outside doesn't match the inside?

I don't know what it's like to be transgender, but I do understand how his distinction from the norm, his inability to live up to gender roles for what is acceptable for a boy, turned him into a modern day leper, shunned by society and forced to do what he had to do to survive.

And those are exactly the people that Jesus reached out to.

CHAPTER 16:

EX-GAY 101

I'm on the verge of *thirty*, and despite the prayers, men's Bible studies, Promise Keepers, Focus on the Family, New Life Clinic, a Jewish psychoanalyst and a Christian men's mentor, counseling with my pastor, an obsessive commitment to "sexual purity," a degree in psychology, and sorting Hugh Hefner's dirty laundry at the Playboy Mansion, I'm still sexually broken.

I'm starting to panic.

I'm ready for serious reparative therapy with a *real* ex-gay therapist.

You don't go to a family doctor if you need brain surgery.

You go to a specialist.

Joe Dallas is the author of *Desires in Conflict: Hope for Men Who Struggle with Sexual Identity*—the first ex-gay book I read five years ago. It captured well my own struggle and has served as a foundation for my pursuit of change. After all, Joe was once active in the "homosexual lifestyle," and is now a self-proclaimed heterosexual with a wife and teenage sons.

Joe is also the poster boy for James Dobson and a featured speaker with the Focus on the Family "Love Won Out" conference where he is quoted as saying, *"If someone as deluded as I was can be brought out of homosexuality then surely anyone can."* Although in his book, *Desires in Conflict*, he does warn, *"So let me emphasize from the outset that I don't pretend to know a universal 'cure' for homosexuality. Nobody does"* (pg. 10).

When I leave a message at his private counseling practice in Orange County, I am surprised when he calls back personally. I can't believe it was so easy to actually talk to him and wish I'd called him years ago. I briefly tell him my story, and we set up an appointment.

I am off to see the wizard.

Since I've been working as a director's rep, my job satisfaction has increased dramatically. It's more responsibility, but I have business cards, an office, client dinners, and an expense account.

I'm in Charles's office because I need his permission to take Tuesday mornings off to make the journey to Orange

County to meet Joe, a request made awkward by the fact I've recently learned Charles is gay. Charles keeps his cards close, his personal life a mystery to most at the office, but I was curious and asked a coworker instrumental in hiring Charles if he had a girlfriend. Asking my gay boss if I can take time off to see an ex-gay therapist feels weird.

"How were the holidays, Bryan?" he asks.

"Not bad. I was in Texas seeing the family," I say, making small talk.

"I was stuck in an ice storm west of Fort Worth. You might have seen it on the news?"

"I saw it firsthand. I was stuck in it, too!" I say, shocked by the small, small world.

"Where were you going?" he asks, mirroring my surprise.

"San Angelo. My mom lives in San Angelo. You?"

"Ranger. I just made it through to my dad's, but there were hundreds of cars stranded."

"Are you from Texas?" I ask, surprised I wouldn't have known that by now.

"Born in California, but raised in Texas."

"Where's your accent?"

"I've lived in Chicago, Portland, and Amsterdam since, although I'll always say *y'all*."

"You and me both," I say, feeling a Texas-connection with Charles.

"So how can I help you?"

"Well, I wanted to see if it was cool to take Tuesday mornings off to take a writing class?"

"I didn't know you were a writer."

"Isn't everyone in this town?" I downplay. "Anyway, I can probably make it in by noon."

"How long is the course?"

"Oh...it's, well several months. But I may take, you know, another one," I stumble.

"Sure. I don't see why not."

"Great. Thank you," I say, moving toward the door to let myself out.

I hate that I lie, but I really don't want him to know I'm sneaking off to Orange County to meet with an ex-gay counselor. I'm not sure how he'd respond, since his sexuality is a side note and not his whole identity—like Adam. If Adam were to discover I'm meeting with Joe Dallas—former president of *Exodus*, the man behind the *"Change is possible"* newspaper ads that had so outraged him—in his view, that's tantamount to meeting with the enemy.

But Charles is a different shade of gay.

As I'm leaving his office, Charles surprises me by saying,

"Would love to read something you've written one of these days." In Hollywood, no one likes to read.

With my hand on the door, I turn and look back. "Well, maybe one day you will."

When I arrive for my first session, I find Joe's office located in an old Victorian house that has been converted into a Christian counseling center. The lobby is filled with religious magazines, *Christianity Today* and *Charisma*, along with pamphlets published by Focus on the Family.

I don't find the middle-aged women behind the desk to be overtly friendly as they busy themselves with paperwork and phone calls. I always assume since it's a Christian facility, the employees will be filled with the love and joy of Jesus Christ. It's always a letdown when I find they are just human beings with sanctimonious dispositions. By telling them I'm here to see Joe, it feels like I'm outing myself, triggering extra anxiety. The facility is clearly headquarters for several Christian marriage and family counselors—and not an ex-gay treatment facility. Joe rents office space, which I discover isn't even in the main house, but in the garage out back.

When Joe emerges, I notice he looks older and grayer than the picture in his book. It's always strange meeting someone in person after you've been studying his or her words for years. His book has been my gospel, so to meet the actual author is intimidating.

As he leads me behind the house to the dilapidated garage/office, I recall when I first read his testimony; I questioned whether he ever had a healthy relationship. Much of his experience seemed to consist of wildly promiscuous sex and adult bookstores, so I wondered if his real issue wasn't homosexuality, but sexual addiction—equally destructive and just as common among heterosexual men. Despite my doubts, I want to believe he has morphed into a card-carrying heterosexual, and not a homosexual sex-addict hiding behind a heterosexual-marriage.

His story gave me hope. If someone as promiscuous as he could change, surely God could work with me, as my testimony is rather tame in comparison. I've been following Joe's prescription for change. If God can change Joe Dallas, surely he can change me.

The converted garage doesn't feel converted. It's filled with garage-sale leftovers and a dank musty smell that can't be healthy to breathe. I wonder why Joe counsels his patients in the garage, away from the main house. Since it's a Christian counseling center, I can almost hear the staff saying: *"Joe, you can have an office here, but we don't want the homosexuals in the main house. You can have the garage out back. And could you also have them park down the street and enter through the back—we don't want to offend our clients."*

He's very serious as he pulls out a notebook, making me feel like I'm interviewing for a job. I know he's married, and supposedly straight, but I can't get the visual of him dancing to the "YMCA" in some gay disco with leather pants, shirt unbuttoned, and chest hair on full display.

"So what led you to call me?" he asks, studying me with intensity.

"I'm beginning to fear that my soul mate probably doesn't menstruate," I say, fidgeting on the lumpy baby-blue sofa with springs that have sprung.

He looks up from his notebook, shifting in his seat.

Starting with our first session, and for the next nine months, my story spills out of me. I tell him everything. I've become a professional patient, all too familiar with my psychological topography, but hoping Joe can locate the so-called "root causes" he refers to in his book.

Theories are convenient and sell books, but I need *answers*.

When I tell Vince, as straight as they come, that I am seeing an ex-gay therapist, he voices his skepticism of the ex-gay movement. In other words, he thinks I'm brainwashed.

"And how do you know this guy still ain't gay?"

"He has a wife and kids!" I say, defending Joe.

Vince laughs, shaking his head. "You think that's proof? Do you know how many repressed gay dudes are married?"

"No. Do you? Have you done some sort of survey?"

"Bro, just because a guy's married don't mean he's not thinking about a dude when he's doin' his wife. A leopard can't change his stripes."

"Leopards don't have stripes," I correct him. "Tigers have stripes, leopards have spots."

"Exactly. A gay person trying to be straight is like a leopard trying to be a tiger, ashamed of his own spots, ashamed of the way God made him," he says, smiling. "Be proud of your spots, you big homo," he plays me, and I appreciate his analogy and humor. He knows how much I've suffered, how much I'm still suffering. "Bro, if I could be gay, I would. Be a hell of a lot easier. I wouldn't have to deal with women and all the bullshit. I just like pussy too much."

I can't help but chuckle.

Vince is the one friend who has offered complete acceptance—not based on a condition of change. His conviction is that homosexuality is just a part of nature and that there's nothing wrong with being gay. But the message that being gay is a disease and a sin is so ingrained in my brain that to suddenly embrace it as a neutral aspect of my being seems impossible.

About three months into conversion therapy with an ex-gay guru, I'm standing in my kitchen shirtless wearing slacks while frantically ironing a white *Hugo Boss* dress shirt.

I'm late for my first Hollywood movie premiere. Kate has landed a big role in a movie opposite Keanu Reeves, and I've been invited to the premiere in Westwood at the Fox theater. As I impatiently wait for the iron to heat up, I grab a beer, noticing the time: I should have left five minutes ago.

I take a manic swig of beer and somehow, perhaps in my haste, the long neck beer bottle hits my front tooth—and *crack!* Half of my front tooth falls onto the ironing board.

It's one of those moments where the brain goes through denial.

No way that just happened.

No way that my front tooth is laying on top of my dress shirt.

No way that—*oh my god, that's my front tooth on the ironing board!* I panic, grabbing my tooth and bolting to the bathroom, and although I'm holding my tooth, the jagged edge prickly against my fingertips, I *still* think when I look in the mirror there will be a tooth.

There's no tooth!

When I smile and see the missing black hole where my front tooth should be, I feel faint. No way I'm attending Kate's premiere with a missing front tooth! I look like I'm wearing one of those Halloween fake teeth inserts, which can drastically change your look.

My tongue investigates where my tooth should be, and my armpits start leaking. My mind races for a solution leading me to the kitchen junk drawer for Super Glue. It's at least worth a try. I do have reservations about having glue inside my oral cavity, but with minutes to spare, it's worth the risk. I frantically apply Super Glue to the tooth, affixing it to the other half inside my mouth, and for sixty seconds, I plead with God that the glue sticks. When I remove my hand, I'm relieved my tooth doesn't fall out. To the naked eye, it even appears normal. I'll just try not to smile too much. I take the Super Glue, just in case, and race off to Westwood.

As I approach the theatre, minutes to spare, I'm taken aback by all the media hoopla. There are barricades to keep screaming fans out, cameras clicking, and reporters interviewing actors on the red carpet. I spot Kate giving an interview to *Entertainment Weekly*. She looks glamorous. I notice her mom standing in the background, and as I approach the rope, security stops me. I wave to Kate's mom, who lights up when she sees me, giving me the "just a minute" gesture.

After Kate finishes the interview, her mom points to me, prompting Kate to walk off the red carpet. "He's with me," she tells the guard who lifts the rope. She gives me a quick hug whispering in my ear, "I'm glad you're here. This red carpet thing is torture." Another reporter is asking for an interview, so I join her mother in the shadows of the media spotlight.

"Hey, mom," I smile, giving her a big hug. "I chipped my tooth on a beer bottle about half an hour ago. So if at any time you notice my front tooth is missing, you've got to let me know."

"Let me see," she says, seemingly amused.

I smile. She examines my teeth looking perplexed. "It looks normal. How did—"

"Super Glue. If it can hold a construction worker to the ceiling by his helmet, surely it will hold my tooth, at least for tonight."

"I'm glad you're here," she says, patting me on the back like a long lost son.

Kate's mom and I shadow Kate as she makes her way down the red carpet, an obstacle course of reporters with cameras. Once successfully down the carpet, Kate welcomes some other friends smart enough to wait at the end of the red carpet. There are maybe seven of us, and together we are a mini-entourage. We join the flow of traffic entering the theatre lobby, and I'm relieved my tooth is sticking. All is going smoothly until I look up—and who do I see joining the flow of traffic merging with our line, immediately exposing the cracks in my façade?

Penny…and *Nate*!

I do a double take, *is that really*…yep, it's definitely them, and as they approach hand-in-hand, looking like a glamorous Hollywood couple, I wonder how to escape without making a scene. Unless I duck behind Kate's mom, who is maybe five feet tall, or jump the rope and rush the exit, my path crossing their path is inevitable. I take a deep breath, put on my seat belt, and watch as Penny notices me first. I watch her nudge Nate who looks my direction, the surprise on his face mirroring mine. As they merge closer, I hope I can come across normal.

"Oh my god, what are you doing here?" Penny asks.

"You mean who let me in?" I joke. "I went to high school with Kate."

"Oh my god, she's so pretty," Penny says.

"She gets it all from her mom," I say, introducing Kate's mom to Penny and Nate.

"Nice to meet you," Penny says graciously, just as the line starts moving fast. Kate, who is maybe ten feet in front of us in line, turns and calls for us.

"I'll meet you inside," I say, to Kate's mom.

"I'll save a seat," she says, entering the theatre as I kick myself for not going with her.

Nate looks stunned. I'm equally flustered. There are people swarming all around, everyone there to be seen, which is both amusing and annoying. Penny is seemingly distracted by all the glitter as Nate gives me a penetrating look with a slight grin on his face. I wish I could snap my fingers and vanish. Nate breaks the uncomfortable silence, "You going to the after party?"

"Yeah. Are y'all?'

"We may check it out," he says.

"Cool. Hopefully, I'll see y'all there," I say, making an awkward exit.

I enter the theatre and find my reserved seat next to Kate and her mom.

During the movie, my mind is reeling as my soul slips into chaos.

The premiere party is held across from the Fox theatre on the top level of a parking garage boasting panoramic views of Westwood Village. It's decorated and catered first class with ice sculptures, open bars, and food fit for royalty. As I scan the fancy spread of shrimp cocktails, Maine lobster, and filet mignon, I wonder how I'm going to eat and keep my tooth glued on.

Gloria Gaynor prepares for a live performance of her infamous song, "I Will Survive," featured in the movie as I sit at Kate's reserved table with her mom, her agent and manager, and some of her friends. I excuse myself and walk the party, preemptively scanning the crowd, but I see no sign of Nate. I start to relax and breathe again. It's better that I don't see him. I don't want to get roped into that drama, so I order a beer and stand off to the side, taking a break from all the social stimulation. I have nothing against people, but these events are draining.

"We got to quit meeting like his," Nate's voice startles me back to reality. I turn to find him smiling, looking like a Hollywood star. His look is piercing, as though he sees right through me, temporarily disabling my defense against feeling the feelings that have been buried.

"I agree," I say, noticing he's alone. "Where's Penny?"

"She's stalking Keanu."

We both smile and there's an awkward tension.

"Good to see you, Bryan," he says, our eyes connecting in a way that is unsettling. I don't respond. I like seeing him, but it's easier when I don't, on account of what surfaces when I do.

"How's married life?" I say, throwing a cold towel on any covert flirting he may be doing.

He just grins, moving to the bar, noticing my empty beer. Nate orders three beers, hands one to me, leaving him holding two: one for him and one for Penny.

Nate motions for us to walk off to the side as Gloria Gaynor sings in the background. "Did you eat?" he asks.

"No. I don't have much of an appetite. Actually, I'm starving, but my front tooth happens to be attached by super glue," I confess, showing him the tooth.

"You can't even tell," he marvels, inspecting my smile.

I feel my tooth with my tongue, and I hope it sticks at least through the night.

"So, how you been?" he asks.

"Great!" I lie. It's as if Super Glue is holding my life together and at any moment it could all fall apart. He doesn't buy my forced, poorly acted response. Neither do I.

I take a deep breath, considering, "I'm..." I trail, as emotions surface.

And already the glue is losing its hold.

"I'm...well, I've been walking the straight and narrow since you and I, you know... I even started seeing an ex-gay therapist, but it hasn't led to the Promised Land leaving me thirty years old and a disillusioned ex-gay in the closet, which is overrated. And a bit isolating."

My sincerity touches him; I can see tears forming in his eyes. He doesn't say a word, but communicates nonetheless, and suddenly I don't feel so alone.

And suddenly we're not alone: Penny crashes our conversation with a plate of chicken wings. "There you are! I couldn't shake Keanu. I just wanted to introduce myself and say I liked the movie and all that crap, and all of a sudden it's like I became his entire focus! And I'm all—*hello, do you see the ring?* I'm married! But that didn't stop him. Oh, not Keanu. He thinks he can just take whatever he wants because he's Keanu, like I give a crap. Although he *is* cute, and we did share a brief, although meaningless, lip-lock. He's not as good as I expected, and the chemistry just wasn't there. Not on my end," she plays, looking at Nate adoringly. "Did you get me a—"

Nate hands her a beer on cue. "Thank god! I'm way too sober for this shit!"

She takes a swig of the beer as Nate and I can't help but be amused by her.

"So, anyone want a chicken wing?" She offers the plate, and I pass, as does Nate. "I haven't eaten all day so I could fit into my dress, but now that we're here and my dress is on and I've already made my entrance and everyone is drunk, I'm going to pig out. Sorry," she says, delicately picking at a chicken wing like a lady. "Excuse me as I gnaw like a rabid carnivore."

I nervously chug my beer, searching my brain for something to say and come up blank.

"Bryan!" I hear Kate's voice. She's motioning me over where she's talking with Keanu.

"You should go! It's Keanu for crying out loud!" Penny jokes.

I'm hesitant. "Well, I'll be back. Y'all aren't—"

"We're so outta here," Penny says, looking at Nate who shrugs as though he's wearing a straitjacket—which he sort of is.

"Good to see you, Bryan," Nate says, shaking my hand awkwardly.

Penny hugs me, trying not to get chicken wings on my white dress shirt.

I join Kate. As she introduces me to Keanu as her high school friend, I can't help but watch Nate and Penny walking hand-in-hand toward the exit. I notice Nate look back at me, and with one lingering look, he confirms all my ex-gay counseling isn't taking.

As Kate and Keanu continue to talk, my mind goes numb. Everything goes into slow motion and before I know it, I'm being pulled into a limo with Kate and her entourage. I remember champagne being popped, driving down Sunset Boulevard, and entering the House of Blues where a table is reserved for dinner, which is odd because it's close to midnight. After eating food I don't remember, the limo takes us to a house in the Hills for an after-after party filled with Hollywood types, but by now, the glue holding me together is starting to give way.

After an hour of milling about, I pull away from the social stimulus. Standing in the backyard of some strange Hollywood home looking out at the city lights, I feel like an outsider.

"You're not having fun?" Kate approaches.

"I'm just tired," I say, covering the drama brewing. "You were great in the movie."

"Really?" she asks, insecurities exposed. "You're not just saying that?"

"You were great, and you looked hot."

"I shouldn't have cut my hair."

"You should be very proud. You've come a long way since our waffle cone days," I say, giving her a hug that takes me back to the day I consoled her after the TV pilot wasn't picked up.

Kate calls me a cab, and after being dropped off at the parking garage in Westwood where I parked the Volkswagon GTI I bought from my roommate (a step up from the Metro), I collapse in the driver's seat, exhausted and scared. I think about Nate, imagining what *might* have been had I not left him standing on the beach in Malibu four years ago—and how easy it is to romanticize *what might have been*. With Nate, a missed opportunity has now become just a fantasy. The reality is that I made a choice. In my mind, it was a choice between Nate and God. And I chose God. My crusade, driven by faith and hope, has required cutting myself off from experiencing love. And when I think about this, all the emotions bottled up inside start to leak.

I wiggle my front tooth, and it comes out in my hand.

I think about how utterly alone I feel—not just alone, but lonely. My relationship with God, the one I've been praying to since a child, the one who I've been trying to chase, has become elusive. I replay the night in my head, trying to sort through my confusion and my life.

There's something missing. And not just my front tooth.

§ § §

After nine months of making the trek to meet with the ex-gay wizard, my disillusionment begins to crest. Joe claims to have *changed*. He's written books, he gives seminars—his whole ministry is based on the concept that change is possible. So, of course, I've been hoping he'd share the secret. I've been waiting for an *"Aha!"* moment when it all becomes clear, the roadblock to my hetero-urges removed, questions answered, and mystery solved.

But since meeting with Joe weekly, I actually have more questions than answers.

There is no doubt his entire theology is built on the premise that the Bible is the inerrant, infallible, and holy word of God. In his fundamentalist worldview, the practice of homosexuality is an unnatural sinful act, on par with pedophilia, bestiality, and polygamy.

"Take First Thessalonians, Chapter 4, verses 3-4," Joe says, citing scripture from memory to make his point. "Paul said, *'For this is the will of God, even your sanctification, that you abstain from fornication and that each of you learn to possess your vessel in honor.'* If you're a Christian, your body belongs to God, not you. It's a vessel of the Holy Spirit. One day you'll stand before the judgment seat of Christ and answer to Him for the way you've managed the body he gave you. It's not always easy. I know. It's every man's battle. God created sex, but he intended it to be shared between a man and woman and in the sacred context of marriage."

"But what if you're not married!" I say, beginning to lose my cool.

"The Bible says that for some, celibacy is a gift from God."

"And for those that burn with passion, the Apostle Paul suggested that it's better to marry."

"Yes, he did."

"So for a gay guy to deal with his lust in a godly way, his only option is to marry a woman?"

"Well, providing he has developed or can sustain an attraction to females."

"I may be going out on a limb, but my guess is that *ten out of ten* gay guys *aren't* attracted to females. That's what makes them gay! But you obviously think gay people can *change!*"

"From my experience, it depends on how long and deeply ingrained. If someone has always been exclusively attracted to the same sex, that person will probably always wrestle with some degree of homosexual attraction. But that doesn't mean that person cannot also experience heterosexual attraction, move into marriage, and have a normal marital life if he chooses. Or live a celibate life. I think heterosexual potential can grow even in the midst of homosexuality."

"Heterosexual potential?" I say, my eyes rolling, as I deflate on the lumpy sofa.

He looks at me thoughtfully, not saying anything, before jotting notes in his notebook.

He's very sympathetic to the plight of a struggling ex-gay and not judgmental in the least.

But after almost a year, week after week, spewing my life story, I'm beginning to crack. I still don't have the answers. *I've been following the yellow brick road and everything!*

"You have to tell me the truth. Does a naked woman turn you on?" I say, bluntly.

"I'm attracted to my wife."

"That's not what I asked. What happens when you see a *Playboy?* Does it turn you on?"

"I monitor very closely what I allow my eyes——"

"I know! But does a naked female spark actual *lust* in your body?"

"When I repented in 1984, I didn't pray for God to make me heterosexual. I prayed that I could be obedient to Him. Whether I would develop heterosexual feelings or marry a woman wasn't even a consideration. I just knew I was living outside of God's will."

"Okay, let me put it this way. Are there times you're still attracted to guys?"

"Well," he says, uncomfortable with the focus on him. "I'm sure it could be possible, but I don't put myself into situations where those impulses might be stirred."

"So, you're saying you still have *homosexual potential?*"

"It might be similar to how an alcoholic might feel going to a bar. Sure, some of the old feelings may stir, but that doesn't mean you have to take a drink."

"But they say an alcoholic is always an alcoholic. One day at a time and all that."

"Yes. That's true."

"So, if homosexuality is like alcoholism, then it follows that a homosexual is always a homosexual," I say, leaning forward to make my point. "And you claim to be straight."

"I am a Christian man committed to keeping my vessel

pure for the Lord's purpose. I spent many years struggling with lust, using pornography, and acting out in ways that were so far outside of God's will. I finally woke up and saw how I was misusing this gift of sexuality."

"But what if it's something we're born with? Must we repent of the way we're created?"

"Just because an inclination is innate, doesn't mean it's healthy or godly. We're all born with imperfections—we're sinful by nature—so just because something feels normal, doesn't mean that you were born that way. Even if one is born gay, it's doesn't follow that it should be accepted out of hand as good. No one would argue that a child born with a defect such as a cleft palette is exactly the way God intended. We come into the world with imperfections."

"So, homosexuality is an imperfection to be corrected like a cleft palette?"

When I get home that night, with doubts brewing, I pick up the phone and dial 411 to see if there's a listing for Doug. It's been seven years since I met him, and five since I last saw him at Stratton's. I find a listing in Orange County, writing down the number and staring at it for the longest time. I don't know what I'd say and question the wisdom of even calling—it's not exactly the ex-gay thing to do. Around midnight, with my roommates crashed, I dial the number, surprised when a male voice answers that definitely isn't Doug. I almost hang up.

"Is Doug there?" I ask, thinking maybe I have the wrong number.

The voice on the other end is hesitant and almost suspicious. "Uh...may I ask who's calling?" the voice asks, which makes me really want to hang up.

"Uh...Bryan," I say, feeling the need to explain my existence. "I'm a college friend."

"Hold on just a second," the voice concedes, although reluctantly.

I hear a muffling on the phone and finally a voice that rings a bell. "Hello?" Doug says.

"Hey. It's me," I say. He knows my voice.

He responds in a way that sounds like he's acting, "Bryan. How you doing? Long time no talk," he says in a fraternal, platonic way.

After a brief, awkward, strained conversation, I give him my number, hanging up completely shaken. Whatever connection we once had is gone—in fact, it was just weird.

The next day he calls, and his tone is completely different. He's back to the Doug I remember, and I discover the voice that picked up the phone is his *partner of three years*!

"We have a house together and dogs so you can't call

me. I don't want to mess this up, and he'll want to know who you are, and I'd rather him not know. I never told him about you."

"I just called to see if you wanted to grab a beer. It's been awhile."

"Dude, I can't. Jason was already thrown by your call. I played it we were frat brothers, so it's cool, but you can't call me again," he says, drawing a cutting boundary.

My heart sinks. My mind tangles. This is Doug, the one who vowed to play it straight until the day he died. A relationship with another dude didn't fit the plan he had for his life.

I guess plans change.

§ § §

I've long dismissed the conclusion of the American Psychological Association: *"The reality is that homosexuality is not an illness. It does not require treatment and is not changeable."*

The fundamentals of my faith have also put me at odds with the American Psychiatric Association, which *"opposes any psychiatric treatment, such as 'reparative' or conversion therapy."* They warn: *"The potential risks of 'reparative therapy' are great, including depression, anxiety, and self-destructive behavior, since therapist alignment with societal prejudices against homosexuality may reinforce self-hatred already experi-enced by the patient.*"

What does a man intent on pleasing God do when the church-endorsed solution to his problem comes with an APA warning? And with my own immersion into reparative therapy leading to a call to a suicide hotline and a psychiatric file riddled with depression, anxiety, and self-destructive behavior, I can't help but question whether *reparative therapy* is destroying me.

I've been following the yellow-bricked road, but at the expense of my psyche.

After almost a year of counseling with the ex-gay guru, I conclude Joe doesn't have the golden key. I even question his own change since he admits in the right circumstance, which he monitors and controls, even he is susceptible to homo temptations. How can one claim to be ex-gay and still have gay feelings? The ex-gay path has led me straight to a dead end.

Pulling back the curtain, I find the wizard is no wizard after all—just a man, a man on the wrong side of the rain-bow, a man no longer friends with Dorothy.

And when I look down, I find my heels already clicking.

CHAPTER 17:

LIKE A VIRGIN

After running into Nate at the premiere and subsequently discontinuing ex-gay therapy, instead of waving the white flag, I'm standing outside of a Rite Aid in Hermosa Beach debating with my new girlfriend, Ashley, which one of us will go in and buy the condoms.

I've rented a cheap motel room on the boardwalk for our big moment: Ashley and I are about to do it for the first time. She's a twenty-nine-year-old virgin tired of holding out for marriage and I'm a thirty-one-year-old disillusioned ex-gay still holding out for a miracle.

My intimacy with Ashley thus far has been clinical and exploratory (she'd never seen a penis close up; I'd never seen a vagina with the lights on). Our intimacy has felt much like playing doctor, which, when you happen to be thirty-some-thing, seems sort of backward.

To learn the finer points of female sexual satisfaction,

I sought out the counsel of Janice, the office lesbian, who taught me an oral exercise that required spelling out words with my tongue. At first I was just doing the alphabet, but soon became bored and began forming words, and then sentences. My oral trick had evolved into a complex and advanced form of communication.

"Ashley, can you hear me?" I spelled out with my tongue.

She moaned.

And then I decided to tell her my truth.

What better way to warn your girlfriend you're gay than through her vagina? "Ashley. This is not about you. But I am definitely gay," I communicated orally, but non-verbally.

Her moaning stopped: "Definitely what?"

Based on the bizarre ways she kept resurfacing in my life at a time when my ex-gay crusade seemed a bust, I thought maybe God was pulling a bunny out of the hat. That's how it happens in the movies—just when all hope is lost, a break-through leads the protagonist to victory. When the Karate Kid got his leg swiped during the climactic fight, it looked like it was all over, but then Miyagi did some magic and the Karate Kid triumphed with the one-legged Crane kick.

When I met Ashley, I was already standing on one leg.

The first time we met was at an Irish bar in Santa Monica for a birthday gathering of a girl I knew from church. Ashley was introduced as a former sorority sister of said birthday girl at Pepperdine and a writer/director, having just completed her first feature film. She was bubbly and cute with curly blonde hair, blue eyes, and a fair complexion. I enjoyed her company, but I didn't ask for her phone number; she gave it to me anyway.

I never called.

The second time we met was in my kitchen on a humid night in July when the house I share with Grant and Logan, friends from church, was overflowing with a diverse bunch of Christian singles singing peppy praise songs in my living room. My roommates are active in a Christian social club for the twenty-something evangelical crowd, and since I'm now thirty-something, I mingled with a few familiar faces, but lacked the enthusiasm I had in my twenties to meet and greet. I felt like a high school kid at a junior high party and went to the fridge for a beer, an act bound to rattle some cages. *"Lord, we lift your name on high"* I sang, grabbing a Guinness. *"Lord, I long to sing your praises!*—anybody else want a beer?"

Ashley did. So did the multitude of Jesus freaks standing in my kitchen, straining to hear the Olympic track athlete giving his testimony in our living room. I witnessed my stock of beer disappear, halfway expecting Jesus to show up and replenish the stash. According to the Bible, when Jesus was at a wedding party and they ran out of wine, he turned water into wine—his first miracle. When a turn of the faucet failed to yield Amstel Light, I went to the store.

Ashley asked to ride along with me.

On a beer run together for the Christian singles occupying my house—filled with the Holy Spirit, but thirsty for a pale ale—I felt a connection to Ashley, as if we were tuned to the same channel. She was quick-witted, funny, and absolutely smitten by me. I'm usually naïve, but she was definitely flirting. Our conversations seemed to dance with humor that only she and I were capable of appreciating. We returned with beer, relieved the "up, up" was winding down. My roommates had rallied the troops for an impromptu camping night in Malibu, and I immediately quelled all recruitment tactics by reminding them I had to be at work in the morning. Ashley was on board but needed a sleeping bag, so Logan, who grew up warming his backside against campfires in Oregon and brushing his teeth in fern-lined fresh water streams, suggested she borrow mine, which is really a hand-me-down from him. So I offered her my sleeping bag, warranting an exchange of numbers, marking the second time she gave me her number. And as she programmed *my* number into *her* cell, I knew she'd infiltrated the walls.

My phone started ringing—not in a *Fatal Attraction* way. She just "wanted to return the sleeping bag." I let her calls go to voice mail. After a week, I left a message kindly letting her know she could leave the bag on our front porch anytime.

I didn't mean to be rude. I was simply protecting her from falling for someone unable to reciprocate her feelings. The phone calls stopped, and she left the bag on the front porch.

A couple of months later, I joined a group of church friends for a concert featuring Christian artists at the Greek theatre in Griffith Park, an outdoor venue tucked away in the Hollywood hills. We had backstage passes granting us access to the VIP area where we enjoyed drinking wine on the outdoor private deck, which we reasoned was exactly what Jesus would do.

About a half hour before the concert, I looked up and had to do a double take when I saw Ashley enter the VIP room alone. She saw me about the same time I saw her.

There was no avoiding her.

She approached cautiously, and I stood to greet her.

"What are you doing here?" she asked, guardedly.

"What are you doing here?"

"My roommate is performing."

Her roommate was actually the main attraction, a talented singer/songwriter. I introduced Ashley to my church friends and joined her at the bar. We started talking and drinking until everything faded into the background. When my friends were exiting to find their seats, I promised to join them, choosing to stay with Ashley in the VIP area—where we both felt we belonged. It wasn't until her roommate took the stage that we slipped out to the reserved seats Ashley had in the front row, surprisingly next to her parents, also there to support the roommate. I met the parents briefly as the superstar roommate took the stage. After the concert we began searching the mass exodus filing out for my friends, until one of them, Brenda, found me.

"Oh my god! We've been looking everywhere! Everyone's in the car waiting."

"I can give you a ride home, if you want," Ashley offered, smiling flirtatiously.

It was only after Brenda left that I learned Ashley came with her parents, who seemed more than happy to give me a ride home. We jumped into the back of her parent's black Mercedes sedan and Ashley's dad started driving. The whole night felt magical. When they dropped me off, Ashley gave me her phone number for the third time.

"This time call me," she said, flirting like a schoolgirl.

"I will."

And I did.

We started making plans and going out on dates, and I began to see a glimmer of hope. *Maybe I can make it work with a woman.* I'd connected with Ashley in a way I hadn't with previous women. To my roommates, it appeared all the ex-gay counseling was taking hold.

After all, I had a girlfriend!

After several months of dry humping, Ashley and I decided we were ready for sex, leading us to this moment of playing *"Rock! Paper! Scissors!"* in the parking lot of a Rite Aid.

Her paper covers my rock and I'm off on a hunt for Trojans!

As I browse the condoms, although I'm thirty-one, I feel like a teenager. When I approach the Hispanic girl at the counter with the condoms, I'm so embarrassed that I have to take another stroll to fill my cart with other things. For many, buying condoms is like buying milk. For me, it's a guilt-ridden affair, as it means I'm having sex, which is a sin, unless I'm married.

And I'm not. Not yet...

I return to the parking lot with a pocket full of Trojans to find Ashley pacing, a mixture of excitement and fear. She's waited almost thirty years for this moment.

We walk to the motel hand-in-hand and although pre-marital sex is still a sin in our fundamentalist tradition, at least we're in a relationship, and for my sake, at least it's with a female. If this is something that goes well, then who knows? Maybe...

In preparation, I stealthily ordered the *Better Sex Video* series by the Sinclair Intimacy Institute—a heterosexual boot camp packaged in a three-volume VHS tape series (with bonus tape). I didn't want my evangelical Christian roommates, Grant and Logan, to know Ashley and I would be doing it, so I intercepted the mail the week the tapes came in discreet packaging.

Unwrapping the tapes, I read the covers with giddy anticipation: Volume 1: "Better Sexual Techniques" promised to *"…sharpen your sexual communication skills with the most updated sex facts from America's leading sex educators and counselors."* Volume 2: "Advanced Sexual Techniques" illustrated *"…specific positions and techniques for deeper penetration, for oral sex (fellatio and cunnilingus), anal stimulation, manual genital stimulation for men and women, plus demonstrations of male and female orgasm."* Volume 3: "Making Sex Fun: with Games and Toys" demonstrated *"…how incorporating adult toys can give a lift to love."*

The bonus tape, *"10 Best Kept Secrets to Sexual Satisfaction"* featured a happy hetero-couple on the VHS jacket with the caption: *"Sex. The More You Know, The Better It Gets."*

And that is my hope. After all, knowledge is power.

The couples demonstrating the techniques were billed as ordinary people, not actors or porn stars. While it may sound appealing to learn from typical couples, when I cued the first tape, I saw the drawbacks of watching typical couples have sex. These weren't people you'd ever want to see naked, so watching them demonstrate advanced sexual techniques was almost too much.

But in the hopes of tapping into my "heterosexual poten-tial," I forced myself to watch.

I didn't tell a soul I ordered the tapes, hiding them in the back of my closet and watching only when my roommates were out. And I definitely didn't tell Ashley. I didn't want to give her any indication that sex with her was something I needed to study for. I genuinely wanted sex with her to be great, even fantastic, something I'd want to do again and again. And again.

When we make it back to the Sea Sprite Motel in Hermosa Beach, it's early evening, and we have a box of condoms, a bottle of wine, and a king-sized bed. It's show time.

The room is a small apartment: kitchenette, living room, and bedroom with sliding doors that open right up on the busy Hermosa Beach boardwalk—dog walkers, bikers, tourists, and the homeless literally inches away on the other side of the glass. When the drapes are open, nine out of ten people passing by look inside, making it feel like we're in a fish bowl.

The room is in need of a demolition/update and suffers from an uninspired renovation that must have occurred before I was born. Finished in a palette of sea tones, there are pictures of seagulls affixed permanently to the coral pink walls, and the bedding has prints of seashells. This is a non-smoking room, but there are cigarette burns on the dresser and the stains on the ocean-blue carpet are disturbing. But it's the bed that makes me the most nervous, inspiring troubling visions of all the strangers who have come before us. I hope to God they wash the sheets.

It's not the Ritz-Carlton, but it's cheap, convenient, and charming in a weird *"I lost my virginity at the Sea Sprite and all I got was this stupid T-shirt"* kind of way.

Once inside the room, I open the sliding doors to air out a strange odor, a combination of Lysol and ass. The sounds of the ocean and the view of the Hermosa pier almost make up for the dingy, depressing room that I question is really worth ninety-nine bucks a night.

I'm relieved it's just one night.

"It looked better in the pictures," I say to Ashley, who is exploring the amenities, which takes two seconds because there are none.

"It's charming...and the location is great. You can hear the ocean," she says, finding the silver lining, just as a gang of intoxicated frat boys walk by, acting like intoxicated frat boys.

I close the sliding glass doors and draw the drapes for privacy, while Ashley excuses herself to slip into something more comfortable. She bought something from Victoria's Secret for our special occasion—something that is supposed to make me go wild with desire. And I pray to God it will. I try adjusting the florescent lighting to create a more romantic glow, but it's impossible. In the kitchenette, as I open the bottle of wine, a cockroach emerges from the drain and I instinctively turn on the water, watch it disappear, and then flip on the garbage disposal creating an unsettling crunchy sound. I move swiftly to the bedroom to set the stage.

"How you doing in there?" I talk to the bathroom door, gulping wine.

"The barb wire bra is a little tricky," she says, making me laugh.

Ashley burned a CD mix of "our songs" and other songs to define our evening, and I place it in the CD player to set the mood. When Madonna's "Like a Virgin" plays, I laugh out loud.

She sticks her head out the bathroom door. "That one's a joke," she says, smiling and quickly closing the door so I don't get a peek of her secret from Victoria.

I sit on the lumpy mattress, Madonna singing "Like a Virgin," as the real virgin prepares herself in the bathroom. Ashley is ready to get it over with already. She wanted to wait until she was married—her virginity a gift to her husband—but as she neared thirty years old, her virginity went on wholesale. Not that she'd just give it away to anybody, she's waited this long so at the very least it should mean something. And with me, it means something. We've done everything but intercourse, so really we're just taking it one step further. And although I've been diligent in doing my hetero-homework, I'm not exactly enthusiastic about taking the final exam.

The *Better Sex* videos were enlightening, but did little to bolster my desire for "the other."

Surprisingly, I learned more about gay sex than straight sex from the hetero *Better Sex* Videos, an entire section devoted to the man's prostate—the elusive G-spot for guys. It was shocking to watch women being taught the proper way to stick their finger, or sex toy, up their husband's ass to reach the obscure spot. Most men don't even know where their prostate is until they're older and an enlarged prostate begins bullying their bladder. But the hetero-experts at the Sinclair Intimacy Institute know all about the erogenous anal zone of men, with a whole line of "anal stimulators" to help the wife reach her husband's button. In their catalogue, I was stunned by how many of the toys looked like penises, with names such as *Swizzle Stick*, *NJoy Pure Fun Anal Plug* (medium and large), and *Men's Anal Pleasure Wand*. If a woman really wants to please her man, she'll spring for the *Rump Shaker Anal Vibrator* or the *Anal Foreplay for Couples CD: The Ultimate CD for Anal Curious Couples*. Anal curious couples? It follows that gay men don't need toys. And from the clitoral geography lessons, a woman doesn't need the male anatomy to reach her button. Strangely and unwittingly, the tapes make a case for gay sex.

I'm nervous about the sex part, especially with a virgin woman who has waited thirty years, but even more anxious about the consequences of having sex part: the commitment I've made to Ashley and myself. *What if I'm unable to be the man she thinks I am or the man I hope to be?*

Jesus may love me, but my relationship with Him hasn't made the fact that there is a woman in the next room preparing to have sex with me any more alluring. In light of how I kept pushing her away before finally going out with her, I've been thinking maybe God is trying to tell me something. Maybe Ashley is meant to be my wife, "the one" I've been praying for since I was a teenager. Maybe there is hope for me after all. Maybe...

As I contemplate the potential divine element in my relations with Ashley, she emerges in a silky black negligee with white fringe, and I can see why Victoria kept it a secret. It looks like a provocative French-maid Halloween costume, one that comes with a duster and maybe a whip.

"It looked better in the store," she says, pulling at it self-consciously. "The lighting is always better in the dressing room."

"You look beautiful," I say, assuring her. And she does, but it doesn't necessarily incite a riot in my hormones, which has nothing to do with her. Jenny McCarthy in the same outfit would produce the same tepid response. Ashley walks self-consciously over to me. "You really do look hot,"

I say, stroking her ego, which I learned from the tapes is good foreplay.

"Where's your outfit?" she jokes. "I went to all this trouble, and you're wearing jeans?" She takes a seat next to me on the king-sized bed as I hand her a glass of wine.

"My bad. I forgot to pick up my rhinestone G-string from the dry cleaners. You'll have to deal with my birthday suit," I joke, lamely. "Cheers," I say, toasting my glass.

"Cheers," she says, smiling nervously, clinking her glass against mine.

The next morning, I wake to the sound of a homeless person urinating in the flowerpot outside the motel window. It takes a moment to get my bearings, my eyes investigating the semi-dark room: an empty bottle of wine, torn condom wrappers on the bedside table, and my clothes and Ashley's costume strewn throughout the room. A sliver of morning sun peeks through a slit in the curtains, illuminating and dancing across Ashley's blissful and angelic face.

She's no longer like a virgin, and I'm still kind of...*gay*.

For a person with a natural inclination toward members of the opposite sex, the very idea of having sex with someone of their own gender is undoubtedly disgusting, maybe nauseating.

It makes no sense whatsoever.

And that's the feeling I have waking up next to Ashley. Having sex with a woman makes no sense whatsoever. Not only was I a participant, like an actor on a set, but also an observer, the director making sure the actor was doing what he's supposed to. I moved through the full arsenal of advanced sexual techniques I'd learned, most surprisingly feeling competitive with the guys in the videos. Physically they had nothing on me, and if *they* could move a woman to bliss, then I *definitely* could. At one point, I even thought I had the potential to be an incredible lover if I applied myself, but when I made it south of the border, it proved, once again, to be a total boner shrinker. It was only with the help of the *Better Sex* video tutors, who became more attractive in my imagination as the night went on, that I was able to perform. I hated that I had to picture a dude in order to put wind in my sail, but the fear of never making it out of the harbor, especially with an eager virgin, required desperate measures. Even though much of the night felt like holding my nose and taking my medicine, I was determined to make it worth Ashley's wait, even if it was all an act. And while I might have passed the final exam, it's crushing to know I had to cheat. The *Better Sex* videos have a money-back guarantee, and as I consider returning them, Ashley's eyes open and look at me sweetly, the sunlight highlighting the sea-tone blues in her eyes.

"Good morning," she says, reaching out and gently caressing my arm.

"Good morning," I say, masking my dilemma.

Maybe I need to give it more time. Maybe it's like eating tomatoes. I used to hate them, but grew to tolerate them and eventually to really like them. Maybe that's how it is with the female fruit. Maybe it's an acquired taste.

"That was amazing," she gushes. She kisses my face and neck, before moving down under the covers leading to a sobering truth that I can no longer gloss over.

In order to perform with a woman, I have to pretend she's not.

CHAPTER 18:

THE BIG APPLE

The next month, on a gray day in March 2001, I'm riding the elevator up inside the Empire State Building. Once I make it to the top, I plan on jumping.

Howard pledged if I hadn't made it to New York City by the time I was thirty, he'd take me.

I'm thirty-one.

I had arrived in a limo with Howard yesterday, and already my unresolved issue has reached a feverish pitch, leading me once again to the edge—except this time it's 102 floors up. The turmoil is so unbearable that instead of climbing the stairway to Heaven, I'm taking the lift.

The night before I left for New York, Ashley accompanied me to Macy's on Third Street Promenade in Santa Monica to help me pick out fancy New York clothes. Howard and I would be seeing several Broadway shows, requiring dressy attire, which my closet is purposefully lacking. That night, while browsing Macy's clearance rack, I told Ashley how much she meant to me and that I believed we had a future together.

Now, less than forty-eight hours later, I'm on the verge of throwing that future away.

As the elevator climbs into the sky, I dig in my pocket and retrieve a matchbook from the trendy restaurant Howard and I dined at the night before: the matchbook is the source of my dilemma. Scribbled on the cover burns a phone number that has taken all my strength today not to call. My resolve is beginning to dissolve, throwing me into an unexpected tailspin, and as I ascend toward the heavens, I contemplate my options. I want more than anything to dial the number, but know that by doing so, my decision has consequences.

It surely won't go over well with my girlfriend.

The night before, I attended my first Broadway show, *The Producers*, with Nathan Lane and Matthew Broderick. It hadn't officially opened and was still in previews. After the show, we had 10:30 p.m. reservations at a trendy restaurant called Asia de Cuba, at the time rumored to be one of the hottest restaurants in New York City. Howard had always talked about the energy in New York City, and when we entered this swanky restaurant, I had little doubt we were at the epicenter. It was buzzing with beautiful people. We were greeted warmly by a tall, dark, and striking, twenty-something jock, sharply dressed in a black-on-black suit.

"Good evening," he said, with an accent I guessed to be Latin, maybe Brazilian, or from somewhere in South America—someplace exotic.

Howard told the stud we had reservations, and after checking the book, he grabbed two menus and led us into the dining room. Living in Los Angeles, I've seen some attractive humans, but the guy strutting us to our table was in a class all his own.

As we took our seats at the center of the restaurant, I was stimulated by the energy in the room, or maybe it was Rico Suave handing me a menu. His eyes were sensual and when they looked at me, it made me nervous. "Enjoy your dinner," he said, with a charming smile.

I didn't want Howard to catch on to my fatal attraction, but I couldn't help but steal a glance of the Latin as he walked away, exposing the fault line in my resolve. We both took in the sleek, modern dining room: expansive ceilings and a soaring two-level seating area enveloped by billowy white curtains, high-backed white banquettes, and seductive lighting. The centerpiece was an impressive fifty-foot long illuminated alabaster table for large parties or communal dining. A bustling bar upstairs offered a bird's eye view of all the action and a twenty-five-foot tall hologram of a lush mountain and flowing waterfall was mounted on the back wall, adding to the enchantment.

"It's designed by Philippe Starck," Howard said, commenting on the interior design.

"Who's that?" I said, showing my ignorance.

"A famous French designer; designs everything from furniture to clothing to architecture. He also designed the Mondrian hotel on Sunset. There's an Asia de Cuba there as well."

"Oh, I've been to that one," I said, recalling the night I met Kate, as well as a certain endowed soap star at the Sky bar.

Howard studied the menu as I spotted the Latin a couple tables over conversing and laughing with some guests. He looked up and caught me staring, and I quickly looked away.

"The Pan Seared Ahi Tuna with crunchy wasabi mashed potatoes and chimichurri sauce is excellent," Howard said, reading from the menu. "Although I'm leaning toward the Grilled Chipotle Glazed Strip Steak with gingered chickpea fries and calabaza melon slaw."

I glanced over the menu but was unable to focus. It was my first night in the Big Apple, and I was distracted by all the stimulation, not to mention the Latin.

"What looks good?" he asked, catching me looking at something not on the menu.

I refocused, hoping he didn't notice the object of my attention, which was going to be a true test because the Latin appeared to be looking back. "The Ahi sounds great," I said.

"Should we do Cosmos since we're in New York City?" Howard asked.

"Sure."

A busy blonde waitress appeared, giving off a model vibe, and I began to think the staff had been selected from a casting call. She was composed, professional, and recited the complicated specials from memory, which was impressive, before asking our drink order.

"Two cosmos," Howard said.

"Excellent. I'll get those started," she smiled and was off.

I took it all in, trying not to come across like I just got off the boat.

Howard started his career in NYC, struggling in those early years. When he returns, he likes to go first class, which explains the limo, the fancy hotel, and the expensive restaurants.

The waitress dropped off the drinks, and Howard offered a toast, "To New York City."

"To New York City," I said, raising my glass. "Thanks for the trip of a lifetime."

All my discipline in controlling my wandering eyes was going out the door, and when I took the first sip of my first New York City Cosmopolitan, I noticed the Latin checking me out. I quickly broke his gaze and focused my attention back on Howard, my heart skipping a beat.

I began to think the Latin was more than just a host, maybe he was the manager: one minute he was behind the bar helping the bartender or helping deliver food to tables, the next he was making rounds, ensuring guests were happy. He appeared to be the grease that kept the place running smoothly. He had to be a model—one I had no doubt would be successful.

"I think it's good to get the lay of the land, so I arranged a tour for you tomorrow morning that will take you to all the major sites in Manhattan," Howard said. "It's only a few hours, then an eight o'clock show, with dinner at Joe Allen afterwards. They have incredible meatloaf."

Howard loves the theatre, making annual trips to New York and London to see as many shows as possible, usually two a day. "You mentioned Kate is here," Howard said. "She's welcome to join us for dinner either night. Just let me know so I can adjust the reservations."

"I'll call her tomorrow. She said her work schedule is crazy."

Kate had been living in New York for the last few months, working on a television pilot, and when we first arrived, I called her. She was on location in Queens and wanted us to drop by the set, but there wasn't time before the show. Hearing Howard mention Kate was surreal. I wouldn't know Howard if it wasn't for her. While I was at UCLA, Kate was always talking about her "acting coach, Howard." It was her referral that opened the door to his acting empire.

Howard excused himself to the restroom, and as I sipped my Cosmo, I saw the Latin looking at me. With Howard gone, I held the stare until I felt a vibrating sensation in my pocket.

It was my cell phone.

I turned the ringer off before the show and when I pulled it out under the table, blood rushed back to my brain when I saw Ashley's number. It's rude to answer at the table, so I let it go to voicemail, slipping the phone back in the pocket of the slacks she helped pick out.

Ashley's call inspired me to rein in my lust for the Latin who was opening a bottle of wine a few tables away. As he pierced the cork with a corkscrew and began unscrewing, he looked at me the entire time. There was no denying this turned me on, as the vibrations in my pocket weren't coming from my cell phone. It only takes a spark to get a fire going, and I wished I could just douse myself with ice water. My pastors, Bible study brothers, and Christian counselors would conclude that the devil was luring me into a trap, the Latin, an agent of Satan there to thwart my progress as a heterosexual. I have a girlfriend, so obviously I was being tempted to take a bite out of the Big Apple. But it was too late, I was under the spell of the Latin with the corkscrew, and when he popped the cork, I could hardly control myself, my entire body vibrating. Although Ashley and I have been sexually active for the last month, there was no denying that even in a Victoria's Secret negligee, she couldn't compete with a Latin dude wielding a corkscrew.

Howard returned just in time, and I tossed down the last of my Cosmo.

"You're supposed to sip," Howard joked. "This isn't a frat party."

I'd never had a Cosmo before. At bars, it was not something I ever ordered. I always ordered beer, usually Guinness. But in New York City, I was opening myself up to new things.

"Shall we order wine?" Howard asked, catching me staring at my empty Cosmo glass.

"Definitely."

After an amazing dinner with Howard, I excused myself

to the restroom. "It's upstairs, toward the back," Howard said, pointing me in the right direction.

The energy of my first night in New York City made me feel alive and daring, or maybe it was the Cosmo and the wine, but as I walked to the restroom, I made sure the Latin noticed.

He did.

We exchanged a look as I walked up the stairs. I was afraid to look back. If he was there, it could lead to crossing a line—a line that kept moving with every second. It's one thing to flirt from a safe distance, but as I approached the bathroom, I began to regret my flirt with disaster.

It was too risky. Especially with my gay acting coach downstairs! Howard knew me as the conservative Christian with a girlfriend who gave him a Holy Bible for his birthday. If he were to discover I was flirting with the macho maître d', he'd see behind the role I've been playing. I entered the bathroom and locked the door and began begging God for strength. As I washed my hands and splashed water on my face, I took a look at the man staring back at me in the mirror, still unsure if I could live with him and his desire for corkscrews instead of negligees.

I took a deep breath, said another quick desperate prayer, and exited the bathroom to find the Latin waiting for me, his smile disarming my defenses.

"Hey," I said, unsure really what to say. Our eyes had already said plenty.

"I'm Hector," he said, extending his hand.

I took his hand and he had a firm grip. "Bryan."

"Nice to meet you," he said, thick with an accent.

The chemistry was volatile, my mouth forming words without double-checking with my brain. "I have a girl-friend, but I really want to ask for your phone number. Is that strange?"

"You have girlfriend?" he said, suddenly hesitant.

"She's in California. She has no idea that, well, you know..." I trailed off, saying the rest without words. He grabbed a restaurant matchbook, scribbled his name and number and handed it to me with a sly grin. I'd never met anyone named Hector. I hastily returned to the table with the matchbook in my pocket and a dilemma burning in my brain.

"Do you want dessert?" Howard asked, perusing the dessert menu.

"Anything chocolate," I said, picking up the menu.

"Latin Lover?" Howard asked.

"Excuse me?" I said, suddenly paranoid.

Howard pointed to the menu and the first dessert was named, *Latin Lover*. "Flourless chocolate cake with chocolate-layered mousse and white chocolate coffee anglaise," Howard read from the menu, and I began to breathe again.

"That's the one for me," I said, closing my menu.

"If you are going to have the Latin Lover, then I will have the—" he couldn't finish before Hector approached our table, triggering a panic attack inside of me.

"Gentleman, how was your dinner?" he asked, cordially.

"Excellent," Howard replied.

"Very good," I said shyly, hoping Howard didn't sense the subtext.

"Could I bring you something from our dessert menu, compliments of the house?"

Howard looked at me, gesturing for me to order first.

"Uh...I'll have the..." I said, fumbling with the menu, as if I'd forgotten what to order. "The Latin Lover." That prompted a slight grin from him, and I quickly looked away because his seductive eyes were hypnotic and if I looked too long, Howard *would know.*

"Excellent choice," he said. "And you sir?" he asked Howard.

"What's your sorbet of the day?"

"Coconut. It's very nice."

"Perfect. And a Cappuccino," Howard ordered politely.

"Excellent," Hector said with a tantalizing smile before strutting away, leaving me with sweat pouring out of my pits and high blood pressure.

"The service here is fantastic, don't you think?" Howard commented.

I nodded in agreement, taking a long drink of ice water.

The elevator doors open on the 86th floor observation deck of the Empire State Building and the view of the New York City skyline is breathtaking. My plan to jump is foiled by the iron bars enclosing the observation deck. Instead, I approach a coin-operated viewfinder, fish out a quarter and scan the city, overwhelmed by the vastness. There are so many buildings!

I locate various landmarks from the tour that morning, the World Trade Center one of them, which on this cold March morning in 2001, dominates the skyline. At the top, it is eerily quiet, even peaceful in contrast to the frenetic streets below. I'm amazed that from this vantage I can see Pennsylvania, New Jersey, Connecticut and Massachusetts. As I take in the view, my phone vibrates in my pocket, and it's Kate. I ask where she lives so I can locate her in my viewfinder. She tells me she lives on West 57th street near Central Park and has the afternoon off if I want to stop by. I have the rest of the day to myself, as Howard made other plans to give me time to explore. I write down Kate's address, deciding to walk to give me time to think.

As I wander the streets, I'm shocked more people aren't killed by cab drivers. When I make it to Times Square, I stop in my tracks. I've seen it so many times on TV, my senses bombarded by the advertising, video billboards, traffic, and tourists. I sit on a bench, wishing I'd worn different shoes. I'm wearing my fancy New York clothes—slacks, a sweater, and dress shoes not made for walking the streets of Manhattan. I pull one off, blisters already forming. I sit a moment, taking it all in, absorbing the sights, sounds, and smells of New York City.

I feel alive and invigorated. I think about Ashley, whom I spoke with during my tour this morning. She was glad to hear I was having a good time and told me she missed me.

I hate that I don't miss her as a certain matchbook burns in my pocket.

All day I've been at war with myself.

I want to call the number on the matchbook, but by doing so—*wait a second! I'm not married. There's no ring on my finger!* Not yet anyway. And if Ashley and I walk down the aisle together one day, it's better to get the Latin Lover out of my system now. All my friends who have married had wild bachelor parties, the groom granted one last night with naked females gyrating all over them before committing themselves to just one woman. Hector could be my last hoorah before I commit myself to a woman for life. Besides, an experience with Hector is geographically desirable since we live on opposite sides of the country. It would be easy to have an anonymous encounter and get it out of my system for once and for all.

I take the matchbook out of my pocket and anxiously dial the number, pacing back and forth in Times Square. When I get his voice mail, I leave a message. "Hey, Hector. This is Bryan. From the restaurant last night," I say, my voice shaky. I leave my number and hang up with my adrenaline pumping and my mood lifting. The ball is now officially in his court.

"You've been walking this whole time?" Kate asks, examining the blisters on both my feet.

"I got a little lost," I say, running my finger over the blisters, "Should I pop them or—"

"Don't touch them!" she warns, leaving the room and returning with Neosporin, a needle and Band-Aids. She plays the role of nurse as I observe her apartment. On the 19th floor of a fancy high rise on West 57th, I peer out expansive windows with partial views of Central Park.

"Do you want to or do you want me?" she asks, eyeing my puffy blisters.

"You seem to know what you're doing."

She takes a lighter to the needle to sterilize it as my eyes go to a large 3x5 foot canvas showcasing an abstract painting in progress. She notices me checking out her work.

"I've been expressing myself lately," she says, mocking her artistic expression.

"It's good," I say, trying to make sense of it: words of a poem, abstract figures of people, objects from nature, the sun, moon, and stars. "I'm trying to interpret what you're expressing here," I say, as she lances a blister and cleans it with a rag as if she's been doing it all her life.

"What do you think is going on with me?"

I study the painting as she applies Neosporin to my wounds. "I'd say you're lonely, depressed, and not taking your meds."

"Exactly," she says, covering my wounds with Band-Aids. "It's been hard living here. I'm just so burnt out working. I have maternal urges, and my clock is ticking and all that."

"You want kids?"

She nods and I sense her frustration and desire to start a family.

It's weird to think I once imagined being the father of her child. I didn't necessarily spend a lot of time indulging this option, no more than any other guy who contemplates the consequences of a broken condom, but if I had a chance to reproduce, I'd want Kate to be the mother. She's naturally nurturing, and I have no doubt will make an incredible mother.

"What about you?" she asks, bandaging my feet like I'm a kid with a booboo.

"Well, I have a girlfriend."

"Really? That's great. Who is she?"

"Her name is Ashley, and we met through church friends, sort of. She's a writer and a director and just finished an independent film that she's submitting to festivals."

"Wow. That's great!" she says, genuinely happy for me. "There. You're all fixed up," she says, admiring her work on my bandaged feet. "Is she someone you could marry?"

This question stumps me, the vibration going off in my pocket further complicating my response. "I don't know. We'll see. Too early to tell," I say, standing up abruptly.

It could be Hector calling me back.

Or Ashley.

"I'm gonna use the bathroom," I say, excusing myself.

"Do you want some tea?"

"Sure," I say, closing the door to the bathroom. I check the voice mail and my stomach drops like I'm on a roller coaster when I hear Hector's voice saying he looks forward to meeting. I put the phone back in my pocket and exit to find Kate heating water in a kettle on the stove.

"Chamomile, Earl Grey, or English Breakfast?"

"Uh...Earl Grey is fine," I say, moving over to the bay window. The view is amazing: New York City skyline, Central Park, and all the people scurrying around like ants.

As the kettle heats up, so does the crisis in my head. I want to tell Kate. I want to tell her I answered Doug's ad the day we went rollerblading through Beverly Hills almost a decade ago. I want to tell her about Nate and the steps I'd taken to un-love him, and then seeing him and his wife Penny at her premiere. And I want to tell her about Hector. *I want to tell her everything.*

My conflict has formed festering blisters on my soul.

As the kettle whistles, words of truth begin forming on my tongue.

She hands me a mug of Earl Grey and a scone, joining me on the window seat, softly blowing on her hot tea. As I prepare to expose the ugly sores on my psyche, I open my mouth, but the words get stuck: *what if she feels betrayed that through all of these years—from dipping cones at sixteen to sipping tea and scones at thirty-one—I've been acting?*

"How are your feet?" she asks, relishing a rare moment of tranquility.

"Better. Thanks."

My feet will heal. The rest of me, I'm not so sure.

I leave Kate's and walk to Central Park; the streets are manic so I retreat into the park to think and pray. The bandages are helping, but walking is painful, so I find a bench. Dark clouds are suffocating the sun, and it's getting colder. Spring hasn't sprung. I watch two squirrels chase one another as I chase sanity inside my brain. Who do I call? Do I call Hector?

Or do I call Ashley?

I dial Ashley, hoping that a conversation with her will pull me from the edge. She's glad to hear from me, and I give her my impression of the city. After hanging up, I decide I won't call Hector back. I take a cab to the Waldorf-Astoria in midtown Manhattan to spare my feet. When I arrive, I find Howard already dressed for the evening, reading the *New York Times.*

The Waldorf-Astoria hotel, an Art Deco landmark, is rich with history. Everyone who is anyone has slept here. But when I first entered our suite with two full-sized beds, it just seemed dated. It feels like we're staying in a museum and any minute the Queen of England is going to pop out of the closet and begin serving tea and toasted crumpets.

"How was the day?" he asks.

"Great," I report enthusiastically. I tell him about the tour and the sights. "Kate won't be able to meet," I say. "She has an early call but told me to tell you hello."

That night we see another Broadway show, followed by dinner at Joe Allen, a restaurant popular with the theater crowd. Although physically present, my mind is a million miles away. I'm thinking about Hector, and how I really want to meet him again, but know if I do...

I'm sitting across from my openly gay acting coach, whom I have the utmost respect for, and I'm unable to talk honestly about the gay part of me that I've cloaked with my evangelical Christian identity. Instead, we talk about the play and New York City. He talks about how poor he was when he first started his acting studio and last year's experience of directing a one-man show on Broadway and the thrill of actually seeing his name in lights on a Broadway marquis.

Howard is one of my favorite people on the planet, and yet I can't tell him the truth about me. It's not that I fear he won't accept me. On the contrary, he would undoubtedly accept me.

The problem is *I* can't accept me.

After dinner, we take a cab back to the hotel, and although I'm tempted to call Hector, I resist. I haven't called him back since he returned my call earlier while at Kate's. I go to sleep praying I'll be able to be as strong the next day, my last day in New York City.

* * *

I wake up thinking about Hector. I can't get him out of my mind.

There's something about New York that feels so... anonymous.

I call Ashley, and after I hang up, I know I have to meet Hector. I work it out in my head that this will be my last experience. Ever. After this, I'm done with all this homo-erotic bullshit.

I'm going to marry Ashley.

Like a bachelor looking for his last yahoo before settling down, I promise myself that this will be the last time. I call Hector, and he's glad to hear from me, bummed I hadn't called back the day before. I tell him it's my last day in New York and I have plans for an 8:00 p.m. Broadway play and 10:30 p.m. dinner reservations. He's willing to meet me afterwards.

We make plans to meet at Grand Central Station at midnight.

I meet Kate later that afternoon at a trendy spa in the basement of a department store on Madison Avenue where she's having a pedicure. She suggests I could use one as well and makes an appointment for both of us. I feel sorry for the Chinese woman stuck washing my calloused and blistered soles. As we get our feet scrubbed, I talk more about Ashley, not letting on that I'm meeting a Latin dude at Grand Central Station at the stroke of midnight.

During the play and dinner with Howard, all I can think about is Hector.

After Howard and I return to the hotel shortly before midnight, I tell him I'm not ready to crash, and since it's my last night in New York, I'm going to take a walk. I slip into the night, uncertain where my adventure will take me. The brisk night air makes me feel alive as I begin to roam the streets like a caged animal freed to follow its most primal instincts. I walk toward Grand Central Station, calling Hector to let him know I'm on my way. He's already there, but suggests that since it's past midnight, the adjacent Grand Hyatt might have a better ambience.

I enter the magnificent lobby with mirrored ceilings, a large, calming waterfall, and a comfy seating area with club chairs. It's late, so the sprawling lobby is empty—except for Hector, reclining in a club chair dressed in jeans, an athletic fleece, and baseball cap.

"Hey," I say, intimidated by his good looks. I can't believe I'm actually seeing him again. He stands, extending his hand, looking like an Abercrombie and Fitch ad. We shake hands like old friends, and I sit opposite him, trying to act casual, but manic inside. He reclines confidently, an Adidas duffel bag at his feet, and he's looking at me slyly with a mischievous grin.

"So who are you?" I ask, smiling through my discomfort.

"Hector," he says with an accent. "Hector is Latin for anchor."

This intrigues me because I feel like a ship in a storm. "Where's your accent from?"

"Cuba," he says, contradicting my guess of Brazil.

"Cuba?" I say, surprised. I don't really know anyone from Cuba: Gloria Estefan and Elian Gonzalez, but that's it.

"Where are you from?"

"Texas originally. But I've been in California for over a decade."

"So your girlfriend doesn't know that..." he starts, but I'm already shaking my head. He looks away, troubled that I have a girlfriend who doesn't know I'm meeting a stranger at midnight. "You look for one night stand," he says bluntly, his accent thicker than I remember.

"Uh...well, I'm not sure what—"

"I'm not into one night stand. It's cheap," he says, laying it on the line.

"Well, I live in California. And I have a girlfriend," I say, reiterating two telling facts that illuminate my motives, which are obvious and cheap.

"What's your last name?"

I hesitate. "I'd rather not tell you my last name," I say, guarding my anonymity.

"You don't tell me your last name?" he says, growing impatient. "You want anonymous sex and that doesn't interest me," he says, standing to leave.

"Christopher," I say. "My last name is Christopher."

He looks at me shaking his head, torn between staying and going, and then slowly sits. "A one night stand is like licking icing off cake," he says. "It tastes good, but it doesn't satisfy."

"So, what are you saying?"

"I want the cake."

We're at a standstill.

"Are you...well, are you gay?" I ask, cringing when I say the word "gay."

He looks at me baffled, gesturing his place opposite me in the Grand Hyatt past midnight. *Duh.* He isn't bi-curious or living on the down low, he is openly gay and out to his family, who are all fine with his being gay. He is the youngest of eight children. He doesn't have any hang ups or shame about being gay—it's just a neutral part of his being.

This gives me pause: I've never been with a gay guy before. I prefer guys with girlfriends. The fact he's gay would be a deal breaker if I lived in New York, a threat to my cover. But since I live in California, I decide to make an exception. He lives with a cousin in Brooklyn and came to New York City for modeling, which makes sense. I'm surprised to learn he's twenty-four years old, seven years younger than me, and the more we talk, the more I'm aware of the age difference. He reminds me of me at that age when I returned to Hollywood to chase my dreams, full of optimism and hope. Now I'm a jaded and bitter thirty-one year old, so I can't help but view his youthful ambition as naïve. He had two casting calls earlier, so has his modeling book in his bag, and when I ask to see it, he pulls it out proudly. After thumbing through a few pages, I have no doubt he will make it as a model. In fact, he might be the perfect specimen of the male species.

"I did Swatch campaign and have billboards all over the city," he says proudly. "A big one on 46th and Madison, you see?"

"No, but that's great," I say, trying not to drool on the pictures of him in a bathing suit.

After talking for over an hour, the tension has built and we begin exploring options of where we might go to be alone. Going to his cousin's place in Brooklyn is out, and I can't exactly take him to the Waldorf-Astoria, so we leave the hotel and start walking down Park Avenue.

Although cold outside, the sexual tension is boiling.

We finally settle on a ratty old hotel on a side street. I offer to put it on my credit card, although I cringe at the thought this night will be forever recorded in my credit records. I don't want the hotel desk clerk to know I'm with a dude, especially since I'm checking in without luggage, so I ask Hector to wait outside. After I get the room key, I go to the decrepit, filthy room and call Hector with the room number. In minutes he's at the door, both of us examining the room, questioning if we might catch something from lying on the bed. We walk over to the window, which offers a tremendous view of the grungy rat-infested alley.

"The view rooms were extra," I say, chuckling nervously.

"We're not here for the view. At least that view," he jokes, stripping to the nude in less than two seconds, revealing a body that would've made Adonis insecure. His skin is smooth, like a swimmer's body, with makes me think that man grooming is mandatory for models.

I drop my slacks, and I'm sporting the New York City themed boxer shorts Ashley and I found on the sales rack at Macy's, featuring cheesy pictures of New York landmarks. He notices the boxers, chuckling at the Statue of Liberty over my crotch, her torch rising.

"I've never seen the Statue of Liberty this close," he says, before lighting my torch.

There are no mental games. I don't need to watch a video to know what to do. But given the smoldering passion and desire that led us to this moment, the ecstasy proves fleeting and unsatisfying. As the flame flickers out, I'm lying in bed with a now familiar stranger in a seedy motel room in New York City, as a tidal wave of regret and shame overtakes me.

What did I just do?

I wish I could have jumped from the Empire State Building.

I have to get out of here. It's after 3 a.m. and Howard and I are leaving at 8 a.m. for the airport. I need to get back to the hotel. I need to... "So, I have to go," I say to Hector.

"No? Really?"

"You can stay as long as you want, but I have a flight in five hours," I say, grabbing my clothes and hurriedly dressing. He sits up looking like a male nude ready for an artistic rendering, before jumping out of bed and throwing on his clothes. "You're not going to stay?"

"Not without you. You crazy?" he says, looking at the depressing room. We dress, and then slip downstairs and into the street. I'm not sure how to end it and neither does he, but the ball is in my court. His eyes look at me differently, and I sense a sadness that catches me off guard.

"What's wrong?" I ask.

He looks away, seemingly surprised by his own emotions. "I just feel like I'll never see you again."

I don't know what to say, so I give him a manly type hug, the kind two straight guys give in public with the pat on the back. And I feel cheap, just as Hector predicted.

"Next time you're in New York, you have my number."

"I do," I say, knowing it will soon be deleted.

"Good luck with the girlfriend and everything."

I take one last look at him and walk away, hailing a cab to the hotel. And from the back seat of the cab, tears already swelling, I regret taking a bite out of the Big Apple.

Once back at the Waldorf, I sneak back into the hotel room, relieved to hear Howard snoring. In the bathroom, I change out of my clothes, placing my New York boxer shorts in a laundry bag for disposal later. I don't want any reminder of this night. I take the matchbook with Hectors name and number, tear it into a million pieces, and flush it down the toilet. I also delete his number from my cell phone. If I could erase my memory, I'd do that as well.

As I slip into my bed, I'm careful not to wake Howard sleeping soundly in the other bed. I lie there, disgusted with myself. Not only have I broken trust with Ashley, I've humiliated Hector by forcing him to play by my dehumanizing rules of anonymity. This realization brings tears, escalating to sobs that I muffle with my down-filled Waldorf pillow. The driving need that fueled the evening wasn't a desire to rebel against God, but rather a desperate attempt to meet needs not being met by Ashley, the need for intimacy and companionship that aren't inherently sexual. But by debasing sex to a purely physical act of the flesh, I actually crippled my ability to be intimate with another human being in a meaningful way. On this night I had hoped to temper future temptations, but fear I've done nothing more than temporarily numb my pain and further magnify my shame. I look at the clock, and it's almost 4 a.m. We're waking in three hours. I'm exhausted, but too upset to sleep. My life is spiraling out of control, and I wish I could die.

I pray, as I have many times before, that God will simply snatch me as I sleep.

Three hours later, I'm discouraged that I'm still on Earth and breathing.

Howard is awake, and he asks about my evening. I cover by saying that I went for a walk around the block and had a drink at a bar down the street. "Nothing too crazy," I lie.

Through the smoked glass of a super-stretch on our way to the airport, I watch Fifth Avenue blur by as Howard does the same, the limo feels vacant with just the two of us.

New York has been a roller coaster. I'm drained and

tired and afraid—afraid of what the future holds, afraid that I can never be the man Ashley deserves, afraid playing a role will eventually steal my soul. Because my fundamentalist faith doesn't allow for a healthy expression of my innate sexuality, I'm limited to one-night stands and anonymous encounters that can never be fulfilling and are potentially destructive. I'm reminded of all the high-profile evangelical pastors and conservative politicians caught pants down in gay affairs. They build their marriages and ministries on sand only to have the truth come and wash it all away.

I don't want to be that guy—living a lie, pretending it's true.

The truth always comes out.

And as I watch New York City whiz past me, I realize I'm already that guy.

"That looks like the maître d' from Asia de Cuba," Howard says, pointing to a billboard with Hector's image stretching two-stories tall.

I suddenly feel sick to my stomach, as though I just gorged on icing.

"It does look a lot like him," I say, using my acting skills to act like I hadn't just had cheap relations with the maître d' in a motel. It's overcast, but I put on my sunglasses to mask my drama. Howard observes the city with fondness, having no idea I'm barely holding myself together on the other end of the super stretch. I can barely breathe, my lies suffocating my soul.

I'm lying to Howard. I'm lying to Kate. I'm lying to Ashley.

And I'm lying to myself.

At the airport, I covertly slip the defiled New York boxers out of my suitcase and into a trash bin. It's a symbolic act: I'm throwing away the gay part of me. And although I'm leaving my intolerable queerness at JFK, I know I still have to tell my girlfriend the truth about me.

CHAPTER 19:

THE TRUTH ABOUT ME

I've just returned from New York, and I've called Ashley over for "the talk."

My plan is to tell her the truth.

No more lies. No more half-truths. No more pretending.

"There's something you should know about me," I start, realizing once these words escape, nothing good ever follows.

We are sitting in lawn chairs in the tiny front yard of the house I share with Grant and Logan in West LA. She takes a nervous sip of Amstel Light; it's dusk, and the streetlight just came on, casting a low amber glow across her face, growing brighter by the minute. I look at the dilapidated chain-link fence, considering the one around me that Ashley somehow hurdled. She's made it closer than most, leaving me with no other choice but to expose me—all of me.

I will tell the truth and let the chips fall where they may.

I don't want to hurt her, but anticipate this will be the end, although I'm not ready to give up. "I've had experiences...on both sides of the fence," I blurt out, unsure how to proceed.

Her brows scrunch together. "You mean with guys?"

I nod.

Her first reaction is denial. I see it. She even chuckles as if I'm joking, but the look on my face communicates I'm clearly not joking. I'm panicked, and she senses it.

"Are you serious?" she asks, studying my petrified face.

And then she looks at me as if it's the first time she's ever seen me. I can't look at her, so I stare at the grass wondering how to put out the fire I've started by telling the truth.

She looks away, shaking her head, processing this new information as I suddenly become short of breath, almost faint, as all the blood rushes to my face, prickly hot with shame. Ashley has seen me naked, but never exposed.

"I've had experiences," I say, whitewashing my reality. "Experiences that don't fit in with what I want for my life and what I believe God wants for my life. I want to be a husband and a father, I really do, but at times I've been curious, I guess, and before we go further I felt like you should know. I tell you this only because I see a future with you," I say, making me cringe.

She's gone into a state of shock, her brain attempting to accommodate this new information in light of the person she thought me to be. She cares for me, so she's holding on to whatever hope I give her. I'm not ready to let go of her either. Ashley is the ideal wife: supportive, driven, caring, funny, smart, and completely head over heels in love with me.

"There was a time when I thought, or had feelings that were..." she starts, surprising me. I'm drowning in a sea of shame, and she's throwing me a rope. "I was in junior high and felt romantic feelings for a girlfriend. It was confusing, so I appreciate the curiosity factor, and although I never acted on it, I'd be lying if I said it didn't cross my mind. So, the fact you've had thoughts and even experiences..." she says, clutching to the hope of a future together.

"My roommates know, and even my pastor, so I thought you should," I say, withholding details I'm certain will prompt her to jump the fence and run. If she can handle the truth about me, and still loves me, maybe she *is* the wife I've been praying for since high school.

"I just had no idea," she says. "I'm usually good at knowing that sort of thing, but with you, I just..." she whispers, trailing off, still shocked by the news, but trying her best to be supportive.

I'm breathing normally, and my heart is no longing trying to leap out of my chest. I take a swig of my beer, the streetlight now fully illuminated.

"I'm glad you told me," she says, reaching over and taking my sweaty hand, which forces me to come clean. She's handling the past, but how do I tell her the past includes last week?

"So, while I was in New York..." I say, changing the course of the conversation. "I didn't plan it, but one night I..."

She's hanging on to every word, so I stop my confession because with each word I'm just giving her more rope to hang me. "One night...*what?*"

I look away and my silence speaks loudly.

"One night *what*, Bryan?" she demands, withdrawing her hand of support.

"One night I...well, I..."

"You didn't...?" she gasps, as if the full brunt of my truth knocks all the wind out of her.

"There's no excuse for it, and I regret it. Believe me it was *awful*, which was reassuring in a stupid way," I say, doing damage control. But the damage has been done, and I see it.

"You were *with a guy* when you were in New York?" she clarifies, not hiding her horror.

"And it was one of the worst experiences of my life and only confirmed that I'm definitely *not gay*," I say. "It would be one thing if I enjoyed it, but I didn't. It was wrong and stupid and I'm sorry—and I know me saying I'm sorry doesn't excuse it, but you have to know that it only reinforced the fact that what we have is special," I say, wincing at my own words.

"Special?" she asks. She doesn't know what to do, and for a moment I think she might just get up and run away, a decision that I would completely understand. "I can't believe it," she says, becoming angrier as the truth sinks in. "We were together! The night before you left you told me for the first time you loved me!" And it's true. I did use the L word, which is not entirely inaccurate. I love many things about her, but I'm not *in love* with her.

"How could you!" she yells. "How could you tell me you love me one night and two nights later have sex with some guy in New York City?"

I don't have an answer.

Just then Logan pulls into the drive in his black Chevy truck with Oregon plates, returning from picking up his girlfriend at the airport who has been in Germany for nine months working with a Christian evangelical ministry. I brace myself as I've already opened up Pandora's box.

"Hey!" Logan says, opening the gate to the fenced in front yard with Beth, a perky Texan.

"Hey, Bryan, how are you?" she says, with a thick Texas accent. I try to cover the drama brewing in the front yard, but almost instantaneously Logan and Beth feel the tension.

"Hey, Beth, welcome back," I say, sheepishly.

We all turn to Ashley; she has hands on her hips and in no mood for pleasantries.

"Beth this is——"

"We're breaking up," Ashley snaps. "So you probably won't be seeing me again!"

"We're sort of in the middle of..." I start, and Logan is leading Beth to the front door.

"Sorry, y'all," Beth says, as they both duck for cover inside the house.

Once they're safely inside, Ashley explodes. "How could you? You and I were in a relationship. We had a commitment!"

"I know. I'm so sorry. It was stupid. I don't know——"

"What was his name?" she interrupts, indignantly.

"Why does that matter?"

"What was his name? I want to know his name!" she says, a little too loud for comfort. I look around to make sure the neighbors aren't gathered and watching the spectacle.

She's not giving up until she gets a name.

"Hector. And if it makes any difference, I flushed his number, cleared his number from my phone, and even threw away the boxer shorts I was wearing. It was——"

"I can't believe you," she says, looking at me like I'm a monster.

"I can't believe me either," I agree.

"I can't believe I fell for you," she says, shaking her head, which puts me on the defensive.

"I tried to protect you. As you might recall *it was me* that wanted you to drop the sleeping bag on the front porch, and *it was me* that didn't return your phone calls. My instinct when someone tries to get close is to push them away, but you were persistent and somehow made it over the wall—which made me think *maybe* God had sent you, that you were the woman I've been praying for, the woman I would marry, the woman who would—"

"The woman who would what?" she presses. "Save you? Free your inner heterosexual?"

I don't say anything, but her comment feels like a dagger.

"So, all the times we've had sex, were you faking it?"

"No, obviously not. I'm attracted to you," I say, unconvincingly. "I am!"

"Were you thinking of me when we had sex?"

"Of course," I deflect, not allowing my brain to even go there.

She tries to read me, but she can't, and her anger fades into tears.

"I'm so sorry," I say. "It's tragic. I'm losing you over a one-night stand that wasn't worth it. I know this sounds irrational and pathetic, but it gave me assurance that I can proceed into the future with you without the need to go down that road ever again because it's a dead end!"

"You and I don't have a future. *Obviously.*"

§ § §

Three weeks later, Ashley and I are on a plane to Austin, Texas, where my mom's side of the family is gathering for Easter. In the weeks I've been back from New York, Ashley has forgiven me and is giving me a second chance. Through it all, we've somehow become even closer.

If I can't be with someone I truly love, she's the next best thing.

I also assured her all the homo stuff wouldn't happen again. I'm done.

I'm thirty-one and it's the first time I've ever taken a girl home to Texas to meet the family, so I think my mom is already planning the wedding. My mom and Auntie Ann pick us up at the Austin airport, and they take to Ashley right away. The first night we have a family dinner at a cliff-side Mexican restaurant with panoramic views of Lake Travis, true Tex-Mex and killer margaritas. Everything is going smoothly; Ashley is getting along with everyone, my

family is treating her like one of the family, and the margaritas are giving me the illusion of hope. Maybe I can make
this work. Maybe I can marry her. Maybe I can…

"I love you," Ashley whispers, taking my hand underneath the table. She looks into my eyes adoringly but I can't
hold her gaze, and I look away, taking a gulp of the Texas-
size margarita.

"I love you, too," I say. She seems to buy it, but I don't.

Even with the numbing effects of tequila, I'm still
playing a role.

I wake up the next morning clammy, sore throat, and a fever,
the torment inside taking its toll physically. Over the next
couple days, Ashley and my mom take turns nursing me to
health, my mom treating Ashley as the daughter-in-law she's
been waiting for all these years.

On Easter Sunday at the country club brunch, my mom
props us up for a battery of pictures. I do my best to mask
my suffering and appear normal, holding hands with Ashley
as we pose with the Easter bunny. Later that afternoon, on
the ride back to the airport, my mom and auntie are chatting
with Ashley, wishing her luck with her film and promising to
visit us in California. It's endearing to see them include her
in our family, but I wonder if they'd be so accommodating if
I'd brought home a dude. They notice I'm quiet, but I excuse

my silence with the fact I'm still not feeling well—which is true. If they only knew what my silence is screaming.

On the flight back, Ashley and I are in 23A and 23B, holding hands, her head resting on my shoulder. There's a false sense of comfort in these small hetero-gestures, as they mask the truth, making me feel less gay. I replay the weekend, which felt like one big charade: Ashley and I held hands, and we posed for pictures; she exchanged email addresses with my mom. We were the perfect couple, except for one rather significant detail: I don't love her.

Not only that, but I'm deceiving her, and everyone else—including myself—into thinking I'm even *capable* of giving her the love she deserves.

I know from the outside, we look normal—a man and a woman—but on the inside, I'm in a heartrending state of turmoil. I'm still living a lie. I'm still playing a role.

I'm still avoiding the truth about me.

§ § §

On a warm day in May, I'm in my office, the door closed, and I'm sitting across from Janice.

"I'm not *flirty* with Charles. What are you talking about? I have a girlfriend!" I say.

"You and Charles should join Karen and me for a double date," she says, teasing me.

"Look, I get it. Maybe asking you for a clitoris tutorial might, in your mind, be a red flag, but really, I come from a fundamentalist background and—"

"You didn't even know where it was!" she laughs, playing me like an annoying sister.

But she's right. A curious dynamic has evolved with Charles over a year's time.

When I'm around him, my soul is at ease. I've been everybody else, but with him, I feel like something closer to myself. Janice has picked up on this. Maybe she sees how my heart quickens when he's around or the way I look up from my desk when he arrives or leaves.

"It's just dinner; we can combine business with pleasure. We'll meet the producers from Chiat Day for drinks, and then Karen can meet the three of us at a restaurant for dinner."

"You're sneaky. I'm on to you," I say, with a smile, seeing right through her shenanigans.

"Great. I'll make the reservations," she says, skipping away.

"Where are we going?" I say, calling after her.

She turns and smiles as big as Texas. "Marix Tex Mex in West Hollywood."

"Are you serious? That's the gayest place in the city."

"It's Tex Mex. You're both from Texas. How's eight?" she says, her plan in motion.

Sitting in Marix Tex Mex, I find Janice's partner Karen sweet and soft-spoken, not as rough around the edges as Janice, who has fun with the lesbian stereotypes. She once showed up at work on her beefy motorcycle, and when she saw me watching, laughed at herself: "I know. I'm such a cliché." Karen and Janice met in college on the East coast, both on the field hockey team, and now they're going on eight years. I make it through dinner without breaking into show tunes or groping Charles under the table. I am out to prove her wrong.

But after dinner, as Charles and I watch Janice and Karen drive away in Janice's macho Ford Bronco similar to Vince's, I turn to Charles. "You want to grab a drink?"

"Where?"

From the Marix parking lot, I notice a local bar tucked away around the corner. We enter the dimly lit bar; a DJ is playing chill house music. It has a nice ambience, not seedy or dirty, but more refined. It's definitely a gay bar, but there are no Go-Go boys gyrating or drag queens performing.

Marix Tex Mex is a scene, guys parading around, everyone trying to be noticed, but this bar has a low-key vibe. Charles and I lean against a brick wall, beers in hand, enjoying the groovy music. For the first time all night, I let my guard down.

"I know she likes giving you a hard time, but she really does like you," Charles says.

"I know. She's the sister I never wanted."

And then out of nowhere, I reach over and kiss him on the lips, which is the gayest thing I could do. I pull away, surprising even myself by my unfiltered display of queerness in a public place. It's dark; no one is watching, but it's been building for months.

"Sorry about that. I don't know what came over me."

"I don't think that's a good idea."

"Why? No one has to know except—"

A guy with a large camera hanging around his neck approaches. "Hey, guys. Sorry to bother. You two look interesting, and I'm doing a photo expose for *Out*, a gay and lesbian bimonthly publication, and I was wondering if you mind if I take your picture?"

Charles looks at me, the look of horror on his face matching mine.

"I don't think so," I say, looking at the camera like it's Kryptonite.

"Are you sure? I think you'd be very impressed with the publication. It's high quality and—"

"I have a girlfriend," I say, the words a showstopper.

He looks at us differently, no longer the happy, well-adjusted poster couple, but a big dramatic dump of dysfunction. "Oh...well, good luck with that," he says, walking away.

I call Ashley on the way home. I have to tell her. She's awaiting my call anyway.

"How was the client dinner?" she asks, sweetly.

"It was fine. Actually, something just happened and I need to talk to you about it."

"What's wrong? Are you okay?"

"Well, I need to be honest with you because I promised I would be honest and..."

The phone is silent.

"Are you there?

"What is it?" she says, words drenched in dread.

"Something just happened with Charles."

"What do you mean by *something*?"

"Well, after dinner, we were at the bar, and—"

"And what?"

"Well, I sort of kissed him, which was stupid and I don't know why..."

She says nothing. There are no angry words, just sadness steeping that I can hear in the silence.

"Ashley, are you there?" I hear muffled sobs, and I regret doing this over the phone. "Maybe the phone isn't the best—do you want me to come over and we can talk about it?"

"I don't think so. I think you've said enough," she says, and then—click.

I drive to her place in Hermosa Beach. It's after 1 a.m., and I don't want to wake her roommate, so I tap lightly on the window. Her face appears, her eyes swollen and red, and she's not happy to see me. She disappears, and I go to the front door. She lets me into the darkened living room, and without saying a word, we tiptoe to her bedroom. She has one of our CDs of songs playing and a candle burning. There's a half-empty box of tissues on her nightstand. Used ones litter her bed. She gathers and tosses them into a wastebasket and sits on her bed, holding her pillow like a teddy bear. She looks devastated. I sit at her desk chair, not knowing what to say, but knowing that I did this. I did this to her. And now the genie is out of the bottle.

"I had a feeling this might happen. And that it might happen with him," she says.

"What do you mean?"

"The couple of times you introduced me, I saw the way you looked at him. There was a life and passion in your eyes. A look I've never seen before."

"It was just a stupid kiss."

"Was it?" she asks, not nearly convinced. "I just feel bad for you. Your parents. Your *mom*. How are you going to tell her? She...she just emailed me *today*. She's going to be devastated. You have to tell her it wasn't my fault, that I..." she says, fighting back tears.

"Why does that matter?"

"At Easter, your mom asked me to take care of you, and I promised that I would. And at the airport, I almost, I mean I *almost* said to your mother, until the day I..." she says, chuckling nervously. *"Until the day I die.* Can you imagine? If we had married and you had held this from me, *and twenty years later*, we have kids and then all this!" She's still processing, as if the plug has just been pulled, and she's watching her dreams go swiftly down the drain.

The future she imagined, the love she cherished, gone in an instant and sealed with a kiss.

"I still can't believe it. I'm in love with a *gay* guy! That's so typical of me. I lost my virginity to a *gay guy*. I'm sure I'll look back one day and find humor in it but right now— "

"I'm not...*gay* gay!"

"Kissing other guys. Sleeping with other guys. That's definitely *gay* gay!"

This makes me mad because I don't *feel* gay. I just feel like a dude who happens to dig other dudes.

"You're gay."

"Shut up!"

"You're gay, gay, gay, gay, gay!"

"Quit it!"

"G-A-Y!" she spells it out, using words of truth to hurt me.

"What are you doing? Why are you—?"

"You're gay! Just admit it! I need to hear you say it."

"Quit it. You're going to wake up your room—"

"Say it! Say it out loud! You can't even say it!"

"No. You're being—"

"Say it! I want to hear you say it. I want to hear the words. I *need* to hear the words."

"Stop it! I won't do it. You can't make me—"

"Say it!

"NO!

"Say it!"

"Fine. I'm gay! G-A-Y. Gay, gay, gay! You feel better?"

"Do you?"

I stare at my feet, the gravity of everything hitting me hard. And then I start crying, surrendering to a battle I can never win, one that has almost destroyed me. The reality that the gay is not going away, and the pain I've caused her, brings sobs, desperate sobs that come from a place of fear as I am forced to take a baby step toward accepting the truth about myself.

She surprises me by handing me a Kleenex, tears in her eyes as well.

"I'm sorry," I say, choking on my sobs. "I'm so... I didn't mean..."

She motions for me to join her on the bed, a selfless gesture that breaks me more. She holds me in a maternal way, as I cry like a baby, my crusade leading me to the truth.

"It's okay, my little gay boy," she says, petting me, laughing through her tears.

And then I start laughing, a moment of levity for both of us.

§ § §

Five months later, I'm walking the Walk of Fame on Hollywood Boulevard.

In a last ditch effort to cut costs, the production company relocated to a former FBI building in the heart of Hollywood. It didn't work. The SAG strike and the tragedy of 9/11 were two blows from which it could not recover, and as expected, it sank like the Titanic.

I have returned to my office to salvage the wreckage, and I'm taking one last walk.

As I stroll across the stars, I'm shocked tourists actually come here. It's the dirty, unglamorous part of Hollywood infested with T-shirt shops, smoke shops, and vagrants sleeping in dark corners. One star after another lines the sidewalks for blocks, most of the names I don't recognize. As long as the world turns, stars will continue to be handed out. And at this rate, by the time I get my stupid star on the Boulevard, they'll be giving them away in Compton.

I enter a shop, a Mecca for knock-off designer luggage and cheesy Hollywood memorabilia. The Japanese man behind the counter sees me and chirps: "One moment, Mr. Bryan," before disappearing behind a beaded doorway reflecting the likeness of Marilyn Monroe. I pick up a mug with James Dean's image, an icon of Hollywood. I've been in Hollywood long enough to know it's all smoke and mirrors. The reality is not James Dean or Marilyn Monroe. The reality is people like me who come to Hollywood looking for a happy ending, only to discover they only happen in the movies. And only *sometimes* do they happen in real life.

He returns with my suitcase, the one I've been lugging around for years, the one with the missing wheel that once left its mark in the halls of the New Life clinic. The man lifts it onto the counter, and making a karate chop with his hand, spins the shiny new wheel and it whirls effortlessly, giving him an inordinate amount of joy. "Good as new, Daniel-san."

"I'm sorry, did you just call me 'Daniel-san'?"

"Hai. People say, I Miyagi. Wax on, wax off!" he says, getting a kick out of himself.

"Are you an actor?"

"We all actor. World stage. Shakespeare know," he says. "I famous, no?" he says, pointing to his headshot tacked on the wall behind the counter. Of course, how did I miss it? It's even signed. "I come Hollywood find fame and fortune. I chase wind like everyone else. Ha!"

I pay for my new wheel, wish Miyagi luck, and wheel out and onto Hollywood Boulevard. I roll the baggage smoothly, without effort—and not even a scratch on the stars. I wait at the corner and check my watch. I'm a couple minutes early. I notice the tourists swarming the Chinese Mann theatre, taking pictures of the same stars I remember as a thirteen-year-old boy.

I remember looking at these stars and thinking one day I'll end up here. And here I am, not exactly the ending I envisioned as a teenager. Standing over a blank star with no name yet, as I contemplate who might be next, I notice that I'm standing in front of a thrift store chain named *Out of the Closet*, the irony of my geography not lost on me, and I can't help but chuckle.

And then I look up to see Charles pull up in his silver Mitsubishi Montero. I demonstrate how much better my suitcase rolls with two wheels. It was his suggestion that two wheels might be better than one, and looking at him smiling at me, I couldn't agree more. I glide my suitcase to the trunk and throw it in the back with the rest of my earthly belongings.

It's been two months since I got the call from Vince to turn on the TV the morning of September 11th, 2001. As I watched the tragedy unfold along with the rest of the world, Charles called from Hawaii where he was on vacation with friends. It was a vacation he had wanted me to join, but I wasn't yet comfortable letting others—beyond my circle of friends—know the truth about me. I was still working on accepting the truth about me. The world was falling apart that day, and he was the one I wanted by my side. And despite what the world might think, this time I refuse to close the door on the opportunity to love and be loved for who I am.

I jump in the passenger seat, put on my seatbelt, and my eyes go from Charles to the two tickets to Thailand on the dash, our passport out of this crazy town and the beginning of our journey together. Two wheels are better than one, indeed. As we drive down Sunset Boulevard and pass Kings

Road, I glance up at the peak, recalling the horrific night I almost ran off the cliff.

I went home and dialed 1 (800) NEW-LIFE because I thought it was the end for me.

But really, it was just the beginning.

EPILOGUE

I'm with my mom for *"All You Can Eat Catfish"* night at the Wharf, a seafood restaurant in San Angelo, Texas. This is the moment. The conversation I swore I'd never have is about to happen.

It was inevitable. I've been with Charles almost two years.

I hadn't planned it, but my mother forced my hand, giving me no other option but to tell her the truth—the big ol' gay truth that Charles is more than a "roommate." She recently made a trip to the suburb where I grew up to attend a wedding of one of the kids on the block. There she reunited with her old friends, her inner circle in the '70s and '80s; they played Bunko, carpooled, and frosted one another's hair. It's been twenty years—all of us kids are grown, and I'm thirty-three—and so my mom is giving me an update on everyone. Apparently all the kids I grew up with are not only *married* but have produced *grandkids*—everyone except my brother and me, it seems.

"I was telling Martha I guess my boys are going to be the last ones of the bunch to get married. She's a grandmother four times over," my mom says, a comment making me wince.

That's it. I'm done. I can no longer carry the burden. I have to tell my mother the truth about me: I'm not the type of son who will be getting married—to a female—and giving her lots of grandchildren, so she needs to place her bets on my brother, because, well… "I'm not sure that's going to happen—at least for me," I say, surprised I actually said it out loud.

We've just sat down in this wanna-be Red Lobster, and the bubbly teenage waitress has already dropped off hush puppies and two iced teas.

"What do you mean?" my mother asks, stirring Sweet n' Low into her tea with her manicured acrylic nail painted candy-apple red.

How do I tell my mother? Like this: "Well, getting married isn't in the cards for me," I say, searching for the right words—words that seem to elude me.

"What do you mean?" she asks, taking a nervous sip of tea.

"I'm not…well, I'm unable to—I'm sort of female intolerant," I finally just say.

I see it in her eyes. Denial. "What's that supposed to mean?" she dismisses, grabbing a hush puppy and smothering it in butter.

"I mean, I won't be marrying a woman," I lay it all out on the table.

Before my mom can comprehend, the perky waitress, undoubtedly a cheerleader, crashes the table. *"Alrighty, folks, are we having the all-you-can-eat catfish? It's yummy. I've already had all I can eat, thrown up, and gone back for seconds! Just kidding!"* she says, far too chipper for either of us to handle at this moment.

"We'll have the all you can eat," I say.

My mom nods, but I see her going numb.

"Baked potato or French fries?" the waitress asks me.

"Baked potato."

"Everything on it—'the works' as we say?"

"Please."

"And for you ma'am?" she asks my mom.

"Same," she says, looking up at the girl and forcing a smile.

"Alrighty, I'll get that started," she says, before skipping off.

I grab a hush puppy, but I've lost my appetite.

"So what do you mean you're not going to marry a woman?" she asks, almost defiantly.

"I mean...well, I'm with Charles," I finally say. "He's more than a roommate."

And this shatters her.

She starts putting two and two together, and it hits her: tears forming in her eyes, mascara on the verge of running, her dreams crumbling in front of me.

This is the reaction I wanted to avoid.

I stare at the placemat, a stupid animated red lobster with a cartoon face staring at me. Eternal silence as my mom falls to pieces. We're in public, so she's trying to keep it together.

"Are you okay?" I ask.

"What do you think? My son just told me he's *gay*," she says sharply, confirming it's not a good thing to be gay. And quite frankly, I don't feel gay, so when she says the word "gay," as with Ashley, my first reaction is: *Wait a second. It's not what you think!* "Gay" is such a loaded word—*and never used as a compliment.* To use it as a word to describe myself is foreign, although accurate because living with a guy, someone I love, that's definitely gay.

"You had no idea?"

Not only had I moved in with Charles in Hollywood, we spent nine months on an island in the Gulf of Thailand living off our severance in a cozy beach bungalow. I was hoping she'd figure it out. She simply shakes her head, dabbing her eyes with a napkin.

"What about a mother's intuition?"

She shrugs, and if we weren't in public, I think she would be sobbing.

We sit in silence—an extremely uncomfortable silence—until the catfish arrives.

We both nibble, neither one of us hungry.

We've had all we can eat.

Once in the car, we just sit. It's as if someone has died. And in a way, someone did: the *me* she thought I was, the *me* I tried to be, the *me* I never really was, the *me* I could never be.

"I'm still the same person you know. It's just...now you know me better."

She's absolutely numb, staring into space as if she's gone into shock.

"It's not something I chose, mom. I spent the first thirty years of my life trying to change it! I did *everything*! I worked at the Playboy Mansion, for crying out loud! I've been in therapy, counseled with my pastors. If you only knew how much I've suffered because of this..." I say, shivering with emotion. "The time...the time I checked into the psychiatric ward? I wanted to kill myself. I really wanted to die. I was twenty-five and still staring blankly at the pages of *Playboy*. I don't know why. If I could change it, I would have. Trust me!"

She's listening, trying to be strong.

"And it's not your fault. You did nothing wrong. You were the best mom on the block—all the kids called you 'Mom,' so you have to know it's not you—so don't blame yourself. It's just how I am, how I've always been—something I've known since elementary school."

Although she's clearly upset, she does something that surprises me.

"You're my son," she says, through tears. "I love you. There's nothing you could do to ever change that." Her words are so real that I shudder. "I love you, so you have to know that," she says, affirming me again. I believe her, and for the first time, I actually start to take it in.

She knows the truth about me, and though she doesn't understand it, she loves me anyway, and that is powerful. She leans over and hugs me, and although I'm thirty-three years old, I feel like a little boy—her little boy—and I feel lucky.

She's my mom and I silently thank God for her.

§ § §

I'm inside a strip club in Cozumel, Mexico watching a local woman gyrate in my face. It's awkward partly because her body had its glory days back in—well, never (not to mention unsightly C-section scars). But my dad, my brother, my uncle, and my cousin flank me.

We're on a family vacation, and this is "boys' night out."

I should have known we'd end up here. In the six months since my catfish confession with my mom, I've been waiting for the right time to tell my dad. When the local woman named Maria puts her crotch in my face, it seems like the perfect time. As my brother puts more pesos in her privates, I turn to my dad and say matter-of-factly, "I'm just not into the vagina business."

My dad smiles, knowingly, as if he's been preparing for this moment: "And it doesn't change my love for you one iota, son," he says, putting his arm around me as Maria competes for our attention, which is unsettling. Apparently my mom called my dad the night I spilled the beans to her, so he's had six months to prepare. My dad affirms me, making me feel loved, demonstrating beautifully the unconditional love I'd only expect from my Heavenly Father.

He's my dad, and I silently thank God for him.

§ § §

Telling my parents the truth about me was the first step. The rest is an on-going process.

It's complicated—especially when I spent over thirty years playing the role of someone that wasn't exactly me. The truth about me is going to be controversial for some of those who know me, especially in light of the fact that most of my friendships were forged through church.

Many will not understand. Not only that, they will be convinced that I have strayed and rejected the Lord, practicing "homosexuality" and living that so-called "homosexual lifestyle."

This conclusion is flawed; a straight person would never be accused of practicing "heterosexuality" or living a "heterosexual lifestyle." Both can be lived out in life-affirming or life-destroying ways, as the bedrock of any solid relationship is love—since God *is* love. *"God is love. Whoever lives in love lives in God, and God in him"* (1 John 4:16).

Ultimately, it all comes down to this fundamental question: If God is love, how might we as mere human beings be so bold as to call the love and commitments between two human beings of the same gender "sin"? Since we're made in God's image, we are designed to love. I love someone of the same gender. I care for him deeply. Life makes more sense with him.

If God is love, how can love be a "sin"?

The moment I opened myself up to love and to be loved, only then did I find the will to live.

Without love, I am a shell of a person—existing, but not really living.

With love, I have the chance to truly live—while I'm alive.

It really does all come down to that. If anyone hates me

for loving another human being of the same gender, then so be it. They will never hate me as much as I have hated me.

I did not choose this existence.

I have driven myself insane trying to change, but the truth is I haven't. If I can't change the truth about me, I either end my life, or learn to live with it. And if I choose to live, then the only way that makes sense is to live and love honestly: to stop lying, to stop hiding, and tell the truth.

§ § §

As an "ex-gay," I spent a decade of my life forcing something that wasn't natural. I obsessively controlled my behavior, while my mind, body, and soul—everything that makes me who I am—remained the same. I used every tool available, relentless in my pursuit to change.

If change were possible, I would have changed. I'd wager the odds of a gay person turning straight the same as a straight person turning gay—a ridiculous concept to most straight people.

The Religious Right—with which I was zealously involved—get a lot of mileage in their anti-gay political platform by demonizing gay people and making homosexuality all about gay sex. Take sex out of the equation, remove the genitals, and a gay person will still be gay.

Being gay is not a matter of *doing*, but a matter of *being*.

It's so woven into the fabric of an individual that to suggest it can be altered fails to acknowledge the complexity and diversity of God's creation.

The "ex-gay" movement's "hope for change" proved to be nothing more than empty promises based on distorted interpretations of the Bible. Further research exposes more sobering conclusions that Joe Dallas and many within "ex-gay" circles don't talk about.

Michael Bussey and Gary Cooper, the two men who started Exodus International, later denounced the organization they helped create as fraudulent, spending the rest of their lives trying to undo the harm they'd caused. They revealed that many of their clients became depressed, even suicidal when they found themselves unable to change their sexual orientation, and despite all the Exodus propaganda, *not one person* was ever healed of their homosexuality.

In 1987, Jeremy Marks founded Courage, London's first "ex-gay" ministry, but in 2001, after nearly fifteen years of watching people, including himself, struggle in vain to change, he renounced Exodus's methods as failing to change peoples' sexual orientation.

In the 1990s, John Paulk, a former drag queen, became the poster boy of the "ex-gay" movement, appearing on *60 Minutes*, *Oprah*, and the cover of *Newsweek*. But in 2000, he was photographed by Wayne Besen in a Washington, D.C. gay bar, inspiring Mr. Besen's pivotal book, *Anything*

But Straight: Unmasking the Scandals and Lies Behind the Ex-Gay Myth.

The voices in many churches that preach that gay people can be saved from their deviant choice through zealous prayer, divine intervention, and a whole lot of willpower, are leaving scars on the souls of countless victims who are led to believe that not only is change possible, but *required* in order to be loved by God. This message not only puts conditions on the unconditional love of God, but it feeds the prejudice of the church, making the flock feel justified in judging and excluding. The incendiary anti-gay rhetoric coming from those churches lashes away at the psyches of gay kids who can't help but internalize the prejudice of the pious.

It's no wonder gay youth are at a higher risk of suicide. They have few choices: either try to be someone they can never be to fit in, become invisible and hope no one notices, or come out and risk becoming a target—and not just from the kid's own family and church.

For me, the "ex-gay" movement was a deceptive form of soul torture, forcing me to declare war on myself, fueling my self-hatred and internalized prejudice to a psychiatric pitch—obsessed with my sexuality and compulsive in my efforts to eliminate it. All the words, the lies, the false studies heralded by James Dobson, Pat Robertson, and the Religious Right fueled my crusade. But the message that my immutable true colors were unacceptable left scars on my soul.

According to Phyllis Hart, an evangelical psychotherapist, the "ex-gay" movement: "...*has a lethal—or nearly lethal effect on sensitive, deeply spiritual gay Christians who have spent the better part of their lives trying to be heterosexual, in a vain attempt to become something they could not. Survivors of the "ex-gay" movement are often shells of the people they could have become if they would have accepted their gay orientation years before.*"

I often wonder what my life might have been if I wasn't so obsessed with hiding the truth, forcing something that wasn't natural, and playing the role of someone other than me.

I am now an ex-"ex-gay." The ex's cancel one another, leaving me with the truth—a truth I didn't choose, a truth I cannot change, a truth that must be lived out with dignity and integrity.

God help me.

§ § §

It's fourteen years later, and I'm still with Charles. It's fair to say this book wouldn't have been possible without him. He has been an unwavering supporter of me and my story and I simply can't imagine my life without him. I want to thank all the readers who have reached out to me personally with their own stories. Your openness and support has been healing beyond measure. And for those readers who have been actively spreading the word, a special thank you as your passionate reviews on Amazon and Goodreads have been invaluable in earning new readers. I invite you to follow me on Twitter, join me on Facebook or contact me directly via email.

Thank you for investing time in my story.

TWITTER:

https://twitter.com/BryanC_books

EMAIL:

For questions, comments, or to contact the author:

bryanchristopher@me.com

FACEBOOK:

https://www.facebook.com/hidingfrommyselfmemoir/

CPSIA information can be obtained
at www.ICGtesting.com
Printed in the USA
BVOW06s1811081116
467262BV00016B/103/P